REPAIRING FURNITURE

TIME
LIFE
BOOKS

This volume is part of a series offering home
owners detailed instructions on repairs,
construction and improvements which they can
undertake themselves.

HOME REPAIR
AND IMPROVEMENT

REPAIRING FURNITURE

BY THE EDITORS OF
TIME-LIFE BOOKS

TIME-LIFE BOOKS
AMSTERDAM

TIME-LIFE BOOKS
EUROPEAN EDITOR: Kit van Tulleken
Design Director: Ed Skyner
Photography Director: Pamela Marke
Chief of Research: Vanessa Kramer
Chief Sub-Editor: Ilse Gray

HOME REPAIR AND IMPROVEMENT
EDITORIAL STAFF FOR REPAIRING FURNITURE
Editor: Robert M. Jones
Assistant Editors: Robert A. Doyle, Betsy Frankel
Designer: Edward Frank
Chief Researcher: Oobie Gleysteen
Picture Editor: Adrian Allen
Associate Designer: Kenneth E. Hancock
Text Editors: Leslie Marshall, Peter Pocock,
Brooke Stoddard
Staff Writers: Lynn R. Addison, Patricia C. Bangs,
Jan Leslie Cook, Steven J. Forbis, Kathleen M.
Kiely, Victoria W. Monks, Mary-Sherman Willis,
William Worsley
Researcher: Kimberley K. Lewis
Art Associates: George Bell, Fred Holz,
Lorraine D. Rivard
Editorial Assistant: Susan Larson

EUROPEAN EDITION
Series Editor: Tony Allan
Head Researcher: Jackie Matthews
Text Editor: Christopher Farman
Writer/Researcher: Thom Henvey
Designers: Michael Morey, Paul Reeves
Sub-Editors: Charles Boyle, Sally Rowland
Editorial Assistant: Rebecca Smith

EDITORIAL PRODUCTION
Chief: Ellen Brush
Production Assistants: Stephanie Lee, Jane Lillicrap
Art Department: Janet Matthew
Editorial Department: Theresa John, Debra Lelliott

THE CONSULTANTS: Albert Jackson and David Day first met in 1962 as
students at Ravensbourne College of Art and Design, Bromley, Kent.
Both went on to train as furniture designers at the Royal College of Art
and then to collaborate on freelance projects before formally going into
partnership in 1971. Since then they have acted as design consultants for
several large firms, have presented two BBC television series—*Make
Your Own Furniture* and *Better than New*—and have co-authored five
books on do-it-yourself topics.

Alan Bayliss served his apprenticeship with a leading Sydney cabinet-
making firm. He worked as a carpenter and cabinet-maker for 18 years,
then took a Diploma in Teaching from Sydney College of Advanced
Education. Since 1970 he has been a teacher of cabinet-making at Sydney
Technical College.

Lawrence R. England Jr. works in L. R. England and Sons, a family
cabinet-making and woodworking business established by his
grandfather in Boston in 1900. The firm specializes in the design and
construction of custom-made furniture.

Contents

A joint that endures. The dovetail joint—a sophisticated version of the mortise and tenon joint used in fine furniture—is a sign of quality construction. Flared tongues fit snugly into matching dovetail-shaped sockets to increase strength; joints of this kind can be separated in only one direction. Dovetail joints are used in drawers and cabinets as a way of connecting two panels of wood that meet at a right angle.

Unfortunately, even good, solid, everyday furniture seldom lasts a lifetime. This is not surprising. It gets sat upon, dined upon, leant against, occasionally stood upon. Over the years, as one guest too many tilts backwards on a dining-room chair, or the scuffs and glass marks become too numerous on a coffee table, or the springs of a favourite sofa finally give way, one piece after another gets tucked away in the attic or basement and is usually forgotten.

In days gone by, it would not have even been stored. In the Middle Ages the chest, or coffer, that served as bench, bed and table, as well as a trunk for storage or transport, was discarded when its wooden panels split, warped or were otherwise damaged. It was too crudely made to be fixed. Today, thanks to modern materials and improved methods of joinery, most damaged furniture can be restored to its original state. The repairs can range from simple tasks such as regluing loose joints, removing stains with special-purpose cleansers and conditioners, or re-covering cushions, to such complex and time-consuming projects as duplicating broken parts with a lathe, stripping and refinishing a cabinet, or re-upholstering a sofa.

Deciding whether to repair a piece yourself or turn it over to a professional is only partly a matter of personal choice. The decision depends, of course, on a variety of factors: how much you like the piece, the use you will get out of it when it is repaired, and the cost and complexity of the work involved. However, if the piece is a true antique—loosely defined as anything more than 100 years old—you should definitely have it restored by a specialist, since a botched or unsatisfactory repair could considerably reduce its value.

Whatever additional tasks or techniques are involved, restoring furniture to usefulness generally begins with repairs to the joints and frame; and, in most cases, this means regluing or replacing the parts of a joint. One basic joint of furniture-making, the mortise and tenon, can be made with only a saw, mallet and chisel. Known to the woodworking craftsmen of ancient Egypt and rediscovered by European craftsmen in the middle of the 14th century, the mortise and tenon joint revolutionized furniture-making. It was used as the basis for a new technique, panelled framing, in which thin panels of wood were set into grooves cut into thicker frames, with the result that furniture became lighter and less likely to split or warp.

Over the next century and a half, all well-made furniture came to be assembled by mortise and tenon, or with similar hidden joints that used pegs or dowels rather than rectangular tenons. The pieces appeared in household inventories as "jointed" or "joined" furniture, and the guild of master craftsmen who made it were known, appropriately, as joiners. Sturdy and elegant, such joints still hold together the frames of the best tables, chairs, sofas and beds—unchanged in concept although now the parts are cut with power tools.

Restoring Separated Joints in Wooden Chairs

Chairs have more joints than most other kinds of furniture, and they are joints that have to work under considerable strain. Even a lightweight ballerina puts stress on a chair's joints when she sits. If a man tilts the chair backwards against a wall and hooks his heels over a stretcher, the stress is multiplied. Sooner or later, a joint works loose or separates altogether.

A weak joint should be strengthened, and the sooner it is done, the better. One bad joint puts increased stress on the remaining good joints, and if too many joints loosen, the entire chair will have to be dismantled. This is a prospect to be avoided if at all possible, because pulling joints apart can sometimes lead to further damage. In fact, you should break down a chair into as few subassemblies as the repair permits and, if you can, correct loosened joints without separating them.

Although there are innumerable joints used in chair construction, the two that are most commonly encountered are dowel joints and mortise and tenon joints. For a dowel joint, one end of a chair member is fitted with a separate dowel or it is turned into a dowel shape. The dowel then fits into a socket in a second chair member.

A mortise and tenon joint is the rectangular equivalent of a dowel joint. Here, too, there are two basic styles. In one—the shouldered mortise and tenon—the rectangular member has one end cut away and shaped to fit into a mortise cut into a larger member. In the other, the tenon is flush with one face of the rail or stretcher and is said to be bare faced.

Both dowel joints and mortise and tenon joints must fit tightly for the joint to be strong and endure pressure. Although glue alone usually holds joints together, sometimes a wedge will have been added to fill a gap, and in some cases a nail or dowel will have been driven into the side of the joint to reinforce it further. All these supports must be removed when the joint is repaired, which is not always an easy task. In fact, you may have to balance your wish for a solid chair against the risk of further damage during dismantling. For a prized piece that is still intact, albeit wobbly, it may be best to settle for stopgap repairs and make sure that the chair is not used as frequently as before.

Glue, wedges and dowels also feature prominently in the repertoire of techniques used to fix chair joints that have failed. Tools for these projects are, for the most part, simple. A wooden mallet or a hammer and a block of wood with sheet cork glued to one face are needed for the job of dismantling the affected chair members. Straps that tighten like seat belts, called web cramps, hold repaired joints in position while the glue dries.

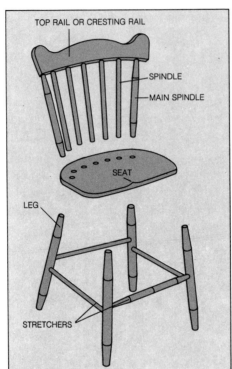

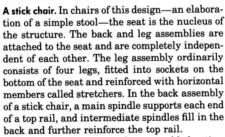

A stick chair. In chairs of this design—an elaboration of a simple stool—the seat is the nucleus of the structure. The back and leg assemblies are attached to the seat and are completely independent of each other. The leg assembly ordinarily consists of four legs, fitted into sockets on the bottom of the seat and reinforced with horizontal members called stretchers. In the back assembly of a stick chair, a main spindle supports each end of a top rail, and intermediate spindles fill in the back and further reinforce the top rail.

Chairs of this type are often assembled entirely with dowel joints that have the dowels turned directly on to the ends of the members. The joints between the stretchers and the legs are usually the most vulnerable to damage.

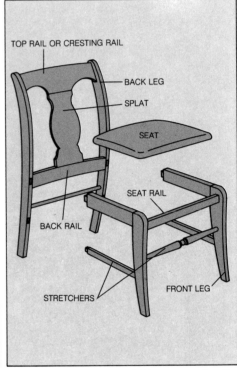

A frame chair. In chairs of this construction, the seat is in effect suspended in a wooden frame and is not a critical part of the support structure. Instead, the design centres on the back legs that run from the top to the bottom of the chair. Usually each of these legs is a single piece of wood. The seat is usually a separate element, resting on four seat rails. The front legs are joined to the side seat rails, and may be reinforced with stretchers on all four sides. The back legs are joined with a top rail and one or more back rails. When there is only a single back rail, a flat wooden member, called a splat, may be inserted between the top and back rails. In many chairs of this design, the seat is upholstered or made of either rush or cane.

In addition to dowel joints, frame chairs often have mortise and tenon joints where the seat rails meet the legs. On some, screws are used to hold the parts together. Usually the joints at the back of the seat, where the side seat rails meet the back legs, are the most vulnerable.

Choosing a Glue and Making It Stick

Timber furniture is made of solid parts, but one of the principal agents holding the parts together begins as a liquid. Scientists still do not completely understand the physical and chemical properties of glues, but furniture-makers and repairers have attested to the powers of glue since 3000 B.C.

An effective glue joint has five layers, as illustrated below, and the weakest of them determines the strength of the joint. In earlier times the weakest layer was the glue itself, but modern glues are so strong that the surrounding wood usually breaks before the glue or the intermediate layers of glue-soaked fibres.

In order to make a well-bonded joint, you must clean the two abutting wood surfaces of old glue, dirt and finish. If the wood is smooth, roughen it by scoring with a knife. If the wood is moistened in the process of removing old glue, allow it to dry. Shape the joint so that the fit is tight, leaving no gaps.

In addition, apply enough pressure to the joint to force the glue into the fibres of the wood. Usually you should pre-assemble the joint dry and clamp it, to make sure that the wood surfaces fit and that you have enough cramps. Then dismantle the joint and apply a thin layer of glue to both adjoining surfaces—on end grain apply a slightly thicker layer than on side grain, which is less absorbent. Reassemble the joint, clamp it and wipe it clean—first with a damp cloth, then with a dry one. Immediately check the joint to make certain that the alignment of the surfaces is correct.

Choice of glue depends partly on the piece of furniture and where it will be used, and partly on preference—even professionals differ on which glues are best to use for furniture joinery. The following glues are most favoured:

☐ POLYVINYL ACETATE, usually known simply as PVA, is a good general adhesive for most indoor furniture. It comes ready to use and, once clamped, sets in 30 minutes, although it should remain undisturbed until it reaches full strength in two days. It should be applied to both bonding surfaces. PVA has low resistance to moisture and should not be used to glue outdoor furniture.

☐ YELLOW GLUE, also called aliphatic resin, is an improved version of PVA. Slightly stronger and more resistant to moisture, it is also more viscous and dribbles less when applied. However, it begins to dry faster than PVA and thus requires swifter clamping. The cramps can be removed after 30 minutes, but the joint should remain undisturbed until it reaches full strength 18 hours later. Yellow glue has good gap-filling properties and is especially good for ill-fitting joints.

☐ ANIMAL GLUE, made from animal skins, nerve tissues or bones, is the adhesive of purists because it was virtually the only glue available for use on furniture from early Egyptian times to about 1900. As restorers of antiques are quick to point out, the glue is reversible; steam and a sun lamp will undo the adhering properties of the glue, allowing a joint to be taken apart. In addition, liquid animal glue allows ample time—as long as 20

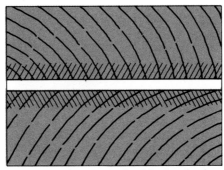

An effective glue joint. A glue joint has five layers: a thin film of glue, two areas (one either side) consisting of wood fibres penetrated by glue, and the nearby wood that is unpenetrated. Chemical bonding between the wood fibres and glue locks the wood pieces together.

minutes—for clamping before it begins to set. But it can be applied only at temperatures round about 20°C; it stiffens in temperatures below 10°C and thins in temperatures above 33°C. Joints assembled with animal glue must remain clamped for six to 12 hours. It cannot be used for outdoor furniture.

☐ PLASTIC RESIN GLUE, sometimes called urea-formaldehyde, is very strong and is used on joints subject to unusual stress. It comes as a powder that must be mixed with water, but once it has dried, the glue is highly resistant to moisture. Plastic resin glue must be applied at temperatures higher than 20°C. It starts to set in five to 15 minutes and, once clamped, it must be kept under constant pressure for five to 12 hours, depending on the surrounding temperature.

☐ RESORCINOL GLUE is available ready-mixed or can be prepared by mixing a powder with a liquid catalyst. It is very strong, has the highest resistance to heat and moisture—it is even used in boat-building—and is the best glue for repairing outdoor wooden furniture. It should be applied at room temperature and left clamped for 10 to 12 hours.

☐ OTHER ADHESIVES. There are a number of other synthetic glues used in woodworking, and new ones are always being introduced, but those listed above are favoured by professionals for furniture repair. The familiar epoxy glues (there are a number of formulations, including some that harden very quickly) work chemically to form a strong bond between pieces of wood, as well as such non-porous materials as metal or glass. However, epoxy is expensive; several less costly glues work at least as well in furniture repair. The contact adhesives, such as those used to laminate thin sheets of plastic to counter tops, set almost instantly. The disadvantage is that they allow no time for adjustments once the glue has been applied to the joints.

Four Kinds of Joint Lock

Looking for obstacles. Before pulling a loose joint apart to make repairs, examine it to see if there is a fastener that you must first remove. Sometimes you must look for subtle clues. A dimple in the wood finish near the joint may indicate that a panel pin is securing the end of a dowel *(right)*. More obvious is a dowel that pins a mortise and tenon joint together *(far right)*, since the end of the dowel is exposed.

Cracks round a joint often signal situations in which the joint should not be pulled apart. Hairline cracks on the sides of a dowel at the point where it emerges from its socket *(right)* usually mean that the dowel has been wedged. Pulling such a joint apart may split the socket. In old furniture, cracks above and below a socket where a dowel enters an oval stile or rail are typical of a special joint called a shrink joint *(far right)*. In this older version of a dowel joint, a knobbed end of dry wood was fitted into a still green socketed member. Since the socket then shrank round the knob as it dried, dismantling these joints would probably split the wood.

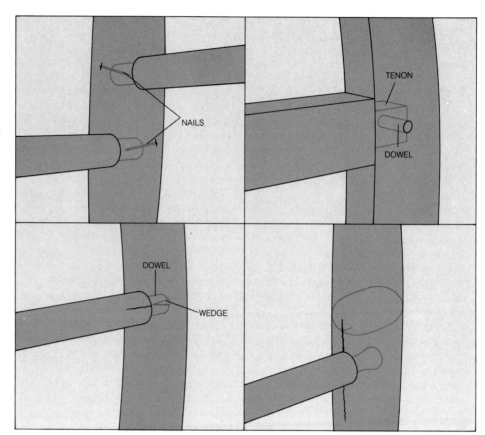

Regluing Loose Dowel Joints

1 Injecting glue. Pull the joint apart slightly and drill a perpendicular hole, slightly larger than the tip of a syringe-type glue injector, into the back of the dowel socket. Jam the tip of the injector into the hole, and squeeze the plunger until glue appears all round the dowel. You may have to drill and inject glue into a second hole if it is difficult to get glue into the first one or if the glue comes out on only one side of the dowel. Smear glue over the exposed section of the dowel, and press the joint back together again. Use wood filler to conceal the hole.

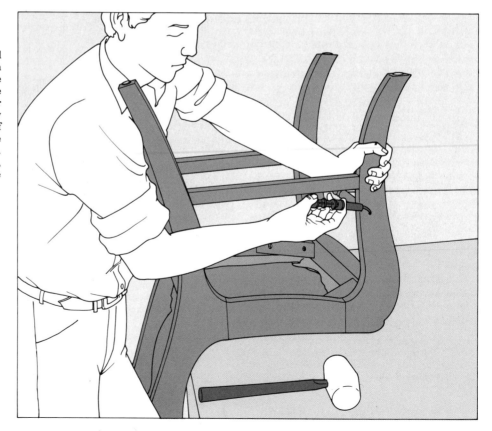

2 **Using a web cramp.** With the dowel in its socket, assemble a web cramp following the manufacturer's instructions, and loop it round the chair so that the loose joint will be forced together when the cramp is tightened. Rest sticks across rails or stiles, as needed, to keep the web strap in place as the cramp is tightened *(inset)*. Tighten the ratchet nut of the cramp with a screwdriver or a socket spanner; if you use a spanner, which is usually easier, tighten the nut only as much as you could if you were using a screwdriver. Tap the joint lightly with a mallet to make sure that the dowel is firmly seated. Let the glue dry completely before removing the web cramp.

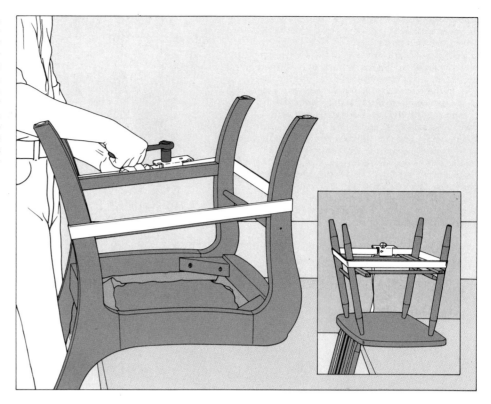

Wedging a Loose Mortise and Tenon Joint

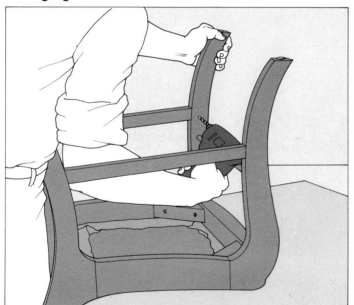

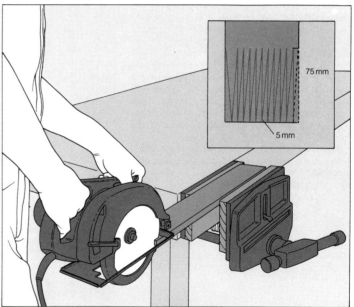

1 **Drilling out a dowel pin.** When a shouldered tenon pinned with a dowel is loose, use an awl to make a pilot hole for a drill bit in the centre of the dowel. Then drill the dowel out, using a bit that has a diameter slightly greater than that of the dowel. If the tenon is bare faced, do not drill out the dowel; instead, fit wedges round the tenon to tighten it *(Steps 2 and 3).*

2 **Making wedges.** Use a table saw, radial arm saw or portable circular saw to cut out hardwood wedges to fill the gaps round a loose tenon. If you use a circular saw, clamp the wood face up in a vice as shown here, and cut along the grain of the wood, not across it. Make wedges about 75 mm long, tapering from 5 mm thick at the butt end to a sharp edge. For economical use of wood, alternate tapered cuts with straight cuts that square off the board again *(inset)*.

11

3 **Wedging the tenon.** Pull the joint slightly apart, and trim thin wedges to fit the gap between the tenon and its mortise. For very loose joints, use wedges on all four sides to keep the mortise and tenon in alignment; for a joint only slightly loose, one wedge is sufficient. Inject glue into the back of the joint *(page 10, Step 1)* and smear glue on the exposed part of the tenon. Coat both sides of each wedge with glue by sliding the wedge through a puddle of glue on a scrap of wood. Insert the wedges into the gaps round the tenon, and press the joint together to seat it. On a shouldered tenon, as shown on the right, the shoulders of wood will drive the wedges into place. On a bare-faced tenon, use a mallet and a small wood block to drive in the wedges. Use a web cramp to secure the joint *(page 11, Step 2, above)* until the glue dries.

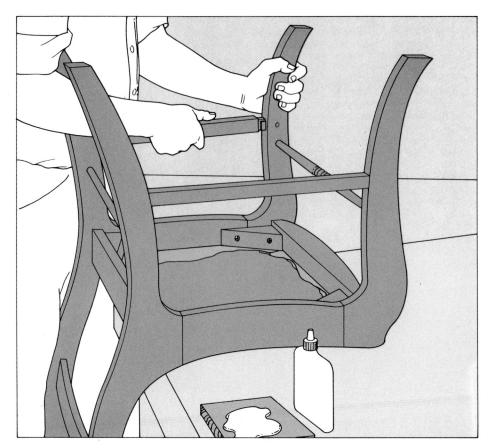

4 **Pinning the joint.** If you removed a dowel to release the joint *(page 11, Step 1)*, cut a new dowel of the same diameter as the drill bit you used but slightly longer than the depth of the hole. Bevel one end of the dowel to make it easier to insert. Use a stick to spread glue inside the hole; apply more glue to the dowel, and tap the dowel into the hole with a mallet. Let the glue dry, then trim the end of the dowel flush with the surrounding wood surface. Finish the end of the dowel to match the rest of the chair.

If necessary, use the same technique to add a dowel pin to a mortise and tenon joint that does not already have one. Drill the hole for the dowel after the glue in the wedged joint is dry.

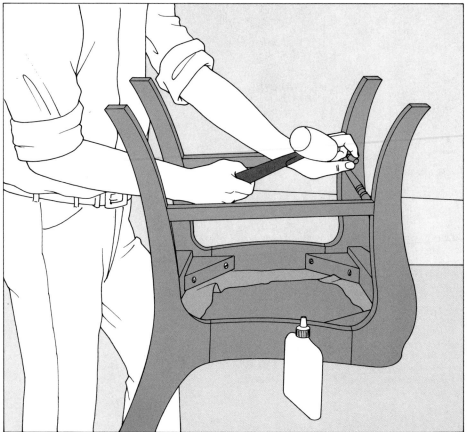

Techniques for Taking a Chair Apart

Using a mallet to loosen joints. Label each part of the chair as a guide for reassembly. With a mallet or hammer, break the bond of glue that holds the parts together. Use a wood or cork block to protect the striking area, and lift that area of the chair slightly *(below)*. Use blows of moderate force, then try levering, if necessary.

Separate the parts of a stick chair by first releasing the leg or back assembly from the seat, as shown below, and then take apart the sub-assemblies as needed. On a frame chair, begin by removing the back legs if they are loose, using leverage *(right, below)*; then proceed to the sub-assemblies. If the back legs are not loose, separate only the parts with loose joints.

Using leverage to loosen joints. Cut two pieces of wood, the sum of whose lengths is slightly longer than the distance between the parts to be separated. Trim one end of each piece into a cup shape, to keep the pieces from slipping off the work, and cut a V and an inverted V in the other ends, to join the two pieces where they meet in the middle. Position this lever so that its outer ends are as close as possible to the joints that are to be opened, and place cork pads between the ends and the chair to protect the finish. Apply force gradually, with your hand, to straighten the joint in the middle of the lever. To apply force over spans of other lengths, construct another two-part lever or use a jet cramp.

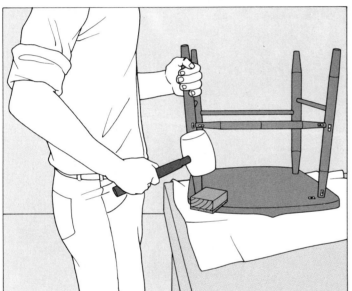

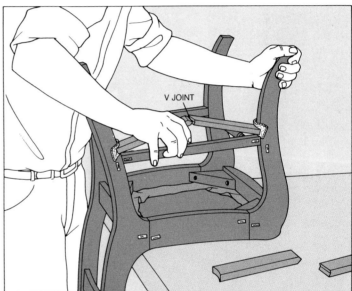

V JOINT

Refitting Dowels in a Dismantled Chair

1 **Scraping glue from the dowel.** Use a knife to scrape old glue from the surface of the dowelled end. Hold the knife almost perpendicular to the wood, but tip the back of the knife slightly forwards so that you will be dragging the blade across the surface of the wood. Use as much force as necessary to remove the dried glue without digging the blade into the wood.

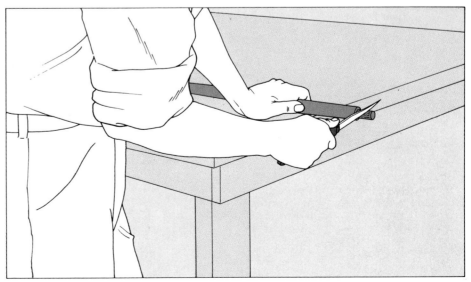

2 **Preparing the socket.** Wrap the socketed part of the chair in cork or cardboard to protect its finish, and clamp it in a vice, socket up. Reach inside the socket with a 6 mm chisel, held with the side of the blade against the side of the socket, and scrape out the old glue. Then enlarge the bottom of the socket slightly so that there will be room for the wedged dowel to expand.

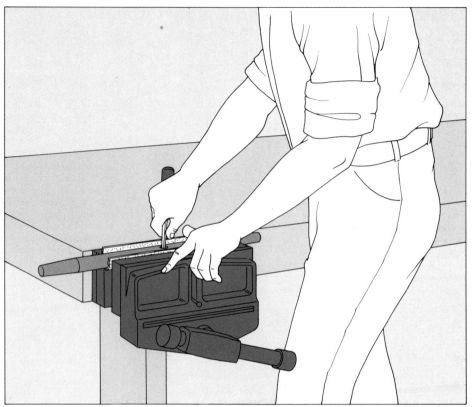

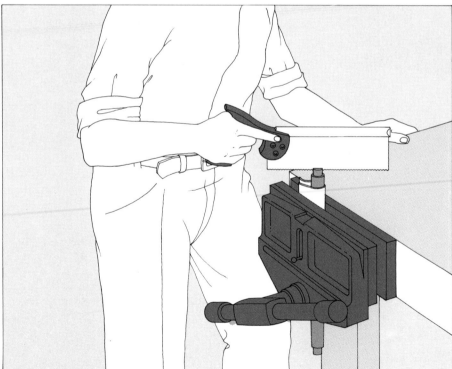

3 **Cutting a kerf in the dowel.** Use a dovetail saw or a small backsaw to cut a kerf in the dowel, stopping just short of where the kerf would be visible. Make the cut so that the kerf will form a right angle with the grain of the socketed part.

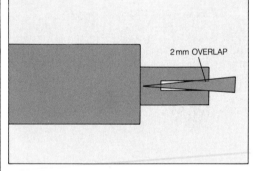

2 mm OVERLAP

4 **Wedging the dowel.** Cut a hardwood wedge *(page 11, Step 2, below)*, and fit it to the kerf in the dowel so that the end of the dowel will spread out slightly when the joint is assembled. First measure the depth of the socket and the length of the dowel to find the clearance between the end of the dowel and the bottom of the socket, usually about 3 mm. Then hold the wedge alongside the kerf, tapered end pointing towards the bottom of the kerf. Position the wedge so that its thickness where it passes the end of the dowel is 2 mm greater than the width of the kerf.

Mark the wedge beyond the end of the dowel, at a distance equal to the clearance depth; mark the other end of the wedge just short of the bottom of the kerf. Cut the wedge at these two marks. Temporarily secure the wedge to the dowel with an elastic band until you have dry-fitted all the other joints and are ready to glue the entire chair back together *(pages 16–17)*.

Replacing a Broken Dowel

1 Drilling a hole for a new dowel. To replace a broken dowel, saw off the broken end and sand it flush with the dowel shoulder. Dimple its centre with an awl, then drill a hole for a new dowel. To drill, clamp the chair part (wrapped in a protective sheet of cork) in a vice, and, with a helper, align a 2 mm bit to enter the wood at the same angle as the old dowel, which in most cases will be parallel to the chair part. Drill a pilot hole with the 2 mm bit, then use a larger bit to drill the hole to the same depth and diameter as the adjoining socket. Bevel a new dowel so that it fits easily into the hole, and trim its extension to three-quarters of the depth of the socket.

To replace a dowel that has broken off inside the end of the dowelled piece, drill it out with progressively larger bits, starting with a 2 mm bit, until the hole is the required size. If the broken dowelled end of a part is simply a tapered extension of that part, it will probably be necessary to replace the whole part.

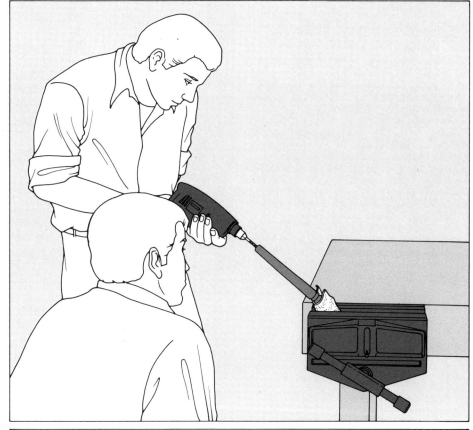

2 Cleaning out the socket. Saw, sand and drill out any broken dowel pieces left in the socket, using the same techniques and drill bits as in Step 1. Position the clamped chair part in the vice so that the socket is perpendicular to the top of the vice, regardless of the angle at which the dowel enters; to check the alignment, hold the joining piece—temporarily without its new dowel—in position against the socketed one.

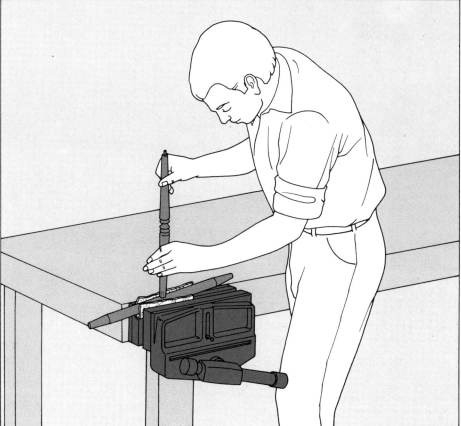

Using Packing Pieces to Enlarge a Loosened Tenon

Applying veneer pieces. To refit a loose mortise and tenon joint, dismantle the joint and cut veneer packing pieces to fit any or all sides of the tenon, depending on where the gaps fall; cut each piece slightly larger than the side of the tenon it will cover. Smear glue on the tenon and packing piece and join the two; place a layer of wax paper over the glued piece and clamp tenon and piece between two wood blocks until the glue dries. When attaching packing pieces to opposite sides of a tenon, glue and clamp both sides as a unit. Remove the cramp and wax paper when the glue has dried, and trim off the excess veneer. Repeat for the tenon's opposite sides if necessary.

Test-fit the tenon in the mortise. If you cannot seat the joint using manual force, pull the tenon out and look for shiny areas where it is too tight. Sand and test again. Repeat as needed.

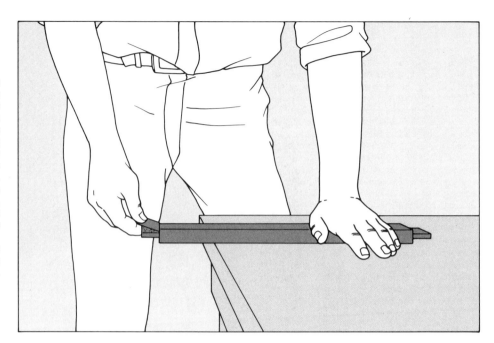

Reassembling a Stick Chair

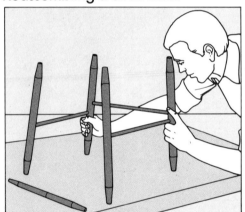

1 **Assembling the legs and seat.** Divide the reassembling of a stick chair into steps, and rehearse them without glue or wedges to prevent any mishaps in the final assembly. If the chair has been completely dismantled, begin by reconstructing the legs and the seat. Make two H-shaped assemblies, each consisting of front and back legs joined by a side stretcher; then join the two Hs with front and back stretchers. Next add the seat, and loop a web cramp round the assembly *(page 11, Step 2, above)* to determine the best way to fit the cramp to the assembly.

Dismantle this portion of the chair and reassemble it in the same order, this time using glue and inserting wedges into any dowels that have been kerfed to receive them. Daub glue into sockets and mortises with a stick, smear it on dowels and tenons, and draw any wedges through a puddle of glue poured on to a scrap of wood. Apply the web cramp and secure it.

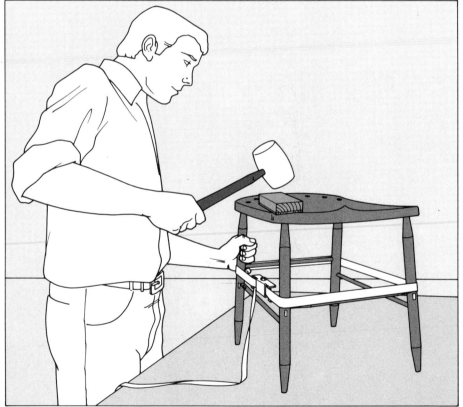

2 **Levelling the chair.** Place the assembled portion of the chair on flat, level surface—such as the top of a desk or a saw table. To check that the surface is absolutely flat, draw a metal straightedge across it twice, the second time perpendicular to the first, and look for gaps beneath the straightedge; there should be no gap greater than 2 mm. Apply glue and, using a wood or cork block to protect the finish, strike the top of the seat over each leg with a wooden mallet, to firm the legs in the sockets. Do the same for the joints between the stretchers and the legs, tightening the web cramp round the legs as you proceed. Let the glue dry.

3 **Attaching the back.** Rehearse the back assembly of the chair without wedges or glue, as in Step 1, fitting the spindles into the sockets. Wrap two web cramps round the back and under the seat so that the cramp winches are behind the back. Then dismantle the back and repeat the procedure with glue, adding dowel wedges, if any. Alternately tighten the winches and tap the top rail with a mallet until all the spindles are set firmly into their sockets.

If the chair has arms, fit the horizontal arm members into the back legs and the vertical arm members into the seat before joining the back assembly to the seat assembly. When you rehearse this final procedure, cut a temporary brace to fit exactly between the two arms near their front ends *(inset)*. Wrap a web cramp under the seat and round the arms, just above where they join the seat, and use the brace to hold the arms apart while you tighten the cramp. For the back of the chair use a pair of web cramps, just as you would for a chair without arms.

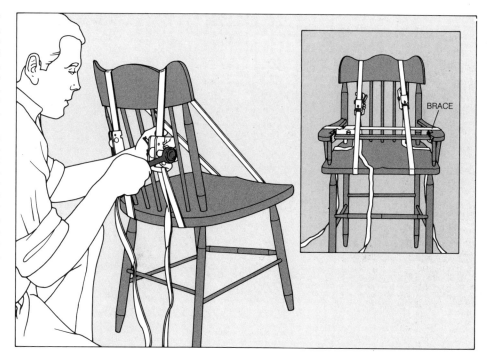

BRACE

Reassembling a Frame Chair

Plotting the stages of reassembly. Rejoin the pieces of a frame chair into subassemblies, and test-fit them without glue or wedges; then repeat this procedure for the final-assembly. Start gluing by joining the back legs with their connecting rails, including the centre splat, if there is one. Wrap one web cramp round this assembly just above the stretcher and another just below the top rail. Alternately tighten the cramps and tap the joints with a mallet until they are firm. Lay the back assembly on a flat surface, and shift the parts until the back lies flat and the two diagonal measurements between the top of one leg and the bottom of the opposite leg are the same. Allow the glue for this subassembly to dry completely before proceeding.

Assemble the front legs and the rails that join them, then join the front and back assemblies with the side stretchers and seat rails, and the arm parts if any. Position a web cramp round the legs of the chair half way between the stretcher and the seat rail. If the chair has arms, put a brace between the ends of the arms, and place a web cramp round the chair at arm level. If the arms consist of horizontal members joined to the vertical stiles with dowels or tenons, wrap another web cramp over the front ends of the arms and under the seat. Place the assembled chair on a flat, level work surface *(Step 2, opposite)*. Tap with a mallet and tighten the cramps until all of the joints are firmly in place and all the legs touch the work surface. Allow the glue to dry before you remove the cramps.

Repairing a Wobbly Table

Although a well-built table should last for many years, ordinary wear and tear frequently takes its toll, especially when the table is used for dining. The joints at the tops of legs are prime targets for trouble. Subjected to severe stress when the legs are kicked or the table is dragged across the floor, they may become loose or even break. Other commonly encountered problems are drop-leaf extensions that sag and sliding extension mechanisms that stick or break. However, many of these flaws can be easily corrected.

Most tables intended for hard use are made with the top attached to a frame: a rectangular substructure of narrow rails that is permanently joined to the tops of the legs. In a few cases, the frame is permanently joined to the top, and the legs are bolted to the frame. Simpler tables have legs attached directly to the underside of the top. These joints may be held together by various means, either alone or in combination: glue, which may fail; tenons or dowels, which may break; plates, screws or bolts, which may loosen. Glue bonds that fail are easily reglued—use the techniques for similar chair joints demonstrated on pages 10–17—but in order to repair the more serious breaks in component parts, you may have to separate the joint and then replace the broken parts. To complete the repair and make it more effective, you can reinforce joints by screwing on either metal corner plates or wooden blocks.

Tables with moving parts that malfunction require other corrective measures. In most cases, you can treat a faulty mechanism on an extension table by cleaning and lubricating the sliding parts, but if parts of the mechanism are broken, bent or missing, it may be necessary to replace them. The manufacturer or a hardware dealer can help you find new parts. For a sagging drop-leaf table, the simplest remedy is usually to attach a wedge, which should be glued to the underside of the drop leaf to take up the slack.

For many of these repairs, it is helpful to have a glue injector so that you can force glue into a confined area. Cramps of one sort or another are also very important tools. You will need G-cramps to close splits, while a sash cramp—a pair of cramping devices mounted on a length of steel bar or pipe—is required to maintain equal pressure on glued frame-to-leg joints. Whenever you use cramps, be sure to pad their jaws with thin pieces of cork or soft timber to avoid marring the surface of the piece you are clamping. Use only the minimum pressure needed to close the glued sections, since too much pressure may force out so much of the glue that you end up with a weak, dry joint.

When the repair involves a broken joint that you intend to fix with a dowelled butt joint *(page 20, Step 1)*, you may want to invest in a dowelling jig to guide the drill, and metal dowel centres; these tools, available at most hardware shops, ensure precise positioning and alignment of the dowel holes. Also helpful are specially grooved dowels, which make stronger glue bonds than smooth dowels.

Getting at a Damaged Substructure

Unscrewing the tabletop. To gain access to a broken joint, turn the table upside down on several layers of cloth or a piece of rug, and remove the top. If the top is held in place with metal shrinkage plates set into a groove in the frame rails *(right)*, remove the screws and plates to detach the top. If the top is attached with screws or bolts to the frame or to corner blocks, remove these fixings *(insets)*. If the repair involves dismantling the joints, use the techniques shown on page 13.

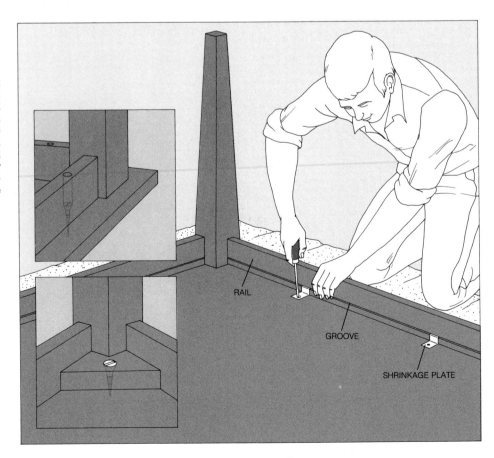

RAIL

GROOVE

SHRINKAGE PLATE

Analysing the Frame-to-Leg Joints

Three types of joint. The most common permanent joint is a mortise and tenon, with a tenon (tongue) on the frame glued into a mortise (slot) on the leg *(below)*. Possible damage includes a split at the mortise or a broken tenon.

Also common is a butt joint that is usually reinforced with dowels glued into matching holes in each of the two pieces *(below, centre)*. These dowels may break; if they do, it will be necessary to drill them out and replace them or to substitute a new joint *(page 20, Step 2)*. Butt joints with dowels are sometimes further reinforced by a corner plate or block *(page 21)*; such a plate or block may also serve to strengthen a butt joint that is made without dowels.

If legs are connected to a frame by mitred joints *(right, below)*, the frame is glued and screwed to the outer face of each leg. The screw heads are sunk below the surface of the frame in counterbored holes filled with plastic plugs. If the screws pull out of a leg, pull or drill the plugs out of the frame, remove the screws, reglue the joint and use new screws of the same length but the next largest diameter. You may have to enlarge the upper parts of the holes counterbored for the screw heads, but do not redrill the lower parts, which are sized to fit the screw threads.

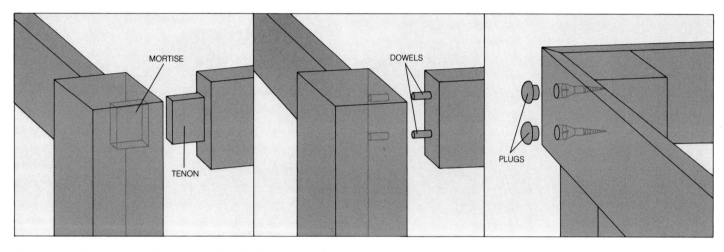

Closing a Split at the Top of a Table Leg

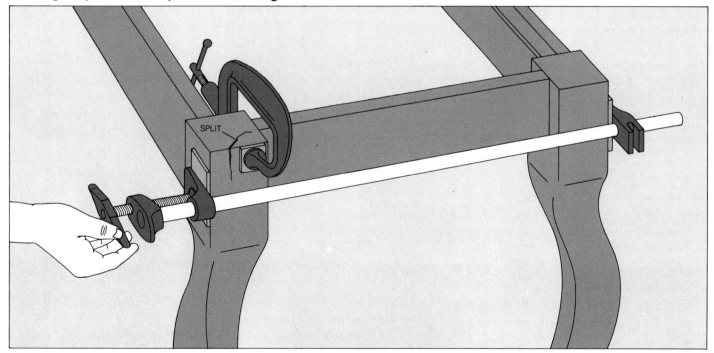

Gluing a split mortise. If a split occurs round the mortise at the top of a leg, inject glue into the split as well as into the hairline opening between the mortise and tenon. Apply pressure with two cramps. First, position a G-cramp across the top of the leg to close the split; then put a pipe or sash cramp across, extending from the outside of one leg to the outside of another, to hold the tenon in the mortise. Allow the glue to dry overnight before removing the cramps.

Repairs for a Broken Tenon

1 Preparing for dowels. When a tenon is badly cracked or broken, convert the joint to a dowelled butt joint; first cut off the tenon and fill in the mortise. Use a fine-tooth crosscut saw—or better, a dovetail saw—to cut off the broken tenon flush with the end of the piece.

With a chisel, clear the mortise of glue and pieces of broken tenon, then measure and cut a wooden plug the same size as the mortise. Coat this plug with glue and tap it into the mortise *(inset)*. When the glue is dry, saw and plane away any wood protruding from the mortise.

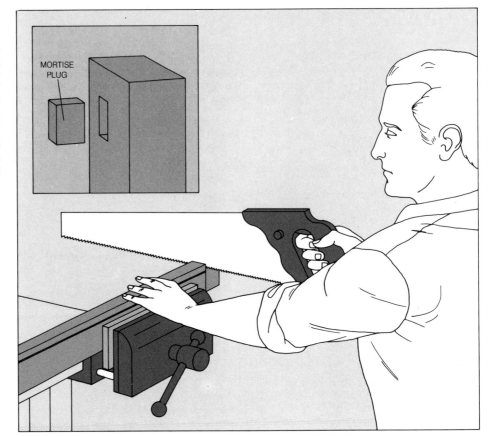

2 Drilling and aligning dowel holes. Mark two pencil lines across the end of the rail about one-third of the way in from the top and the bottom. Centre a dowel jig over one line and drill an 8 mm hole 30 mm into the rail. Repeat at the other line.

Insert the dowel centres into the holes, align the rail carefully in position at the top of the leg, and tap the other end of the rail with a rubber mallet, using enough force to push the tips of the dowel centres against the leg *(inset)* to leave marks. Use these marks to position the jig, and drill two 8 mm holes 30 mm into the leg.

Spread a thin film of glue on the end of the rail and on two 8 mm dowels, each 55 mm long. Tap the dowels into the rail holes with the rubber mallet, then insert them into the leg holes and tap the rail into place. Apply pressure with a sash cramp *(page 19)* until the glue dries.

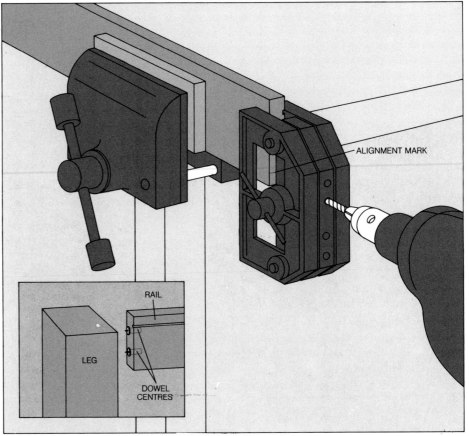

Two Joint Reinforcements

Bracing a corner. To attach a metal corner plate *(below)*, position it across the leg and hold it temporarily in place against the frame by driving one screw on each side. Then drill a pilot hole into the leg through the centre hole in the plate, using a drill bit slightly smaller than the diameter of the screw bolt. Remove the screws holding the plate and remove the plate. Screw the bolt into the leg, gripping the bolt in the centre with pliers and turning it until all threads at the leg end are in the leg. Replace the plate, putting in all the end screws to fasten the plate to the frame. Then put a lock washer and wing nut on to the screw bolt and tighten.

To attach a wood corner brace *(bottom)*, cut a triangular block from hardwood, so that the grain runs from rail to rail, and notch it to fit round the leg. Attach the block to the frame with two No. 8 screws driven through the block and into the leg, perpendicular to the frame, one screw on each side of the leg.

Wedging a drop leaf. To level a drooping drop leaf, mark the outermost point where the supporting slide or gate leg touches the underside of the leaf, scrape away old glue or finish and attach a shallow wedge to the leaf. Cut the wedge from a scrap of hardwood, spread glue on the upper face and push the wedge between the slide and the leaf, adjusting it until the leaf is level. Place a weight on top of the leaf to apply pressure on the wedge until the glue dries.

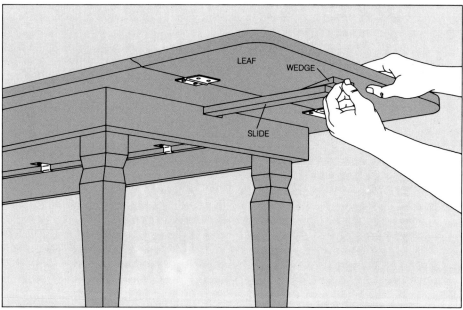

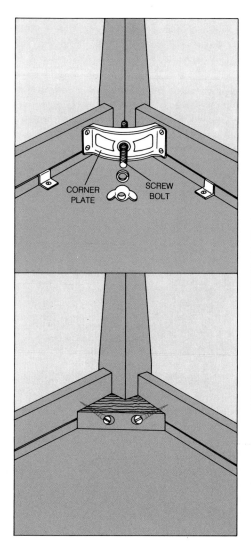

CORNER PLATE   SCREW BOLT

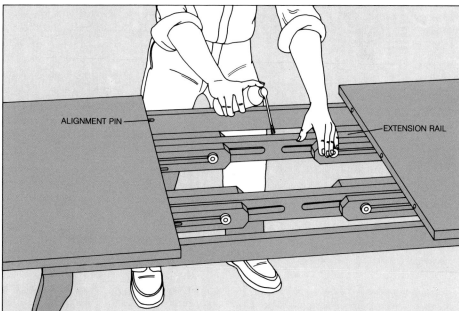

ALIGNMENT PIN   EXTENSION RAIL

Rehabilitating an extension table. To unstick an extension table that refuses to slide on wooden rails, open it until it is fully extended and use a chisel to scrape away deposits of dirt and hardened lubricant from the insides of the rails. Apply fresh lubricant to all accessible moving parts, using either a silicone spray or candlewax. If the extension table has metal rails, use a tapered dowel or stick to clean the sliding parts. Then sprinkle them with powdered graphite.

If a wooden alignment pin on the edge of an extension leaf breaks, drill out the stub and replace it with a hardwood dowel. Glue one end of the dowel into the cleared hole and taper the other end to fit loosely into the alignment hole, sanding to round its end and reduce its girth.

Joints for Beds: Strong but Easy to Take Apart

Although beds appear to be massive and sturdy, they are, in fact, fairly fragile. If you take away the mattress and box springs, all that remains is a rectangle of relatively thin wooden parts, some of them designed to shift slightly to accommodate the changing positions of sleepers, and others designed to separate during removals. Small wonder, then, that these parts can begin to deteriorate.

Some problems with beds have much in common with other furniture ailments—breaks, splintering and warping—and can be repaired as described in Chapter 2. Unique to beds, however, are problems found in or near the side rails (the long pieces that connect the head of a bed to the foot). One particularly vulnerable spot is the joint immediately between the side rails and the bedposts. Here, special hardware—which is used so that the joint can be easily dismantled—often becomes a source of trouble.

Metal fixings for these joints fall into three categories. On many modern beds the fixing comprises a pair of steel plates with interlocking parts; one plate is mounted on the rail, the other on the bedpost. The plates are sometimes set into the wood, sometimes mounted on the surface. Such fixings seldom break, but the wood surrounding them may weaken and split. You can usually correct the problem by repositioning the fixing.

Most older beds have pin-and-hook fixings. Flat metal hooks, much like the hooks on a modern fixing, are set into the end of the side rail and enter a slot on the bedpost, where they latch over metal pins. In some cases, the pins are set directly into the bedpost, and wooden plugs cover their ends. Alternatively, the pins may be set into a wooden block, which is then inserted in a recess cut into the bedpost.

When a pin-and-hook fixing fails, it is usually because the pins have weakened the surrounding wood. If the pins inserted directly into the bedpost pose this problem, the old fixing must usually be abandoned and a new steel-plate fixing substituted. However, if the problem is caused by pins inserted in a wooden block, it is often possible to salvage the fixing by simply replacing the damaged block.

The last type of fixing, found on even older beds and on reproductions, is a long bolt that penetrates the thickness of the bedpost and extends some way into the end of the rail; the bolt is fastened by a nut that is embedded in the rail. The bolt head is sometimes counterbored in the bedpost and covered with a small disc; the nut is locked into place with an application of glue, and the access hole to it—in the side of the rail—is usually filled with a wooden plug. When one of these joints works loose, it is generally either because the bolt head has eaten into the wood or because the nut has broken away from the glue; both conditions are fixable.

As well as their joints with bedposts, side rails have other problem areas. They may bow outwards under the weight of mattress and box springs; or the narrow ledges attached to the side rails, which support slats or box springs, may begin to sag. Mending a sagging ledge is a simple matter of refastening and reinforcing it, but straightening a bulging side rail calls for more elaborate techniques. A general rule to remember, however, is to avoid pulling in the side rails too much; allow 2 mm of space between slat and rail on each side of the bed to ensure a proper fit.

Anatomy of a bed. A bed frame is a rectangle that can be taken apart for moving. The headboard and footboard are permanently fastened to bedposts with glued mortise and tenon joints, but special hardware used at side rail and bedpost joints allow them to be separated. To support box springs or the slats that hold a mattress, there is a narrow wooden strip (the ledge) on the inside of each rail and sometimes also on the inside face of the headboard and of the footboard.

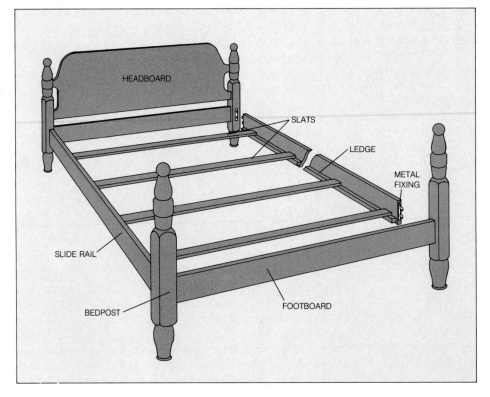

Mending the Detachable Post-and-Rail Joints

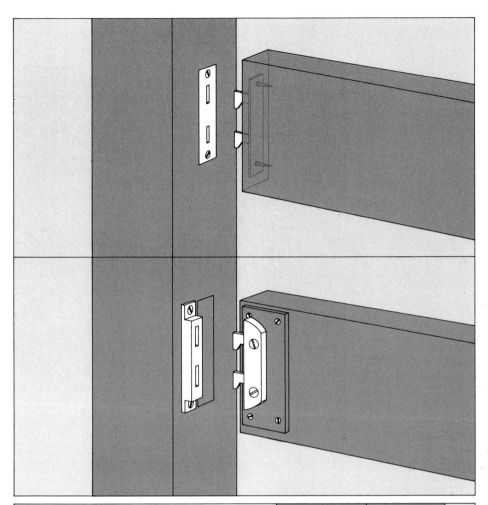

Repositioning a steel-plate fixing. Dismantle a worn interlocking steel-plate joint *(left)* and remove the fixing from the bedpost and the rail. Repair the damaged wood if possible; you can strengthen the end of the rail with a piece of plywood, glued and screwed to the inside. Then remount the fixing parts in new positions on both the bedpost and the rail. To establish these positions, ask a helper to align the bedpost and rail while you hold the closed fixing against them, marking the new positions. Separate bedpost and rail, and screw the fixing parts in place.

If the existing fixing parts are of the recessed type, replace them with a surface-mounted fixing *(centre, left)*. Fill in the old mortises with blocks of wood *(page 20, Step 1)*.

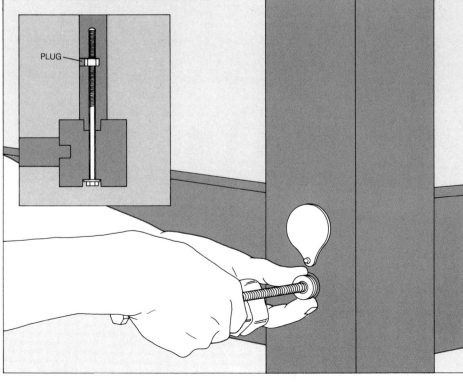

Tightening old-fashioned bolt joints. To tighten a bolt head that has eaten into the wood, remove the bolt and add one or two washers, then put the bolt back in its hole. If the nut inside the rail spins, so that the bolt cannot be tightened, drill or chisel out the wooden plug that conceals the access hole. Remove the loose nut, clean the old glue from the hole, spread epoxy glue round the nut and replace it in the hole. Cut a new plug slightly longer than the access hole. Apply glue, and hammer the plug into place until its end hits the edge of the nut. Trim off any part of the plug that protrudes, and refinish the area.

Repairing a pin-and-hook fixing. To replace a worn wooden block, chisel out the old block and clean the hole in which it rested. Cut a new block to fit the hole, and mark positions for the pins by holding the block against the side of the metal hooks and tracing their outline on the block. Make a slot wide enough and deep enough for entry of the hooks, either by drilling a row of holes the length of the slot and clearing them with a chisel or by sawing a channel the length of the block. Then drill holes for the pins, put the pins in the block, and glue and clamp the block into the hole in the bedpost.

If the pins are damaged, cut new ones from bolts of the same diameter.

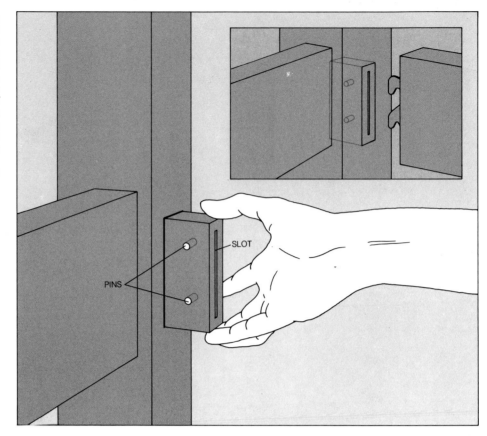

Strengthening a Loose or Sagging Slat Ledge

Adding reinforcement. Unscrew the ledge and gently prise it away from the rail with an old wood chisel, cleaning old glue from both ledge and rail. Fill in the existing screw holes in the ledge and rail with wood filler, then mark off and drill pilot holes for new screws along the ledge and rail, using the distance between existing holes as a guide. Reattach the ledge to the rail, in the same position as before, with glue and screws. Glue and screw several wooden blocks against the underside of the ledge for added support, placing the blocks about 50 cm apart.

If the ledge is badly warped or if it cracks while you are removing it, replace it with a strip of hardwood cut to the same length and width. Prepare the strip as described above, reinforcing it with wooden blocks if desired.

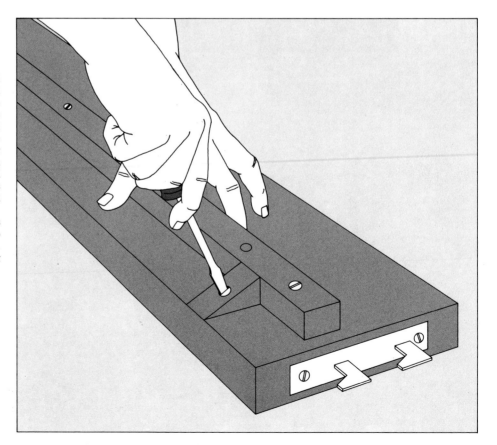

Tying in a Bulging Rail

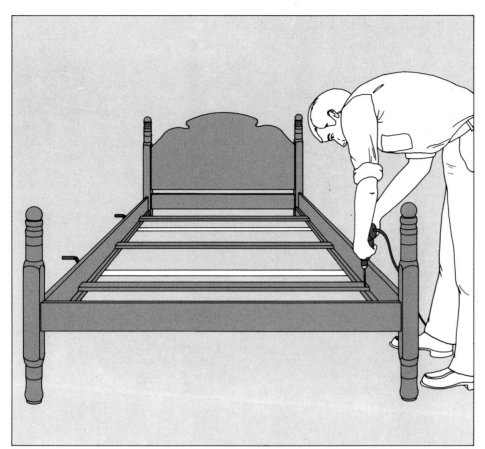

Correcting slight warps. Using two sash cramps, pull the side rail back into line. Space three slats evenly along the length of the rails, making sure that each end of each slat forms a right angle with the rail. Drill a 5 mm hole through both ends of each slat and into the ledge below, leaving a 2 mm gap between the slat ends and the inside face of the rail. Countersink the holes, then insert 5 mm diameter countersinking bolts in the holes, add nuts and tighten. Place the rest of the slats on the ledges but do not fasten them.

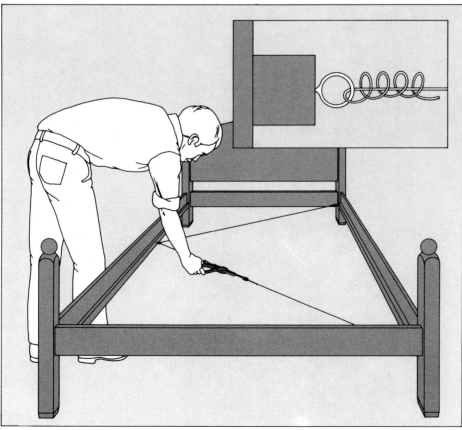

Using a turnbuckle for a bad bulge. Fasten screw eyes to both bedposts on the side opposite the bowed rail, placing the screw eyes at the height of the ledge. Attach a third screw eye to the ledge at the centre of the bowed side rail; the screw eye should be long enough to penetrate the ledge and half the thickness of the side rail. Connect the three screw eyes with two lengths of heavy picture wire, fastened at the bedposts by looping and twisting *(inset)* and joined with a turnbuckle that can be adjusted with a pair of pliers to pull the bulging rail straight.

If the other side rail is also bowed, repeat the process on the opposite side.

Coming to the Rescue of Flawed Cabinets

Though cabinets come in many shapes and are constructed with a variety of joints, they do have some basic characteristics in common. Bureaux, vanities, armoires, desks and china cabinets are all box-like structures *(below)* that are fitted with doors, drawers or both. Since the cabinets are not built to support weight, the stresses on them are different from those on chairs or beds. It is usually the moving parts that wear out or break.

When drawers stick or doors do not latch, look for simple remedies first. A loose nail may be catching on a drawer guide, and you will simply need to drive it back in. Door problems can often be traced to a loose hinge. Tighten the hinge screws. If the screw holes are enlarged, plug them and redrill for the screws.

Some more serious problems, such as worn-out drawer guides, can be remedied without dismantling the whole structure. Most older cabinets are constructed with

wooden guides; frequently the bottoms of the drawer sides serve as runners. Even if these pieces have been kept waxed, the rubbing wood surfaces can wear down or become rutted over a long period of time. Professional joiners restore the drawer sides by reshoeing the drawer—replacing the worn edges with new wood.

A drawer that is coming apart at the joints calls for some judgment in its repair. If all of the joints are loose, knock the whole drawer apart *(opposite page)* and reglue. But if only one joint has worked free, it is usually easier to force glue in and then clamp it together, leaving the rest of the drawer intact. Open up the sound joints of a drawer only if you must; the force needed to separate a joint invites further damage to the drawer.

If the problems of an ill-fitting door cannot be traced to loose hinge screws, the solution may lie in repositioning the hinges—"throwing the hinges", in the par-

lance of professionals. A door warp can sometimes be straightened *(page 37)*, but many cabinet-makers prefer to disguise it by moving the door hinges slightly. With this technique, you may be able to bring the protruding corners of a warped door back into line with the frame. With a similar technique *(page 29)*, you can tilt a sagging door so that it does not bump against the cabinet frame. Trim a door edge only as a last resort—for example, when problems of fit are caused by a distortion of the cabinet's basic frame.

If a cabinet castor is broken or bent, it should be replaced immediately; a cabinet that is not level is subject to stresses it was not built to withstand, and therefore will be more susceptible to joint failure. Replacements are available in many sizes and designs. You may need to increase the size of castor mountings *(page 31)*, but select new castors of a style that complements the design of your cabinet.

Anatomy of a cabinet carcass. The carcass of a typical cabinet is composed of its top, sides and base—either assembled individually on to a frame, or joined to form an interlinked structure, as shown on the right. Most sections are jointed and glued. Other parts are screwed into place. In the drawing, two top rails with triangular fillets provide an anchor for screws driven up into a solid-wood top.

The back of the cabinet, often made from several pieces of solid timber, locates in grooves or rebates in the top, bottom and sides. The cabinet may be raised off the floor on a separate frame known as a plinth, or it may have legs screwed on to the underside.

From the front, most cabinets are enclosed by doors or drawers. Doors are hinged to the end panels and may be flush with or cover the front edges of the panels. In a cabinet containing drawers, the bottom one rests on the base, while the others are supported by drawer rails extending across the front. The runners which enable the drawers to slide in and out are usually attached to the sides of the cabinet, but some are fixed to the drawers themselves *(page 28)*.

Short drawers are separated by an upright post tenoned between the rails and they slide on runners fixed to the centre as well as the sides. A drawer guide located above the central runners prevents the drawers from slipping sideways. Most types of drawer cabinet are provided with stops—small wooden blocks glued to the base and rails—and there are usually dustboards fitted between the drawers.

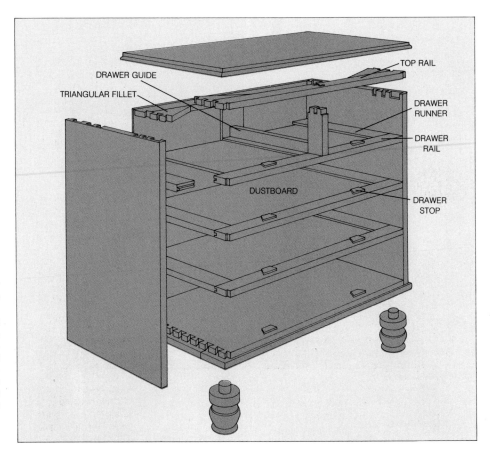

DRAWER GUIDE
TRIANGULAR FILLET
TOP RAIL
DRAWER RUNNER
DRAWER RAIL
DUSTBOARD
DRAWER STOP

Gluing a Drawer Back Together

1 Knocking a drawer apart. To separate a loose dovetail joint, prop a block of wood in the corner of the drawer and strike it with a mallet or hammer. If the joint is very loose, a blow with your hand may suffice. Repeat at the other corners.

Scrape the joint edges with a chisel, cleaning away any dirt and deposits of old glue. Remove the drawer handles to facilitate clamping.

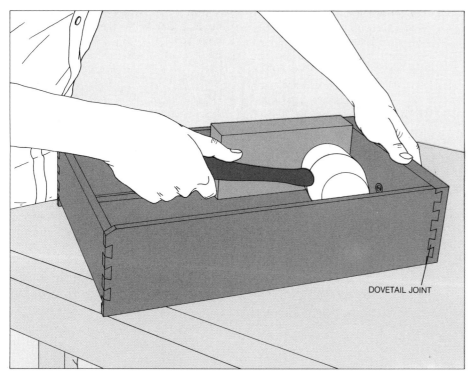

DOVETAIL JOINT

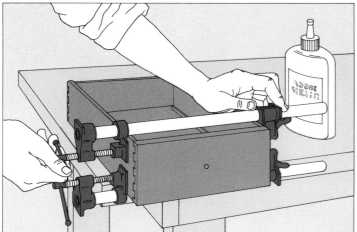

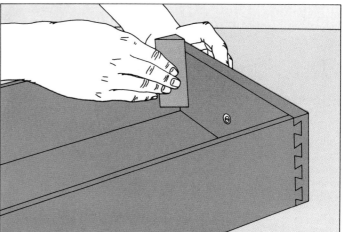

2 Regluing the joints. Apply glue to all joining surfaces and reassemble the drawer. Attach sash cramps on the top and the bottom, 6 mm behind the dovetails that join the sides and front of the drawer. Then rest the drawer on its front, and place a third sash cramp across the back. Measure immediately to make sure the drawer is square: diagonal measurements between opposite corners must be equal. Shift the cramps, if necessary, to square the drawer.

3 Adding glue blocks. To reinforce the joints of the drawer, cut four triangular blocks of wood as long as the drawer is deep, then glue one of them inside each corner. To set a glue block firmly without using a cramp, spread an even coat of glue on two faces of the block and on the surfaces inside the corner. Press the block in place, and rub it up and down four or five times, until the glue begins to resist movement. The rubbing motion should cover only about 6 mm.

Easy Remedies for Drawers that Stick

Flipping a sagging drawer bottom. Using pincers to grasp the nail heads, pull the pins that fasten a warped bottom to the lower edge of the drawer back. Slide the bottom out of the grooves in the sides. You may need a chisel to prise off glue blocks that join the bottom to the drawer front or sides. If the bottom also fits into a groove in the back, the drawer will have to be dismantled.

Turn the bottom over and reassemble the drawer. If the bottom is split and cannot be mended *(page 47)*, replace it with a new piece of thin plywood or hardboard.

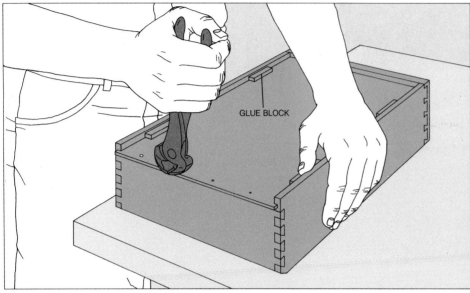

GLUE BLOCK

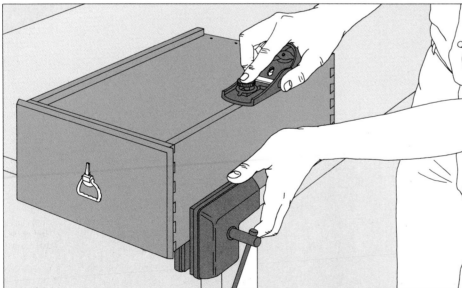

Reshoeing a drawer. If drawer sides that slide along wooden runners are so worn that the drawer does not move smoothly, plane the worn edges and rebuild them. Secure the drawer—or a side if the drawer is dismantled—upside down in a woodworking vice, then plane each worn edge to make it straight. Edges usually wear more at the front than at the back; to restore evenness, you rarely need to remove more than 3 mm of wood. If you are working on an assembled drawer and cannot plane to the ends of the edges, finish these areas with a chisel.

Cut strips of hardwood to the length and width of each side. Glue both strips in position, using straight-edged boards and large G-cramps to secure them until the glue has dried. Then test-fit the drawer and, if necessary, plane or sand the new strips so that the drawer runs smoothly. Rub candlewax along the runners and the bottom edges of the drawer sides.

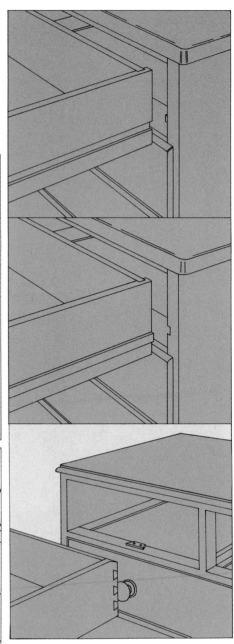

Replacing wooden drawer runners. Though there are several designs, most drawer runners made of wood can easily be replaced if the parts are worn. The drawer sides in the top drawing are grooved to fit over runners attached to the cabinet carcass. In the centre, the configuration is reversed: runners attached to the drawer sides slide in grooves in the carcass. In the third design, directly above, there are no grooves, and the bottom edges of the drawer sides slide on runners attached to the carcass. To replace a runner, remove it, trace its outline, then cut and install a duplicate. Use glue and screws to attach it.

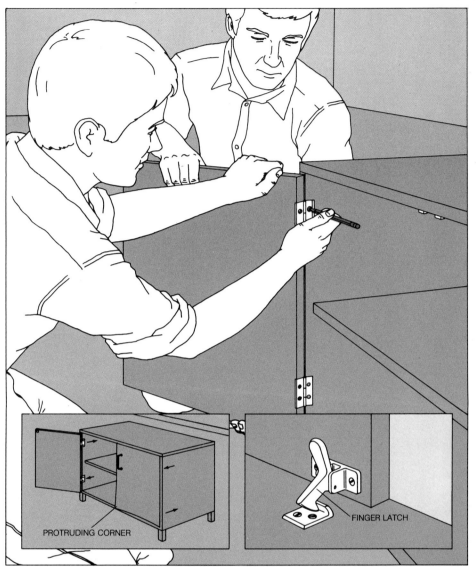

Effective Fixes for Faulty Cabinet Doors

Throwing the hinges. If one corner on the unhinged side of a cabinet door protrudes when the door is closed, the drawer is probably warped. On a flush cabinet door hung with butt hinges, you can remedy this displacement with a process known as throwing the hinges. Unscrew the hinge leaves from the cabinet, plug the screw holes with glue and dowels and, while a helper holds the door in position, mark new screw holes to reposition the loose hinge leaves laterally.

To determine how much and in which direction to reposition the hinges, measure the displacement at the protruding corner. You can compensate somewhat by moving just one hinge a distance equal to the amount of the displacement, but it is more effective to divide this amount equally between both hinges. In doing this, move the hinge that is directly opposite the protruding corner inwards on the cabinet carcass, then move the other hinge outwards an equal distance.

If there is one warped door in a set of double doors that meet at the centre, divide the displacement equally among all four hinges *(inset, far left)*. To determine which direction to move each hinge, follow the directions above for the door that is warped, but reverse the directions on the unwarped door. If both doors are warped, deal with each one individually.

On any double door, instead of moving hinges, you can install a finger latch *(inset, left)* inside the cabinet to secure the warped corner.

PROTRUDING CORNER

FINGER LATCH

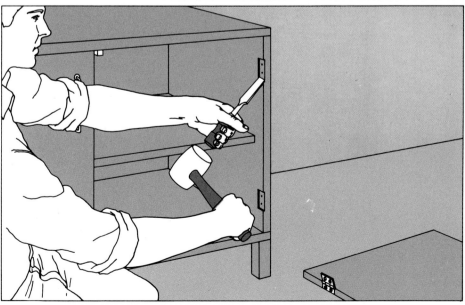

Providing clearance for a sticking edge. If the unhinged edge of a cabinet door sticks as it closes—jamming either just below the top corner or along the bottom edge—make sure that the screws in the top hinge are tight. If they are, unscrew the hinge leaves attached to the cabinet and remove the door. Check the hinges to see if they are worn; if so, replace them. You will have to trim the old housings with a mallet and chisel to accommodate the new housing. Slightly worn hinges, or those that cannot be replaced easily, can be swapped top for bottom. Another possible source of the sticking may be pieces of veneer that have been packed incompetently into the housing. Remove them with a mallet and chisel and fit new pieces of veneer of the correct thickness. If neither of those methods works, the problem is probably due to a twisted cabinet frame. Check that the cabinet is standing evenly. Alternatively, it may be necessary to plane down the edges of the door *(overleaf)*.

Planing a door edge that sticks. After marking the spots that stick and removing the door from the cabinet, secure the door in a woodworking vice. On a rebated door, as shown, use a shoulder plane or a block plane to trim the inside lip. On a flush door, use a block plane to bevel the edge, being careful not to remove any more wood than is necessary where the edge meets the outside face of the door; if you shave away excess wood here, you will only increase the gap between the closed door and the cabinet's front frame.

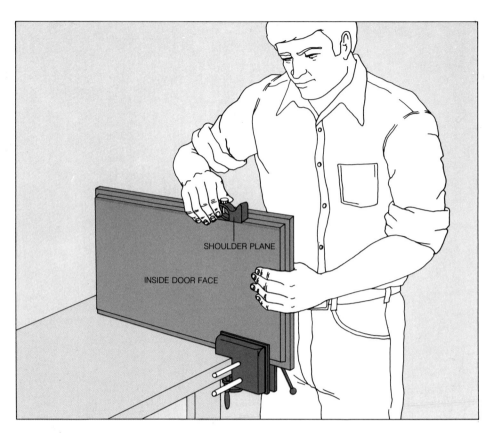

Analysing Castor Troubles

Two basic designs. The commonly encountered types of castor differ primarily in the way they are attached to furniture. Fixed-plate castors are screwed directly on to the underside of the piece they support; they are quite strong and rarely require repair. They cannot, however, be mounted on small areas, such as the bottoms of narrow legs. Here, stem castors are used. The roller of a stem castor is attached to a shaft that fits into a matching sleeve; the sleeve fits into a hole in the end of the leg. Though this design is more versatile, it is also more vulnerable to problems; the shaft may become loose in its sleeve, or the sleeve loose in its socket.

If the furniture design allows it, replace a faulty stem castor with a fixed-plate castor. Otherwise, repair it with the technique shown opposite. Both styles are available in various sizes, either with a wheel or ball-shaped roller.

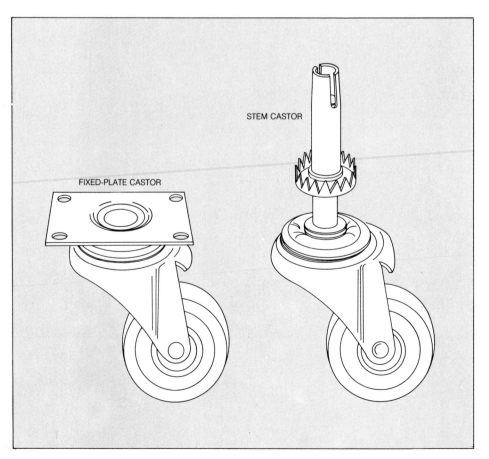

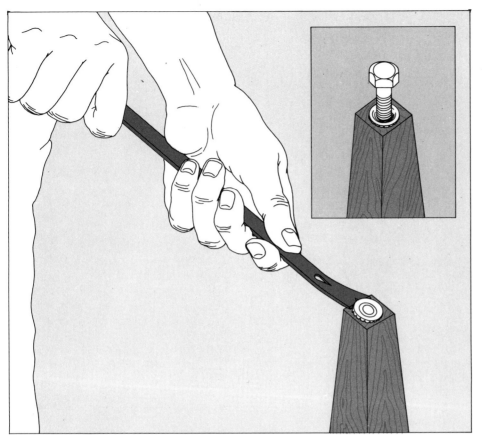

Replacing a Loose Stem Castor

1 **Removing the stem system.** After pulling out the roller and the shaft, try to work the clawed end of a small wrecking bar under the serrated flange of the sleeve so that you can prise the sleeve out of its hole. If this fails, tap a threaded bolt of about the same diameter as the sleeve into the opening *(inset)*, just until it is wedged tight. Grip the bolt with pliers, and work the sleeve loose and out of its socket.

Use a drill to enlarge the old hole to fit the next largest size of stem castor. Wrap tape round the bit to mark the depth of the socket before drilling, and use a dowelling jig *(page 20)* to centre the drill bit. If the leg is too small for you to drill a larger hole, plug the old hole with a glued wooden dowel, and drill a hole for a stem castor a size smaller than the old one.

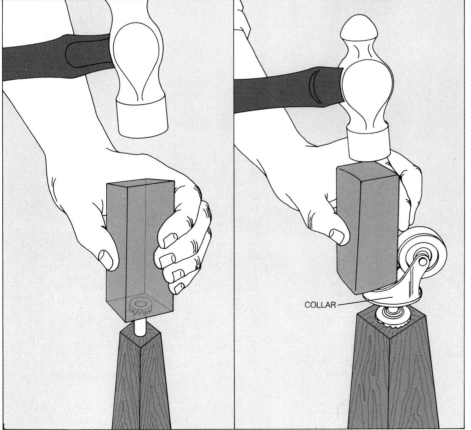

COLLAR

2 **Installing a new stem castor.** Use a hammer and a wooden block to tap the stem sleeve into its hole until the serrated flange bites into the wood *(far left)*. Push the stem shaft into its sleeve; if necessary, tap lightly on a wooden block held against the stem collar just above the roller *(left)* to force the stem into the sleeve. Repeat Steps 1 and 2 to put matching castors on the other legs.

2

Surgery for Breaks and Gouges

A patch of veneer. In the delicate surgery required to patch a wounded veneer surface, a trimming knife is used to cut out a diamond shape, removing the damaged section and exposing the underlying wood. The edges of the cut-out section are bevelled inwards to accept a similarly bevelled patch of matching veneer. Both the bevelled edges and the diamond shape hide the lines of the cut. The patch is glued in place and pressed down with a roller; a light sanding brings it flush with the surrounding surface.

Furniture with broken parts can often be put back together again so that it looks almost as good as new; indeed, given space-age glues, modern power tools and sufficient care, the results can be even better than new. Solid-wood surfaces and veneers can be inconspicuously patched; broken chair legs can be spliced and pegged so that the breaks do not show; rush seats can be rewrapped and cane seats rewoven.

Many of the techniques for doing these repairs have changed little through the ages. The ancient Egyptians knew how to salvage their valuable and elaborately cut veneered surfaces by regluing them, as is revealed by objects discovered in the tombs of the Pharaohs. And the practice of turning new chair rungs on a lathe had become common by the middle of the 17th century.

People have, in fact, been enormously resourceful and inventive in the ways they have devised to patch furniture—not always, however, with aesthetically pleasing results. In the 17th and 18th centuries, for example, it was not uncommon to mend the split wood of a chair seat by nailing crude tin patches over the splintered areas. Cracks running along the grain of the wood were sometimes simply stitched together with leather laces woven through holes that had been drilled on either side of the break. In one classic instance of improvisational mending, the three legs of a delicate 1750 candlestand were refastened to the central column by means of baling wire.

However, in many cases furniture repairs were made with amazing finesse and skill. Each year the Conservation Analytical Laboratory of the Smithsonian Institution in Washington, D.C., examines up to 100 pieces of furniture acquired for its collections. Technicians use chemical analyses and infra-red and ultraviolet light, among other things, to establish the date and origin of each piece. In addition, all repairs that have been carried out are carefully recorded. On a valuable early 19th-century side chair, for instance, there may be as many as half a dozen repairs, ranging from the simple regluing of a chip to the painstaking replacement of an elaborate finial. Some of these repairs are so finely done that only the trained eye of a professional furniture restorer can spot them. It often takes an expert's knowledge of furniture design and wood-repair techniques to spot a skilfully duplicated leg that has been set among three original ones.

As a rule, museums, connoisseurs and collectors express strong disapproval of any repairs to fine furniture that remove or alter original elements of the piece. When it comes to everyday home furnishings, however, you can employ any number of tried and true repair techniques. It is only good sense to patch, mend or replace broken pieces as skilfully as possible, since it is by measures such as these that you restore furniture to usefulness and extend its value and service for many years.

Home Remedies for Bent and Bruised Wood

Furniture made of solid wood, for all its sturdiness, sometimes seems as prone to damage as a new car in a busy parking area. It gets dented, gouged, scratched and chipped and, in addition, it may even be affected by the atmosphere—moisture present in the air can penetrate the wood and cause it to warp.

If the piece is very old and the injuries are only minor, they are often left alone—in an antique, slight nicks and bends can be desirable signs of age and character. However, greater damage should usually be repaired, using a cure that is appropriate to the ailment.

Dents and warps can be steamed back into shape, and nicks and gouges treated according to the finish and the value of the furniture—the more precious the piece, the more painstaking the remedy should be; if the item is particularly valuable, it may be best to seek the advice of a professional. Whatever corrective measure is taken, the result should always be a piece at least as attractive and functional as before the damage occurred.

The simplest repair for slight scratches or chips in solid wood is the wax or shellac stick treatment, also used in repairing a damaged finish (page 73). If the scratch or chip is wide but not deeper than 6 mm, a quick and inexpensive repair can be made with stopper or wood filler. It dries rapidly, comes in tints to match many woods and stains, and can be stained—although not always successfully. It should always be tested with the stain or finish that will be used over it.

A third, more elaborate remedy for a scratch or gouge calls for enlarging the injured area and grafting in a new piece of wood. Shaping this graft has some steps in common with the shaping required for inserting a veneer patch (pages 40–41). When you select the wood, check its age and its colour—as well as the pattern, shading and texture of the grain, which should be as near a match as possible with the wood of the furniture. Also test the planned finish on a scrap of the patching wood before making a final decision.

Most patches will have to be cut by hand to fit, but for damaged areas less than 12 mm in width, you can save yourself time by using a plug cutter—a simple attachment that can be used with most electric drills—to make a plug that matches the grain of the original workpiece.

For any of these spot repairs, begin by thoroughly cleaning the area of the damage, then sand it with very fine sandpaper to remove the existing finish. To flatten a warped surface, however, you may have to remove the finish from the entire surface to get at the root of the trouble; you may also have to take the affected part off its frame. Warping usually occurs when one side of a board is finished and the other side is not, or when the board has not been securely fastened to its understructure. Moisture which penetrates the unfinished side of the board, can cause the edges of the finished side to curl.

Warping can sometimes be corrected if you place the warped board, concave side up and finish removed, on a flat surface, and iron it with an ordinary laundry iron over a damp cloth until the warp relaxes. Alternatively, wait for a sunny day and then place the board, concave side down, on a freshly watered lawn. Within a day, or perhaps two—weights speed the process—the warp should be gone. In either case, the board should be refastened to its support immediately and refinished when the wood is completely dry.

For more severe warping you may have to resort to more involved techniques. If moisture and heat do not eliminate the warp, you will have to cut shallow slots in the underside of the board and attach hardwood battens across the slots to hold down the board's errant edges.

Removing a Dent with Water or Steam

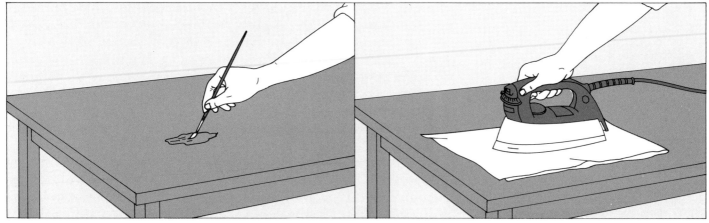

Raising wood fibres. Use an artist's brush or a fingertip to apply warm water to the crushed wood fibres (above, left), taking care not to moisten the surrounding area. On softwoods, repeat the applications of water until the fibres rise; on hardwoods, apply water, then place a wet cloth over the dent and hold an iron set at low heat against it for 15 seconds. Check the dent and repeat the process if necessary. If the dent does not respond, prick it with a pin to channel steam into the fibres. Try to raise the crushed fibres slightly above the surrounding surface.

For tiny dents or dents close to glued joints that might be loosened by steam, isolate the steaming process. Cover only the affected area with a folded wet cloth, then place a bottle cap upside down on the cloth over the dent and hold the iron against the rim of the cap.

Allow the raised fibres to dry thoroughly. Then sand the area and refinish it, using the techniques described in Chapter 3.

A Patch for a Solid Wood Surface

1 Routing the surface. Join four pieces of wood to form a jig for a router, outlining the area to be patched. Clamp the jig in place—directly, as shown here, or, if the jig is not near the furniture edges, by clamping two boards on top of the jig. The jig must be positioned over the damaged area so that its sides will lie at an angle of about 45 degrees to the grain of the wood. The jig should be just large enough to allow the router to take out the damaged wood, leaving the undamaged wood alone. Rout the surface to the depth of the damage, and square off the corners with a chisel. If you do not have a router, cut the damaged area with a mallet and chisel. Make sure that the edges of the recess are vertical and that the bottom is flat.

2 Applying the patch. Tape paper over the cut-out recess and trace the shape of the edges. Cut out this shape to make a pattern for the patch, and tape it to the patching wood, aligning the pattern so that the grain of the patch matches the grain surrounding the recess. Cut the patch slightly larger than the pattern.

With sandpaper or a plane, bevel the edges of the patch slightly inwards *(inset)*, testing it frequently for fit. When it fits snugly, but lies slightly above the surrounding surface, apply PVA and fasten the patch into the recess. Cover it with brown wrapping paper or wax paper; weight it or clamp it overnight. Then sand it level with the surrounding surface, and refinish.

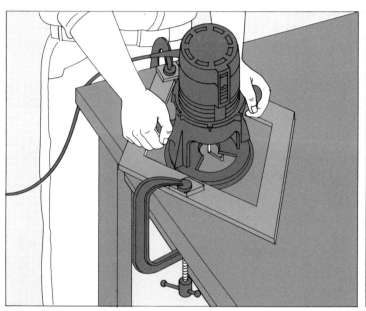

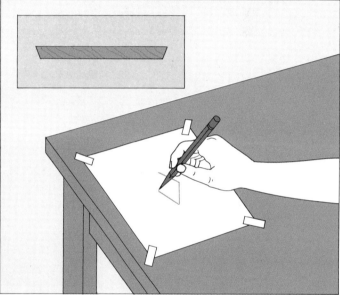

Wood Filler to Repair Edges

Filling in chipped edges. Rub candlewax or wax crayon on a scrap of wood that is long enough to span the area of edge damage, and clamp the waxed surface against the furniture edge, using edge cramps as shown, or cramps with wood wedges for the same effect. (The wax will prevent wood filler from sticking to the scrap wood.)

With a spatula or a putty knife, force wood filler into the damaged area. If it is deeper or longer than 6 mm, build up the filler in layers, giving each coat time to dry. Overfill the depression slightly, to compensate for shrinkage. When the filler has dried, remove the scrap wood, and sand the filler flush with the surface. Apply stain, if it is needed, then a sealer such as a coat of thinned varnish. Complete the repair with painted-on graining if necessary *(page 75)*.

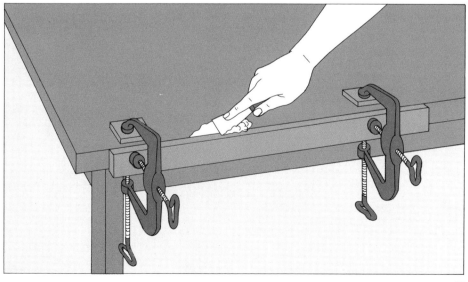

Moulding a missing corner. Using stopper or wood filler and the same basic repair technique as for chipped edges *(page 35)*, rebuild a missing corner by constructing a three-sided mould *(inset)*. If a leg joins the piece of furniture near the corner, leave space for it. Wax all three sides of the mould that will touch the filler. Clamp the mould to the furniture, then fill in the damage.

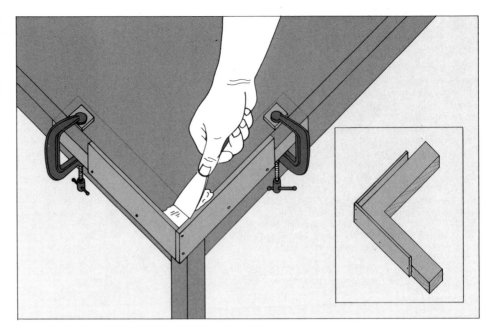

Reconstructing a Broken Corner with a Wooden Block

1 Preparing the corner piece. Using a router or a mallet and chisel, prepare a flat surface for the new corner by clearing away all the damaged wood on the existing corner. Then cut a wood patch to fit against the newly smoothed face of the corner, making this patch about 18 mm longer and 1 mm thicker than needed. Set the patch into place, and slide it backwards and forwards until the grains of the patch and of the furniture are in the best alignment. Mark the patch in this position, then cut it down to size, leaving about 1 mm of overhang at the sides.

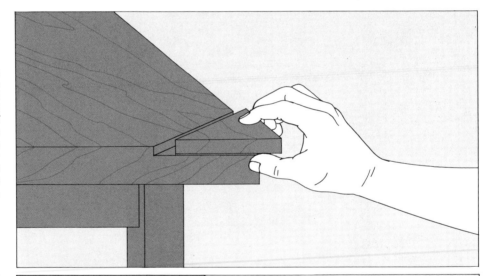

2 Clamping the corner. Apply glue to the horizontal and the vertical surfaces of the cleared corner, and set the corner patch in place. Slide a G-cramp over the patch, and cock the cramp slightly off the vertical until the swivel head on top of the screw is 3 mm closer to the inner face of the patch than the top of the cramp is. In this position, pressure will be inwards as well as downwards. Tighten the cramp.

If the broken corner extends completely through the furniture, from top surface to bottom, construct a three-sided brace like the mould shown at the top, coat it with wax or cover it with wax paper so glue will not adhere to it, then clamp it against the furniture. Wedge the new corner, coated with glue, into the brace. Alternatively, use two special edge cramps *(page 35)* to hold the new corner in place, but check periodically to make sure the corner has not slipped.

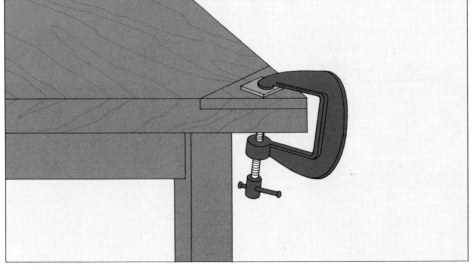

Saw Kerfs for a Severe Warp

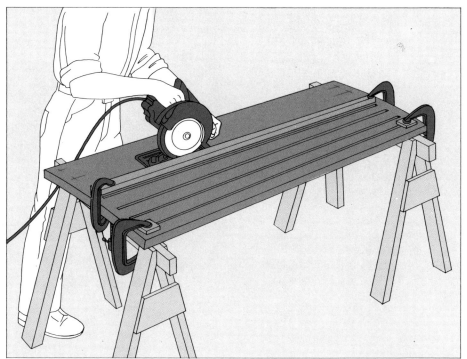

1 Kerfing the underside. When moisture alone does not straighten a warped surface, such as the table leaf shown here, clamp it bottom up against saw-horses as a worktable, and use a circular saw to make shallow, evenly spaced cuts, called kerfs, along its grain, stopping 25 mm short of the ends. To guide the saw, clamp a straightedge against the warped wood, and set the depth of the saw blade to half the thickness of the wood. Start with four kerfs, spaced at even intervals across the warped surface. If the warp persists, make additional kerfs, keeping them evenly spaced, but do not cut them any closer together than 50 mm. Caution: do not saw kerfs in fine antique furniture; they may cause damage and reduce the value of the piece.

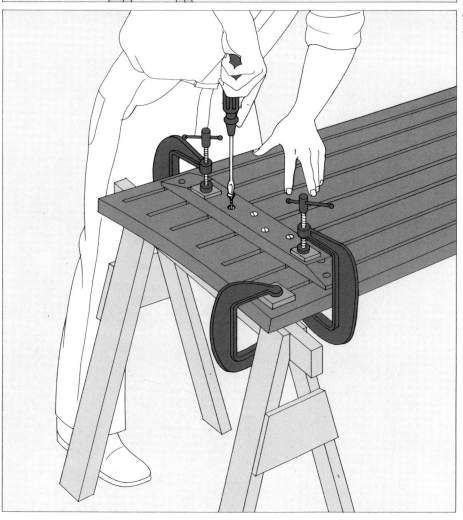

2 Attaching battens. If kerfing alone does not eliminate the warp, cut battens or cleats, preferably out of oak or other hardwood, 20 mm thick, 40 mm wide and as long as the warped board is wide. Bevel the ends to make them less conspicuous and clamp the battens to the underside of the board about 200 mm in from the ends, or in locations where they will not interfere with the legs or frame of the furniture. Drill pilot holes about 150 mm apart for screws that will penetrate the board to within 6 mm of its top surface; by making the holes slightly oval in shape—easily done by overlapping two adjacent drill holes—you can allow for expansion and contraction in the wood round the screws. Position the holes to fall between kerfs. Drive the first screws where the batten touches the high point of the warp. Then tighten the cramps on the batten slightly, and drive screws successively closer to the low edges of the warp. Continue in this fashion until all the screws are in place. Seal and finish the bottom of the board, and refasten it to the furniture.

Invisible Mending for Veneer

The richly coloured, beautifully grained surface of a fine piece of furniture is likely to be a veneer—a thin layer of decorative wood glued over a core of less expensive wood or manufactured board. Sliced from selected logs, veneers are cut with the grain; varied patterns are achieved by cutting across the growth rings at different angles. In modern furniture manufacture, veneer is sometimes peeled from a spinning log in a continuous sheet, the wood unrolling much as paper towels unwind off a kitchen roll.

The unique patterning of veneered surfaces makes them well worth repairing, especially on older pieces that have veneers matched and finished with great care. Fortunately, even severe damage, if limited to small areas, can be repaired with scarcely a trace.

On old veneers the most common problem is blistering, or lifting, caused by the failure of the original animal glue (so called because it was derived from various animals). Because this glue softens when heated, you may be able to repair the veneer by melting the glue with a warm iron and pressing the veneer back in place. Protect the surface from the iron with a damp dish cloth. When the area has been flattened, weight it with heavy books for several hours, until the glue sets. If the glue still fails to adhere, you will have to cut through the veneer, scrape out the old glue and apply fresh adhesive, as shown opposite. Modern glues seldom fail, but surface chips, gouges and burns are sustained by new and old veneers. They are more difficult to repair, requiring patching.

To cut the bevelled edges of a veneer patch, you will need a trimming knife that has a replaceable narrow, slanted blade and pointed tip, of the type craftsmen and artists use. Such a trimming knife is also used for the delicate task of scraping away dried glue and paint in certain areas. Other special items that are useful purchases are a tool with a thin, flexible blade, such as an artist's palette knife, for lifting up veneer flaps; a wallpaper-seam roller or print roller for flattening a reglued blister or a new patch; and a glue injector, a sort of enlarged hypodermic needle, for applying glue in constricted areas.

Craft stores usually have samples of available veneers, so you can select one to match your furniture. Veneer is sold in leaves 150 to 300 mm wide or wider; buy a piece large enough to allow some leeway in selecting the area round the damage that must be cut away to accept the patch.

Although veneers come in many thicknesses, some paper thin, those most commonly found on furniture are usually less than 1 mm thick. On older furniture, they are frequently thicker, 1.5 mm or more; indeed, on a fine antique the veneer may be 3 mm thick. It is best to use a patch of the thickest available veneer, then sand it down to the level of the surrounding surface. In some cases, the existing veneer may be so thick that you will have to glue more than one layer of new veneer to the underlying surface to bring the patch to the correct height. The underlayers need not match the surrounding grain.

Plastic laminates—used on less expensive furniture that is subject to heavy use—are usually attached to the underlying surface with fast-drying contact adhesive. Repair a lifted edge by scraping the old adhesive from both surfaces, spreading new contact adhesive according to the manufacturer's instructions, and pressing the laminate back in place; no clamping is required. Chipped laminate can be repaired the same way if the chip is saved. If the chip is lost, fill the damaged area with filler as shown on page 35.

Getting Rid of a Blister

1 Cutting through the veneer. If the veneer has risen to create a blister in the middle of the surface, cut diagonally across the grain of the veneer through the blister, with a trimming knife, using a metal straightedge as a guide. Make a second diagonal cut, intersecting the first in the middle of the blister to form an X. Avoid cutting directly across the grain; this would leave an obvious line on the repaired surface. For a small blister, you need make only one slit along the grain.

If the veneer has risen at the edge of the surface, you may be able to scrape out the old glue (*Step 2*) without cutting through the veneer. If you cannot scrape the innermost part of the separated area, make a cut through the veneer, either parallel to the grain if the edge lies perpendicular to the grain, or diagonally across it if the edge parallels the grain (*inset*).

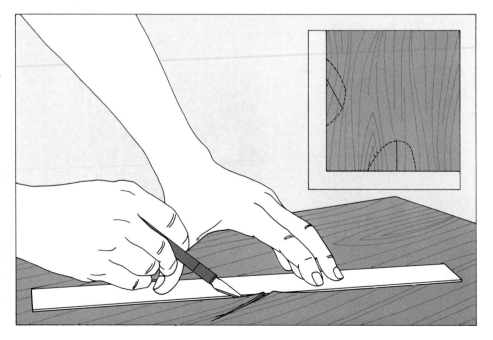

2 **Scraping out old glue, putting in new.** Using a tool with a thin, flexible blade, such as a small palette knife, gently raise one flap of a blister or a lifted edge and, with the tapered blade of a trimming knife, scrape old glue from the bottom of the veneer and the top of the underlying surface. If the veneer is too stiff to bend easily, dampen it with a few drops of warm water. Scrape under other sections the same way, stopping occasionally to blow away particles of old glue.

When the inside of the blister or raised edge is clean and dry, apply a thin coat of PVA to the underlying surface, using a glue injector, a small putty knife or a fine artist's brush to reach inside. Then press the veneer back into place and immediately wipe away excess glue.

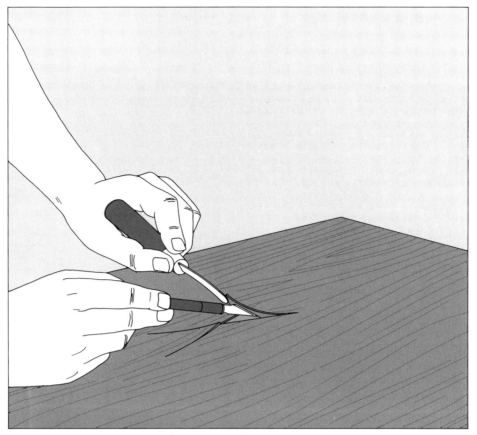

3 **Setting the glue.** With a wallpaper-seam roller, roll the repaired area, first lightly, then again with heavier pressure. Wipe away any excess glue forced out and cover the area with a piece of brown wrapping paper. Place a flat wooden block, slightly larger than the repair, over the paper and weight it with several large books *(inset)* until the glue is dry. Alternatively, you can clamp the repaired area with a sash cramp. Be sure, however, to place protective wooden blocks between the cramp and the workpiece.

Remove the weights and the paper. If scraps of paper stick, gently pare them away with a sharp chisel, bevelled edge down. Refinish the repaired area, using the techniques in Chapter 3.

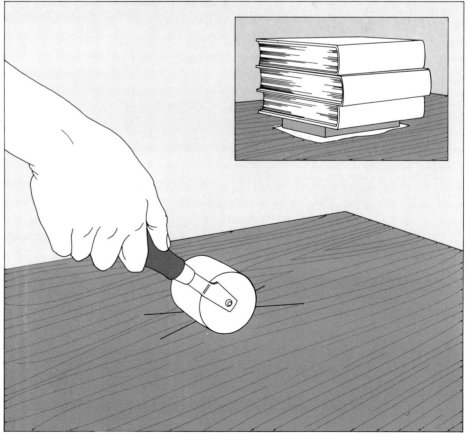

Grafting In a Veneer Patch

1 Cutting the patch. Using a trimming knife and a metal straightedge, cut a patch of new veneer slightly larger than the damaged area. Plan the patch so that its grain will parallel the grain of the existing surface and match its striations as closely as possible. To avoid the obvious line of a blunt cut across the grain, make a diamond-shaped patch, as shown, to repair damage in the middle of a veneered surface, or a V-shaped patch for chipped edges or corners. In cutting the patch, use repeated light strokes of the knife and bevel the edges inwards slightly by tilting the knife tip towards the patch at an angle of about 10 degrees, to make the bottom of the patch somewhat smaller than the top *(inset)*.

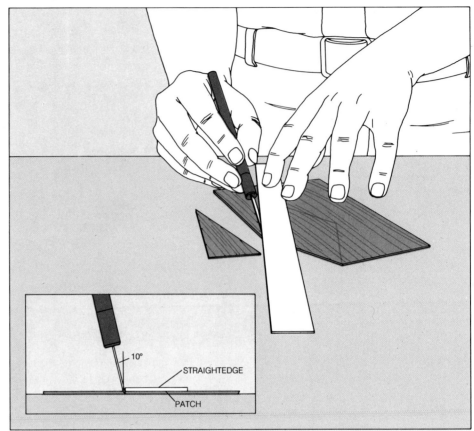

2 Marking the surface. Place the patch over the damaged area, aligning its grain with the surface grain, and outline its shape with a sharp pencil. Use a metal straightedge and a trimming knife to cut just inside each pencil line to make a hollow for the patch. Bevel the cuts 10 degrees towards the centre, as in Step 1. Cut completely through the existing veneer with repeated light strokes, taking care not to cut beyond the corners of the diamond-shaped recess.

As an alternative to Steps 1 and 2, some craftsmen achieve a perfect fit by placing the new veneer over the damaged area and cutting through both layers at the same time. This method is best used with thin modern veneers.

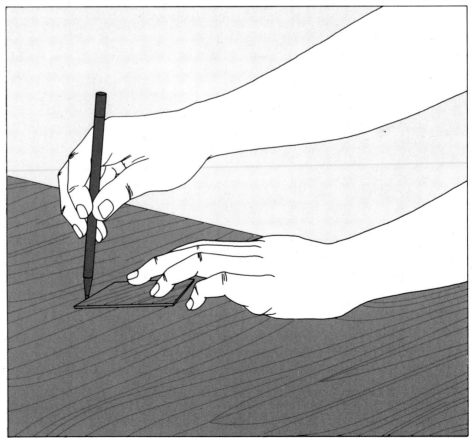

3 **Clearing the recess.** Starting at the centre of the damaged area and working outwards, remove the old veneer inside the diamond recess with a chisel held bevelled side down. If the veneer is hard to loosen, tap the butt of the chisel lightly with a mallet. Use the chisel to scrape any remaining glue or dirt from the bottom of the recess, stopping occasionally to blow away debris.

If the surface under the veneer is damaged, level it with wood filler *(page 35)*. Let the filler dry before you glue in the patch.

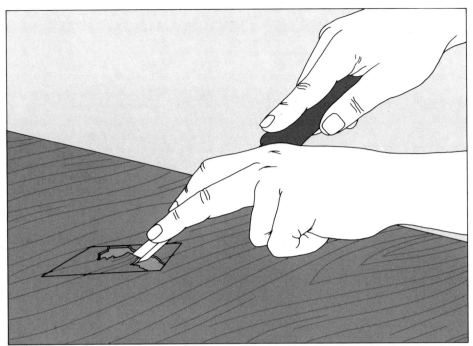

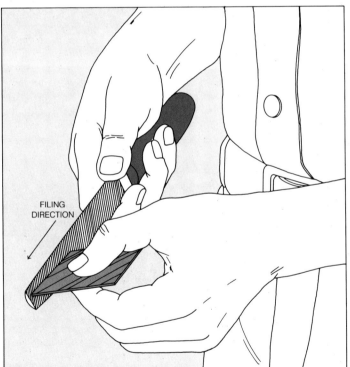

FILING
DIRECTION

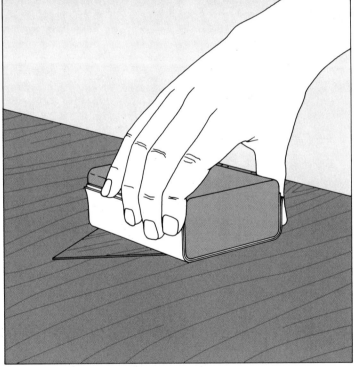

4 **Filing the patch to fit.** Lay the patch over the recess to check its size, then use a fine wood file to trim the edges for an exact fit. Be careful to maintain the edge bevel, and file only in the direction of the grain to avoid tearing the corners of the patch.

When the patch fits, brush a thin layer of PVA on the bottom of the recess, press the patch into place and wipe away excess glue. Roll and weight the patch as in Step 3, page 39.

5 **Sanding the patch flush.** When the glue has dried, sand the slightly protruding patch until it is flush with the surrounding surface, using very fine sandpaper wrapped over a flat, cork or felt-covered sanding block with slightly rounded edges *(page 77)*. Sand in the direction of the grain and use only light pressure to avoid chipping the corners of the patch or gouging the surrounding surface with the sanding block. When the patch is flush, refinish the area you have repaired, as shown in Chapter 3.

Pegs and Splints to Heal a Broken Part

A break in the supporting frame of a piece of furniture creates, in effect, a joint where none was intended, in an area originally designed to accept great stress. The repair of such a break must leave the broken part as strong as it was originally, to be able to withstand this stress; at the same time it must be as unobtrusive as possible.

For certain breaks *(below, centre)*, glue alone will do an admirable repair job. However, since wood that breaks is in many cases dry and brittle, a quantity of glue must be worked into the pores, so that as it soaks in enough will be left on the surface to produce a good bond. Some breaks need additional support—in the form of either dowels or rectangular bracing blocks. When inserted in or attached to the area of the break, these dowels or braces stiffen the joint by providing more surface area for the glue to grip.

Dowels can be hidden within a broken part or inserted into a hole drilled from the outside; in the latter case, the end of the dowel will still be visible. If a part is broken cleanly in two and its centres can be drilled to receive a dowel, a hidden dowel is the better choice of repair. But if a break is at an extreme angle, or it is located at a curve in the part, you will find it easier to insert one or even two dowels

from the outside—and the repair will be just as strong. The diameter of the dowel should usually be half the thickness of the part being mended and its length usually twice that thickness, though the dowel can be longer if more strength is needed.

Braces are used to mend breaks in flat, thin parts, such as chair-back splats or sofa frames. In a visible part, a bracing block should be recessed into a mortise cut to span the break, but in a hidden area, such as one beneath upholstery, a brace can be mounted across the break without a mortise. The thickness of a brace should be half the thickness of the broken part and its length about twice the width of the broken part. Both dowels and braces hold best and last longer if they fit the broken part snugly but not tightly—a piece too loose will leave glue gaps and one too tight will force the break apart or even cause a split in the wood surrounding it.

These reinforcements should be made of hardwood, cut along the length of the grain for strength and flexibility. You can purchase short hardwood dowels ready-made, or you can cut them to any length from a dowel rod of the right diameter. Hardwood to be used for braces can be purchased at a timber yard or scavenged from old, unusable hardwood furniture. It is sometimes

possible to obtain a piece of matching hardwood from hidden parts of the broken furniture piece itself, perhaps the glue blocks or the drawer runners.

Adequate clamping is crucial whenever glue is used. A cramp must be placed so that its force is applied perpendicular to the line of the break, in order to draw the ends together without pulling them out of alignment. Because most furniture is not constructed with perfect 90-degree angles, and because breaks do not always occur in neat, straight lines, you may have to use some ingenuity in devising a special clamping technique for each repair.

G-cramps, for example, can be used to sandwich an extremely angled break or to press a bracing block into a mortise. A G-cramp can also be attached to a curved part to serve as an anchor point for a sash cramp, which runs from the G-cramp to the end of the broken part, perpendicular to the break *(page 45, Step 3)*. A sash cramp that cannot be placed so that it applies force perpendicular to a break will tend to pull the broken pieces out of alignment, making the part bend at the break; by running a second sash cramp from one end of the first cramp to another part of the furniture *(page 44)*, you can shift the force so that the joint dries straight.

Three Common Ways that Wood May Break

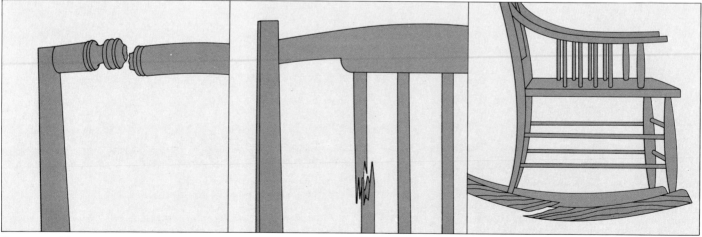

Three types of fracture. A wooden furniture part, held rigid by another part joining it or weakened by deep ornamental turnings, may snap cleanly *(above, left)*. Since there is little surface area for glue to bond, glue alone probably will not mend this kind of break permanently. The repair

should be strengthened with a brace or a dowel. Wood that breaks jaggedly *(above, centre)* is said to have a lot of tooth, and it provides a large, irregular surface for an effective glue bond. This kind of repair becomes the equivalent of a tongue-and-groove joint. Wood that breaks along

the line of the grain *(above, right)* produces a long, angled break that has a large surface area but not much tooth for the glue to grip. Depending on how heavily the piece is used, the repair for an angled break may need to be strengthened by the addition of a dowel or brace.

A Clean Break Rejoined with a Hidden Dowel

1 **Drilling holes for a dowel.** Place the piece of furniture (in this case, a chair with a broken leg) at a convenient height, broken end up. Clamp the furniture to a workbench or saw-horses if it is unsteady and clamp the piece that broke off in a vice, also broken end up. If the pieces are broken cleanly enough for you to use a dowelling jig, drill into their exact centres, as shown. If a dowelling jig is unusable because of the shape of the the break or the piece, you will need to estimate the centres visually *(page 15)*. Use a small bit to drill a pilot hole in each piece, then drill the final holes with a bit the exact size of the dowel to be used. Clean drill debris out of the holes with an upholstery vacuum, or turn the pieces upside down and tap the debris out.

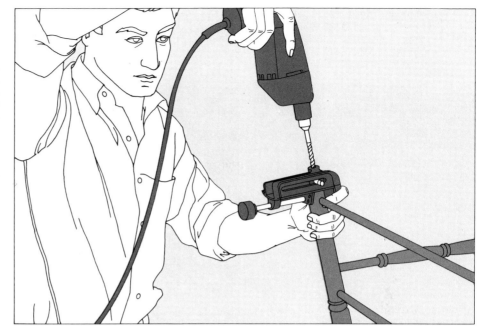

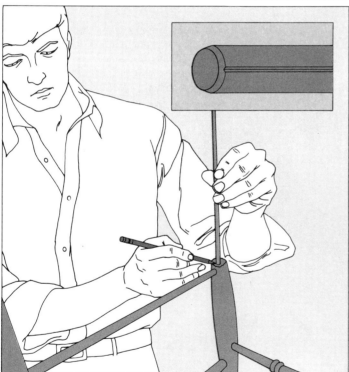

2 **Making the dowel peg.** Insert an undersized dowel or a pencil into each dowel hole and mark the depth on it. Cut a dowel of the right diameter for a snug fit to a length slightly shorter than the sum of the depths of the holes. Bevel the ends of the dowel slightly *(inset)* with a file or sandpaper, and groove the dowel sides with a saw to provide channels that will let the glue spread.

3 **Joining the pieces.** Put glue in one hole and on one end of the dowel, and, with a mallet, tap the dowel into the hole as far as it will go. Then tap the other broken piece on to the protruding dowel which is unglued so you can check to see if the broken ends align precisely. If they do not, file down one side of the dowel or shave it slightly with a trimming knife *(inset)* so that the pieces line up. When the pieces are aligned, put glue on the other end of the dowel, in the other hole and on the broken ends, then tap the pieces together securely. Wipe off excess glue.

4 Cramping. Apply a sash cramp extending from one end of the broken part to the other, running as nearly perpendicular to the break as possible *(right)*. If the cramp cannot be placed exactly perpendicular and tends to pull the pieces out of alignment, apply a second sash cramp at right angles, connecting the first cramp with some part of the furniture opposite it, in order to pull the pieces back into alignment *(far right)*.

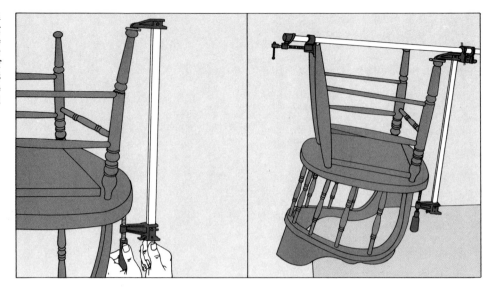

A Visible-Dowel Repair for an Angled Break

1 Drilling the dowel hole. Apply PVA to the broken edges and clamp the pieces together, using two strips of wood and two G-cramps to hold them in place. At the least visible area, drill a pilot hole for the dowel hole through the first broken piece and part of the way into the second, at right angles to the break. Using the pilot hole as a guide, drill a hole the same size as the dowel that is to be inserted. Clean the sawdust out.

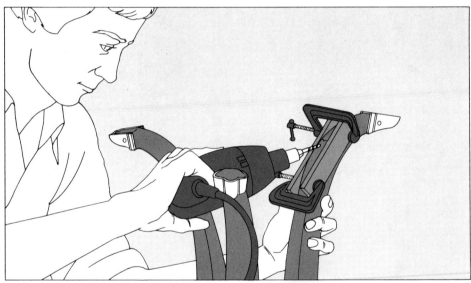

2 Inserting the dowel. Use a dowel grooved as in Step 2, page 43, but in this case cut the dowel slightly longer than the depth of the hole. Put glue in the hole and on the dowel; tap the dowel into the hole with a mallet. Remove the cramps and the supports, and wipe off the excess glue.

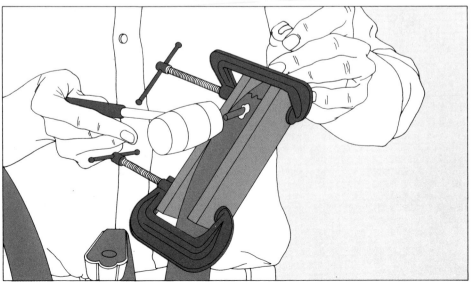

3 **Clamping a curve.** To apply force perpendicular to this break, you will have to attach a G-cramp near the break to use as a bracket for applying force with a sash cramp. Attach the sash cramp in such a way that it runs from the G-cramp to the end of the broken part, spanning the break and remaining perpendicular to it. When the glue has set, use a backsaw and sandpaper to trim the protruding end of the dowel so that it is flush with the surface of the broken part.

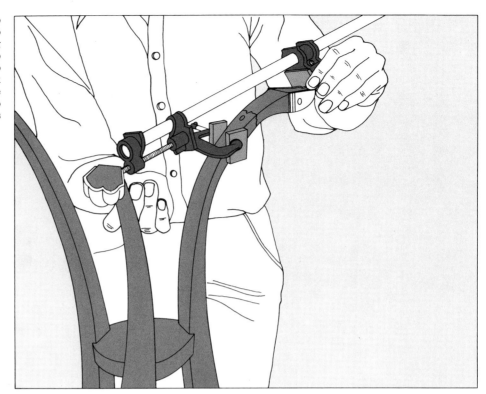

A Mortised Splint for a Flat Break

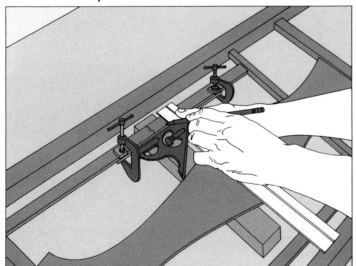

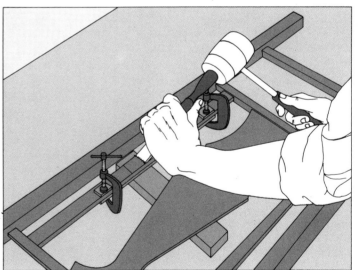

1 **Getting into position.** Clamp the furniture down on a bench or rest it on the floor with the back, or the least visible area, of the broken part horizontal and facing up. Apply glue to the broken edges and join them together. Clamp the area of the break in position, using two G-cramps, one on either side of the break, to secure a strip of wood spanning the underside of the break. If necessary, support the part from underneath with a second scrap of wood, as shown. Guided by a combination square, mark where the ends of the mortise will fall on either side of the break, at right angles to the length of the part.

2 **Cutting the mortise.** Cut the mortise ends at the marks to the planned depth, using a tenon saw. Alternatively, use a chisel, held vertically with its bevel facing the break as you tap it with a mallet. Then, keeping the chisel angled and the bevelled side down, score the area between the cuts every 10 mm to a depth slightly less than that intended for the mortise. When you have scored the area, reverse direction in order to remove the chips, and then pare the bottom of the mortise smooth by shaving it with the chisel, still bevelled side down. Smooth the bottom of the mortise with sandpaper or a wood file.

3 **Clamping the brace.** Cut a hardwood brace to fit snugly into the mortise, then put glue in the mortise and on the back and ends of the brace. Insert the brace into the mortise, wipe away the excess glue and, without removing the original G-cramps and strip of wood, clamp the brace into the mortise securely with additional G-cramps. When the glue is dry, unclamp and sand the brace to match precisely the shape of the part.

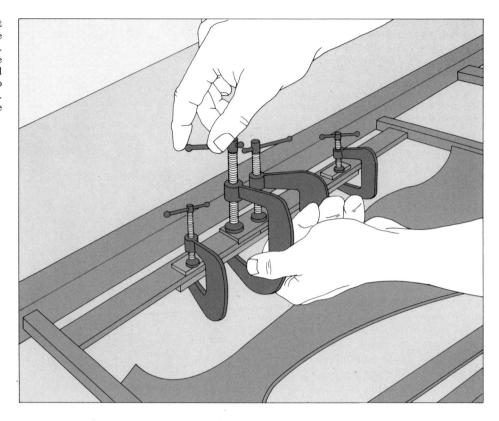

A Screwed-on Brace Concealed from View

A simple strengthener. Expose as much as possible of any concealed broken part; if the break is underneath upholstery, remove tacks or staples *(pages 92–93)* and fold back the fabric about 200 mm on each side of the break, taking care not to damage the fabric. Apply glue to the broken edges and clamp them together with a sash cramp running from one end of the framing member to the other. Drill pilot holes through the corners of a 6 to 12 mm thick rectangle of wood that spans the break on the exposed side of the broken part. Spread glue on this brace and attach it with screws. When the glue is dry, unclamp the piece and retack the fabric.

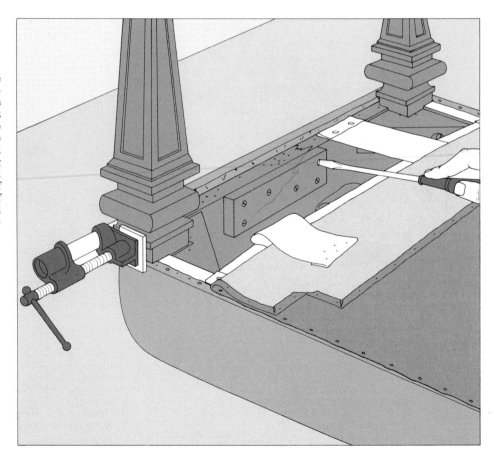

Fixing a Crack in a Tabletop

The boards that make up a tabletop may shrink and draw apart, producing cracks where they were glued together. If such a crack can be drawn closed by clamping, clean the crack with a thin blade and repair the break by forcing glue into the crack with a glue injector *(page 10)*, then clamping the crack shut.

A straight crack that cannot be drawn closed easily with a cramp can be sawn out. Remove the tabletop and draw a line along the crack from one edge of the tabletop to the other, then make a precise cut along the line with a bench saw or a circular saw guided by a strip of wood clamped parallel to the crack. The saw blade cuts out the crack so that the two pieces of the top can then be reglued at the new joint.

A wide crack can be filled with a narrow wedge of wood. Cut the wedge with the grain, from matching wood, and taper it with a file or sandpaper until it precisely fits the crack. Then glue it into position.

As with all glued repairs, apply cramps perpendicular to the break to draw the glued parts together. In the case of a round or oval tabletop, clamping is facilitated by the use of a caul—two crescent-shaped boards that fit snugly round the edge of the tabletop *(right, below)*.

Tracing a caul. To clamp a round or oval tabletop, you will need to cut bands to fit against the tabletop, providing straight edges for clamping. Remove the legs and place the top upside down on two boards extending at least 50 mm beyond the tabletop at each end. Place the boards parallel to each other and to the crack in the tabletop, keeping the outer edges of the boards at least 50 mm beyond the edge of the tap. Trace the outline of the top on the boards, and then cut along these lines with a jigsaw.

Pad the edges of the tabletop with felt, or rubber cut from an old inner tube, and position the crescent-shaped boards—the caul—against it. Apply glue to the edges of the crack, then position sash cramps so that they are perpendicular to the crack from one board to the other. If more than two cramps are used, alternate their positions *(inset)* to avoid warping the top.

A Wedge to Fill a Wide Crack

Filling a tabletop crack. Cut a wedge slightly longer and wider than the crack; sand or file the wedge to fit the crack snugly. Apply glue to both sides of the wedge and insert it into the crack, from the edge if it is a short wedge, and from the top if it is a long one. Tap it in gently with a mallet, leaving any protruding parts until later. If the tabletop is rectangular, apply sash cramps perpendicular to the crack; for a round or oval top, make a caul cramp *(bottom)*. When the glue is dry, remove the cramps and trim any protruding parts of the wedge; use a backsaw to cut the wedge end flush with the edge of the tabletop, and a chisel, bevelled side down, to pare away the part of the wedge that protrudes from the top *(inset)*. Smooth with sandpaper and refinish.

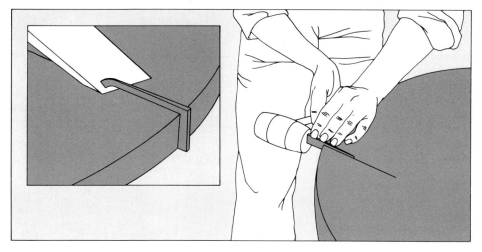

Clamping a Round or Oval Top with a Caul

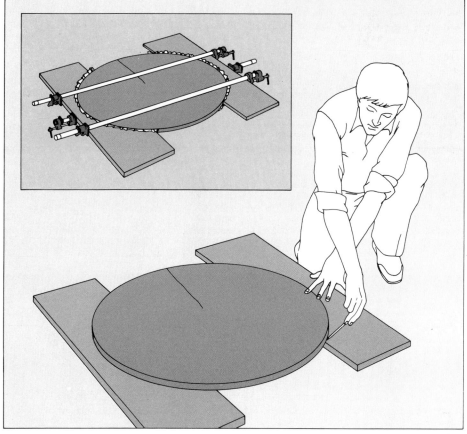

Restoring the Curves of Bentwood

Bentwood furniture is made with solid wooden rods that have been softened by steam and bent into continuous curves that have great strength. The technique is ancient, but in 1842 a Viennese cabinet-maker, Michael Thonet, adapted it to mass production, thereby eliminating much of the joinery of conventional furniture manufacturing. Bentwood chairs and tables are lightweight and sturdy—many of the millions of pieces built since Thonet's time are still in use, and 19th-century examples are valued antiques. Occasionally, however, the severely stressed curves split, requiring special repair.

Most splits occur along the outside of a curve when wood fibres, stretched in the bending process, tear apart. You can repair these splits by steaming the wood to soften the tongue of the split, so that it can be glued back in position. To prevent a recurrence, the mended split may then be reinforced with dowels. Small splits, which can easily be pushed back together again, may need only gluing without either steaming or reinforcing. Repairs to the few joints used in bentwood pieces are made by the same techniques used for other types of furniture (pages 10–17).

Repairing Split Bentwood

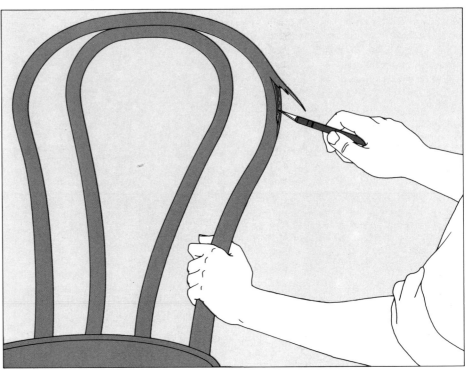

1 **Cleaning the damaged area.** With the tip of a sharp, tapered tool, such as a trimming knife, scrape away dirt, old glue and paint from inside and round the split so that they do not interfere with sound bonding of the glue. Use an upholstery vacuum attachment to remove debris.

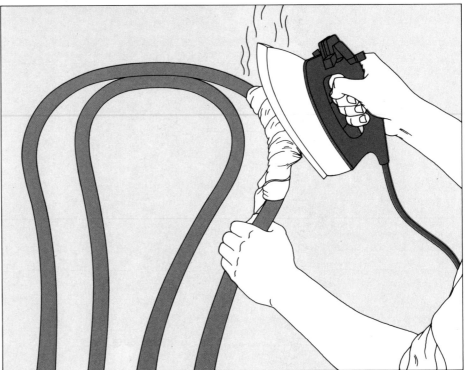

2 **Softening the wood.** Wrap the damaged section with several layers of cloth that have been soaked in hot water, and steam the wood by rubbing a hot iron against the cloth from all sides. A steam iron is best, but you will still have to wet the cloth as it dries by dripping water on to it. Steam until the wood is pliable enough to be pressed back into its original shape. This usually takes about 15 minutes. Then remove the cloth.

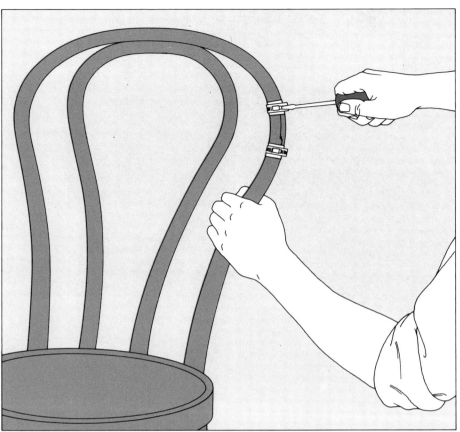

3 **Clamping the split.** Press the softened wood into its original position and clamp both ends of the split with hose clips, protecting the wood under the clips with padding made of several layers of masking tape. Alternatively, use G-cramps to hold the split closed, padding the cramp jaws with small pieces of plywood or cork. Let the wood dry for 24 hours in a warm place.

Remove the cramps and, as the split opens slightly, coat both inside surfaces with PVA. Use an artist's brush to apply glue to the throat of the split. Press the split closed and wipe away excess glue, then retape and reclamp the split until the glue dries, which should take about 18 hours.

4 **Reinforcing the split.** If the split is deeper than one-quarter the thickness of the wood, drill holes for 9 mm dowels at 50 mm intervals, beginning at the deepest point of the split. Drill about two-thirds through the wood, angling each hole differently to create an interlocking pattern.

Cut 9 mm dowels slightly longer than the depth of the holes and glue them in. Wipe away any excess glue, and sand or file the protruding dowel ends until they are flush.

Duplicating Parts by Copying the Originals

Parts of old furniture frequently wear out or get lost, or a part may be broken beyond repair. Fortunately, because most furniture is symmetrical, it is usually possible to duplicate the part by using an existing part as a model—but bear in mind that the two parts were probably mirror images of each other, rather than exact copies, so that the profile of the duplicate may have to be inverted before it can be of any use.

Whatever the part or the furniture style, the process of duplication always begins in the same way: you remove the existing part being used as a model. Though dismantling a piece of furniture to get at a single part may seem troublesome and time-wasting, it is definitely worth the effort. A copy is far easier to make if you can freely turn the part being copied to examine its profiles from different angles.

Sometimes, if the shape is relatively simple and the part has one flat surface, you can use the part itself as a pattern, tracing its outline directly on to the new piece of wood. Professionals often sacrifice the model in order to get a flat surface, cutting the model in half lengthwise, although this obviously means making

two new replacement parts instead of one.

More often, you will have to make a separate pattern, tracing all the profiles of the part—front, back and sides—on to a sheet of paper and using these silhouettes as patterns for transferring the profiles on to a block of wood. When you are duplicating a part on a lathe, the paper pattern will be a negative of the finished shape—that is, whatever line is concave on the model will be convex on the pattern, and vice versa *(pages 56–57)*.

Accuracy is very important when these profiles are traced, especially when a joint is involved or when matching parts must function in unison—for instance, a pair of chair rockers. Use a clutch pencil with its lead extended, so that you can hold the pencil absolutely vertical against the shape you are outlining. A profile gauge *(page 57)*, pressed against the contours of a part, is helpful in making an exact tracing—although a profile gauge is usually not long enough to capture more than one section of a part at a time.

Measuring tools such as a Vernier caliper, a protractor and a sliding bevel are needed to transfer the dimensions of join-

ery parts, such as dowels and sockets, or mortises and tenons. They are also helpful in copying profiles and in checking the shapes of new parts against old as the work progresses. In fact, only when you are using a tapering jig, or are tapering a square table leg, can the elaborate process of tracing and measuring be simplified.

In addition to tracing the outline of the part, you may also have to transfer a carving detail. Tape a sheet of paper over the carving, rub it with pencil or chalk, and then transfer the outlines of the carving to the new part with carbon paper and a sharp pencil or an awl.

The wood to be fashioned for a new part should match the old as nearly as possible, and its dimensions should be large enough to encompass the part with several centimetres to spare. In the initial cutting, you will roughly shape the wood with a band saw, jigsaw or coping saw *(pages 52–54)*, or carve it with a draw knife or a spokeshave *(page 55)*. For shaping the details, you will need gouges, chisels and a thumb plane; a router equipped with the appropriate bit is useful for reproducing missing parts such as sections of moulding.

Transferring Dimensions of Diameters and Angles

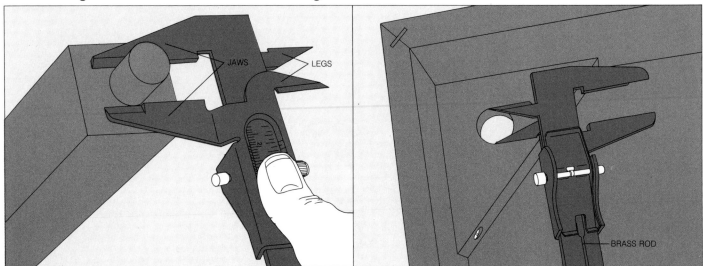

Using a Vernier caliper. To measure and transfer the diameter of a dowel, loosen the caliper screw and open the caliper jaws until they rest against the widest part of the dowel *(above, left)*. Then lock the jaws by tightening the screw, and use the pointed tips of the caliper legs opposite the jaws to mark the dowel diameter on a new piece

of wood. At any setting, the caliper's jaw separation equals its leg separation.

To measure and transfer the diameter of a dowel hole, close the caliper legs and set them in the hole; then open them until they touch the walls of the hole *(above, right)*. Lock the caliper by tightening the screw, as above, and use the

pointed tips of the legs to mark the diameter of the hole on a new piece of wood. To measure the depth of a dowel hole, rest the bottom of the caliper stem against the top of the hole, and extend the brass rod until it touches the bottom of the hole. Read the depth of the hole from the scale on the caliper stem.

Using a sliding bevel. Loosen the wing nut slightly, then position the handle and blade of the bevel against the two sides of the angle that you want to copy *(right)*; tighten the wing nut. Move the bevel to the new piece of wood, hold the handle against the edge and mark along the blade to transfer the angle *(right, below)*.

To measure an angle in degrees, you can use either a protractor with the sliding bevel or a tool that is a combination protractor-bevel *(inset)*. Loosen the lock nut and align the bottom of the protractor plate with one side of the angle to be measured. Align the bevel arm with the other side of the angle, and read the angle in degrees on the plate of the protractor.

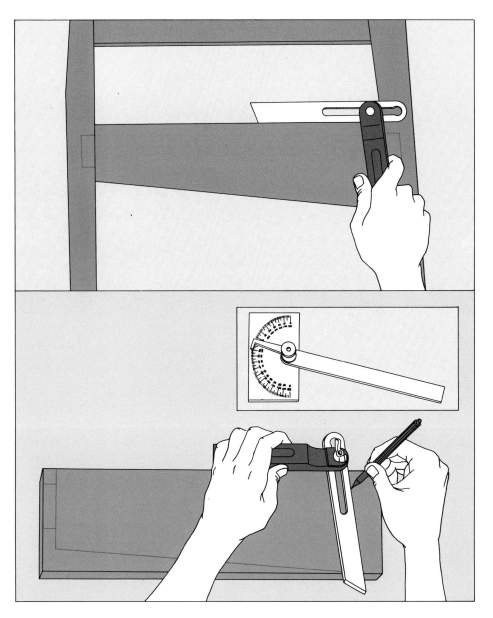

Laminating a New Rocking-Chair Runner

1 Tracing the lamination parts. On a board one third the thickness of the runner, trace three outlines, using the existing runner as a pattern. Arrange the outlines on the board so that the wood grain runs in a different direction in each one; so far as possible, avoid short grains at the ends of the runners, as these are brittle. Or, you can cut the new runner from a single length of thicker wood.

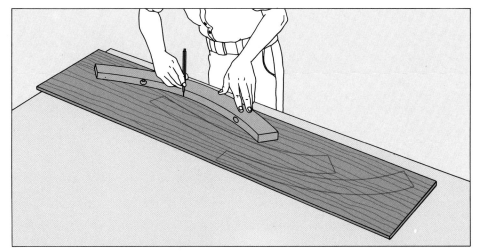

2 **Sawing the runner sections.** Clamp the board to a work surface or saw-horses and, starting at the board edge, cut out the runner parts. Support each runner as the saw nears the edge of the board, so that the piece does not fall and break.

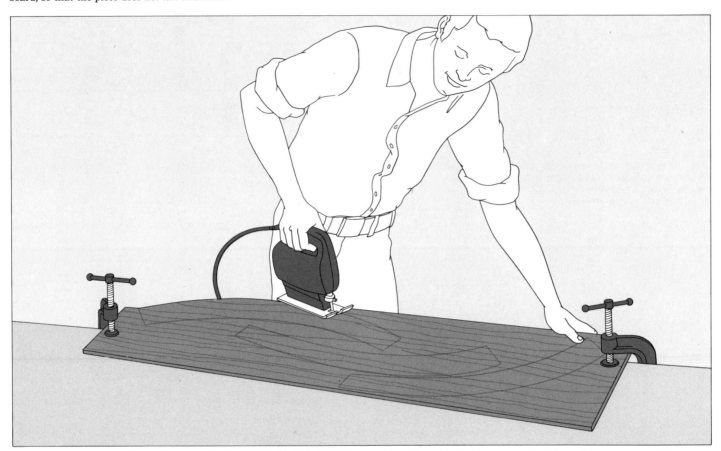

3 **Gluing the runner together.** Spread yellow glue on both faces of one runner section and on the interior faces of the other two sections. Assemble the sections and clamp them between long blocks of wood to distribute the pressure evenly. Allow the glue to dry for 24 hours.

Remove the cramps and smooth the curved surfaces of the new runner with a thumb plane, spokeshave or forming tool *(page 55, inset)*. Then cut the holes for the dowels or tenons that will join the runner to the chair, taking care to position them the same distance from the ends as the holes of the original runner so that the chair will rock smoothly. Spread glue on the new runner and clamp it in place.

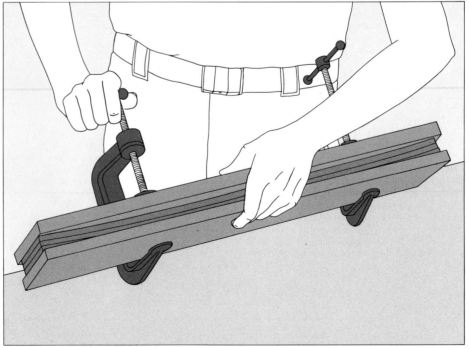

Shaping a Curved Rail for a Ladder-Back Chair

Cutting the compound curves. On a block of wood long enough to accommodate tenons at both ends, trace the curved front, back and top profiles of the new rail. Use a band saw to rough-cut the front and back curves, slicing off the back corners and hollowing out the front. Then refine both curves, working slowly and evenly along the profile to avoid gouging the wood or twisting and breaking the blade. Rough-cut and refine the top profile in the same fashion.

Smooth the front, back and top curves with a thumb plane or a forming tool. Measure the mortises on the chair rails and shape matching tenons on the rail with a dovetail saw and a chisel. If you cut the tenons as short as possible, you may be able to insert the new rail without pulling apart the rails already in place. Glue and clamp the new rail in place.

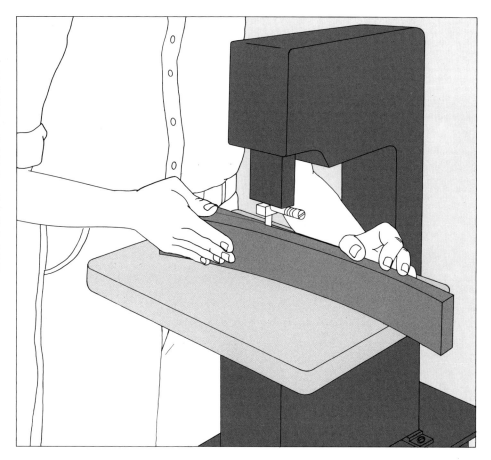

A Compound Rough-Cut for a Cabriole Leg

1 **Tracing the profile of the original.** Place the leg to be copied on its side on a sheet of paper and trace its profile. With a caliper or a rule, compare the measurements of the leg and the tracing; correct the tracing if necessary. Cut out the tracing with scissors and, using a block of wood large enough to encompass the whole leg plus a tenon, position this pattern so that the knee and foot are both touching the corner of the block where the two faces meet *(inset)*. Transfer the profile on to the wood, then turn the pattern over and move it to the adjoining face so that the knee and the foot touch the same points on the first tracing. Then transfer the profile on to this side as well.

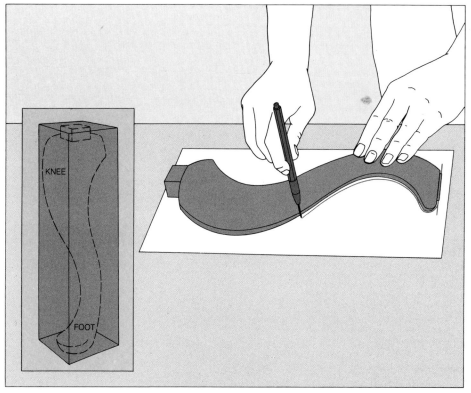

2 **Making the compound cut.** Place one profile, face up, on the table of a band saw and cut along both edges of the profile. Nail the cut-out sections of waste wood back into place temporarily, taking care not to nail into the leg. Then flip the block of wood, placing the other profile face up, and again cut along both edges of the profile. Caution: do not let the saw blade hit a nail, or the wood will kick and the blade may break.

After the last cut, use a forming tool or a thumb plane to shape the rough-cut leg to match the original. Carve decorative details with gouges and chisels, and sand the leg smooth.

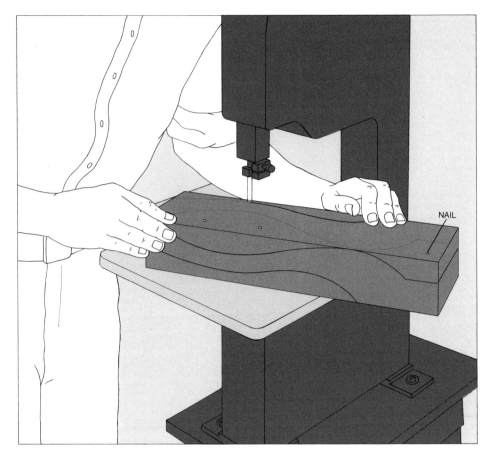

Using a V-Shaped Jig to Cut a Tapered Leg

An exploded view of a tapering jig. A tapering jig can be made from readily available materials: two lengths of 75 by 25 mm wood for the folding legs; a 60 mm fixed-pin butt hinge screwed into one end of each leg; a sliding stay attached to the opposite end, to set and hold the angle of the legs; and a 75 by 25 mm wooden stop on the outer face of the open end of one leg. Reference points, used in setting the angle, are marked on the inside edge of each leg, 300 mm from the hinge end.

To use a tapering jig, you must first determine the taper of the part as a ratio of millimetres per 300 mm. On a leg, for example, measure the width of the leg at the top and bottom, in millimetres, and subtract to find the difference. Divide this figure by the length of the leg, in 300 mm units. The result is the amount of taper in terms of millimetres per 300 mm. Open the jig legs to this amount of taper at the reference points, and tighten down the wing nut.

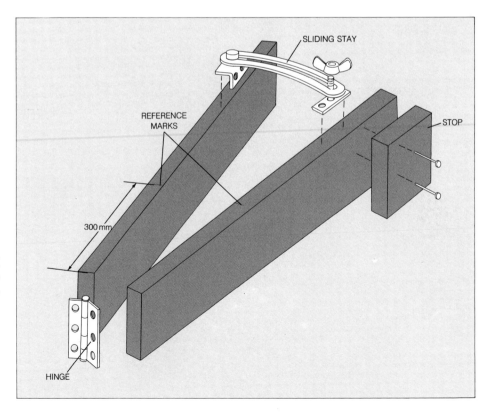

Using a jig for a tapered cut. Start with a block of wood as long as the original leg and as wide as the top width of the leg. Resting the block against the jig, push jig and block through the saw. Turn and cut the other three faces of the block, but double the angle of the taper whenever a tapered face rests against the jig: cut the third side at the same angle as the first, and the second and fourth at double that angle.

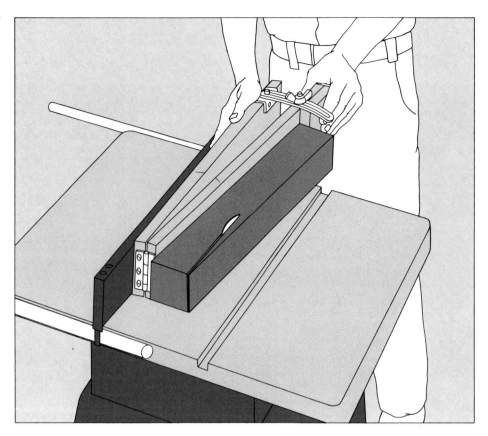

Sculpting a Free-Form Shape with Hand Tools

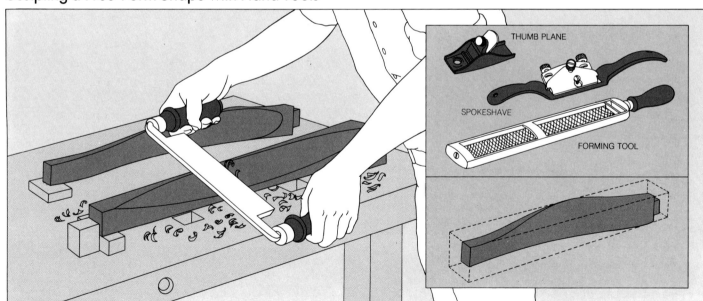

THUMB PLANE

SPOKESHAVE

FORMING TOOL

Using a draw knife to cut a chair arm. Trace the outer limits of the arm's curved surfaces on a block of wood large enough to encompass the overall dimensions of the arm. Secure the block of wood to a worktable and, with the bevelled edge of the blade down, pull a draw knife across the top face of the wood. To take off thin shavings, keep the handles of the knife nearly parallel to the face of the wood; tilt the handles down for thicker slices. Work slowly, and check the measurements frequently against the original, using a caliper and a rule. Turn the wood as needed, sculpting all four faces as you go.

To finish the shaping, use a thumb plane, a spokeshave and a forming tool *(inset, top)* that is fitted with interchangeable coarse, medium and fine plates. Use the thumb plane—75 mm long and held in one hand—to manoeuvre into tight corners and over subtle changes in contour. Use the spokeshave, which can be held in the same way as a draw knife, to give a smooth finish to the surfaces already rough-cut; for curved surfaces, spokeshave blades are available with special convex and concave faces.

Fashioning a Template for Lathe Work

A spindle or leg that is a straight cylinder can be replaced with a dowel of the same size. However, for a shaped leg—or a drawer knob with a convoluted design—using a lathe is the only feasible way to make a duplicate. To do the job by hand takes hours of laborious shaping, first with a draw knife, then with a gouge and chisel, and the results are usually crude.

If you do not own a lathe, you can either hire one or give the work to a professional, in which case you can save both time and money by providing a two-part template. One part is a guide for marking the break points—the highest and lowest cutting points—on the smooth cylinder (right). The other guide is a negative profile of the part, to hold against the work in progress for comparison. If you plan to make your own replacement part, you will need to make the template for yourself.

Making a Pattern from an Existing Part

1 Tracing the original part. Place the part to be copied on heavy wrapping paper spread over a hard, smooth surface, and, using a clutch pencil with the lead extended, trace the front and back profiles. Then, using calipers, compare the cross-section measurements of the original and those of the tracing at each break point; correct the tracing, if necessary, so that it corresponds exactly to the original.

Draw a centre line down the length of the profile. Then draw a second line—this is called the template line—parallel to the centre line and 75 mm outside the widest point on the profile edge (bottom). Draw perpendicular lines, known as break lines, from the break points to the template line. Mark on each break-point line the diameter of the original part at that point; measure with the calipers.

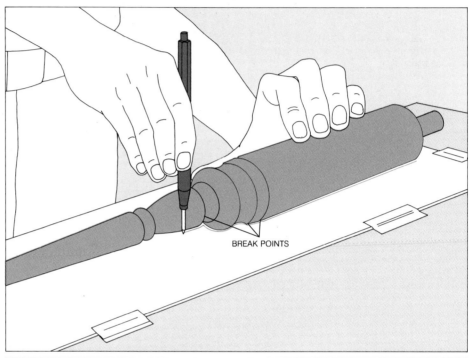

BREAK POINTS

2 Cutting out the template. Using scissors, cut along the centre line and the template line. Glue the tracing to 3 mm thick plywood or hardboard, using rubber cement. Clamp the wood or hardboard to a worktable, and saw along the profile line. If the saw blade will not turn sharply enough to follow the outline, saw as close to the detail as possible, staying outside the line when you depart from it, and finish shaping the profile with a file.

If your original has a squared section, as some table and chair legs do, make the template for the curved portions only. The squared section will not be shaped on the lathe.

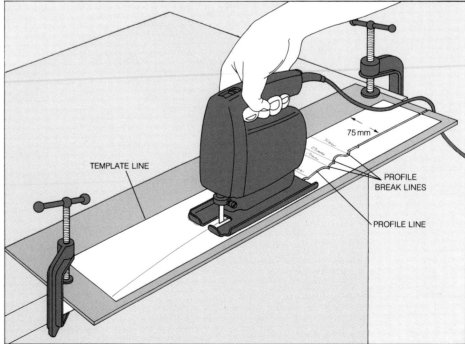

TEMPLATE LINE

75 mm

PROFILE BREAK LINES

PROFILE LINE

3 **Using the template.** Before starting to shape the part on the lathe, hold the straight edge of the template on the slowly spinning cylinder of wood so that you can rest a pencil point at each of the break-point lines to mark these lines on the cylinder. Begin to cut and shape the part, stopping the lathe as you near the end to compare the profile of the wood with the profile edge of the template. Use calipers to make frequent checks of the diameter at the break points, but stop the lathe while you are using the calipers to avoid gouging the wood.

When cutting a part, such as a knob or finial, on which the design is cut into the end of the wood as well as into the side grain, check the side with a template as described in Steps 1 to 3. But check the end profile with a profile gauge *(inset).* Set the gauge by holding it against the original part and pushing the teeth into the design.

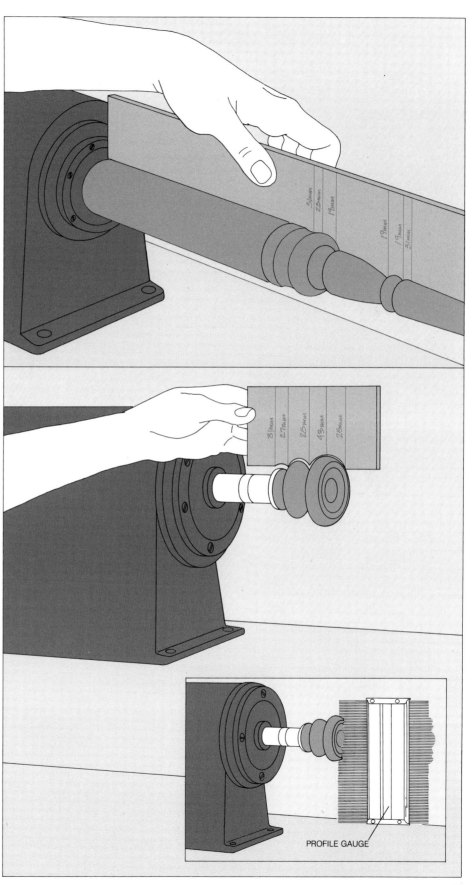

PROFILE GAUGE

Reweaving Chair Seats of Rush or Cane

The techniques for weaving chair seats have been known and used for a very long time. Egyptians were using bulrushes to make seats for chairs and stools some 3,000 years ago. The rush-bottomed chairs associated with rural life had their precursors in light reed and wicker seats made by European peasants in the 16th and 17th centuries, when chairs first came into general use. In the same period, European gentlewomen added caning to their accomplishments, copying the intricate patterns of caned furniture brought from India by Portuguese traders.

Rush and cane seats are still popular, and the techniques and materials for weaving them have changed very little. Natural rush is widely used in modern furniture-making because it is available from various countries, and craftsmen are no longer dependent on a seasonal factor. Artificial rush, made of twisted kraft paper, offers a cheap and attractive alternative. Perhaps the greatest change has been the introduction, in the late 19th century, of pre-woven caning and the tongue-and-groove method of attaching it to the seat. The groove runs round the perimeter of the seat, and edges of the caning panel are forced into it, to be held in place by a flexible tongue made of reed.

Cane furniture fitted with pre-woven caning is much simpler to repair than a cane seat woven from scratch. But even the complex caning patterns are not difficult to reproduce. The process is handiwork, requiring few tools but much patience—hand-caning a typical 350 by 300 mm seat can take as long as 14 hours. Both rush and cane are available from craft shops or from suppliers who specialize in materials for basketry and caning. Most such sources also carry pre-woven caning for tongue-and-groove seating.

For hand-caning, the seat frame must have holes drilled round its perimeter. Pre-woven caning can, of course, be applied only to a chair with a groove. It is sometimes possible to add a groove to a chair that has none, but you should consult a professional furniture-maker about the feasibility of such a step.

Wrapping a rush seat is relatively easy, and tools are basic and few. You will need string or tacks and a spring cramp for securing the strands; a trimming knife for cutting; a mallet for adjusting the strands; cardboard for padding; and a set square of clear plastic for checking that the rows form a right-angled pattern—a sign of a well-made rush bottom. For natural rush, you will also need a blunt screwdriver to prise open the corners for packing, and a rolling pin for smoothing the surface.

Before beginning to wrap artificial rush, dip it in water for half a minute; if left longer, the paper will start to untwist and the rush will be damaged. You should immerse natural rush in cool or lukewarm water for about 15 minutes, being careful not to bend the strands. Alternatively, dowse the rush with a hose or watering can, making sure that the strands in the centre are thoroughly soaked. When ready for use, the rushes should be soft and pliable, never brittle.

Rush weaving is a time-consuming process, particularly for beginners, so it is best to separate the task into two sessions. But do not end the first session in the middle of working a corner: the pattern may be spoiled if the tension of the rushes is lost. Instead, finish the session by leaving a loose end of rush, approximately 350 mm long; dampen this end before beginning again. Alternatively, you could tie off to an untwisted layer and, when starting the second session, tie in with another strand and work in the same direction.

Always use two rushes at a time, of roughly the same thickness and paired butt to butt; if the strands are spindly or of markedly different dimensions, they will distort the pattern. The rushes should always be joined on the underside, since joins made in the top layer will rub apart because of constant friction.

To create a hard-wearing surface, twist each pair of strands together as you work them from one rail to another. Pull and stretch the strands to achieve maximum tension. The design of a seat depends on the careful formation of right-angled corners. If the angles are too wide or too narrow, you will be unable to weave a symmetrical pattern.

Hand-caning is more difficult than rush weaving and is usually done in a six-step pattern with a seventh step to lock the cane to the chair. You will need, in addition to the weaving cane, a supply of wooden pegs—golf tees will do—to hold the strands of cane in the holes, and a small amount of beading cane (cane one size larger than the weaving cane, to be used for binding).

With pre-woven caning, installation is a much simpler process. You will need a hardwood wedge 100 mm long, to drive the caning into the groove, and several hardwood wedges 25 mm long to hold it there. To secure the caning permanently, use a flexible reed tongue with a tapered edge; the taper of the tongue and the wedges should conform to the width of the groove.

Cane strands and pre-woven caning need to be soaked in lukewarm water for 15 minutes before use. Cane strands should be coiled in a bucket, with the shiny sides out. To soak pre-woven cane, which must be kept flat, you may have to use a bath.

Before beginning any weaving project, repair broken chair parts, remove traces of old rush or cane and, if necessary, refinish the chair frame. To remove an old hand-caned seat, cut as close to the frame as possible with a trimming knife, then use a mallet and chisel to cut through the loops on the underside, so that they can be pulled from the holes. On a pre-woven cane seat, clean the groove completely before recaning. You can use a mallet and chisel to remove the old caning and tongue, and vinegar will soften up old glue.

Since weaving takes time, it is important to work in comfortable conditions. Place the chair on a stool or table—padded with a blanket to protect the finish—so that your working level will be easy on your back.

Once woven, each type of seat may need special finishing and care. Dampening cane may raise stray hairs, which should be removed with tweezers or scissors before finishing the seat. For a seat of artificial rush, brush on one or two coats of shellac, and repeat this application once a year to prolong the life of the rush. Natural rush should be left in its original state; it will darken in time to a mellow, attractive tone. Cane also darkens with age, though you can stain it if you wish. For a high-gloss finish, apply a lacquer sealer, followed by a coat of clear lacquer.

A Variety of Weaving Materials

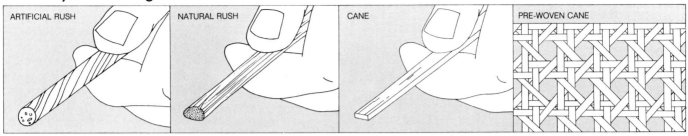

ARTIFICIAL RUSH NATURAL RUSH CANE PRE-WOVEN CANE

Artificial Rush

A counterpart of natural rush, this cord-like material is made from kraft paper, twisted by machine into strands about 5 mm wide. It is considered a most durable seating material, and comes in an array of earthy colours. Artificial rush is sold by weight; approximately 1 kg will cover an average-sized chair seat.

Natural Rush

Natural rush is harvested from a cylindrical, reedy marsh plant which grows from 2 to 3 metres high. It is available in a variety of warm hues, from yellow through most shades of green to brown. Natural rush is sold in bolts of 1 or 2 kg;

1 kg will be a sufficient quantity to cover an average-sized chair seat, provided that all the rush is of good quality and that none has to be discarded.

Cane

Cut from the outer bark of the rattan plant, cane strands come in six sizes suited to the spacing and diameter of the holes in the seat frame. However, since the size variations are slight, you should obtain samples from your retailer and check them against the chair before placing an order. Cane is sold by weight; approximately 80 g will be sufficient to cover a seat 300 mm square with up to 72 holes round the frame.

Pre-woven Cane

Also called cane webbing, this material consists of strands of natural cane loom-woven into various patterns. The traditional six-way pattern shown is sized according to the width of the holes in the mesh; sizes range from 10 to 25 mm. Pre-woven caning is available in rolls 300 to 900 mm wide, from which suppliers will cut pieces to size. Buy such caning to bridge the widest part of the seat, measured from the outside edges of the groove, adding 25 mm for the material to be driven into the groove. The reed tongue, driven into the groove to hold the cane in place, is sold by length in widths based on the width of the tongue.

Wrapping an Artificial Rush Chair Seat

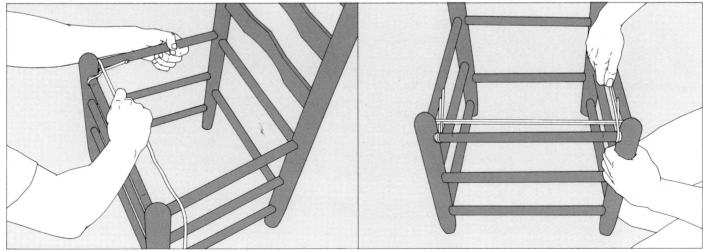

1 Establishing square corners. If the front rail of the chair is longer than the back, mark it in pencil opposite the points where the back rail emerges from the seat posts. Tack one end of a strand of artificial rush to the inside face of the left rail, 75 mm back from the front corner. Bring the strand under, then over the front rail; loop it back under itself, then under and over the left rail *(above)*. Pull the strand across to the opposite side; loop it under and over the right rail, then carry it back under itself, and under and over the front rail.

Tack it to the inside of the right rail, directly across from the point where it is tacked to the left rail. Tack a second strand to the inside of the left rail, behind the first *(above, right)*, and wrap it in the same pattern until you have filled the triangular areas between the front corner posts and the pencil marks. To keep the intersecting runs

of rush at right angles, pull the strand taut across the seat but relax pressure while wrapping the corners. When the chair corners are squared off, hold a set square against the intersecting strands to make sure they are at right angles. If the strands cross the rails too far out, gently tap them back with a small block of wood and a rubber mallet; if they cross the rails too close in, flatten them with a mallet to widen the weave.

2 **Completing a circuit.** After the chair has been squared off, lightly dampen about 6 metres of rush, roll it into a manageable coil and tack one end to the left side rail, just beyond the last squaring-off strand. Wrap it round the two front corners in the same way as you wrapped the corner strands *(Step 1)*, but instead of tacking it to the right rail, continue the pattern to the right back corner, then to the left back corner, and finally to the left front corner, to complete an entire circuit *(inset)*. Continue wrapping until the rush runs out. Then attach a new length of dampened rush with a reef knot, making sure the knot falls on the underside of the seat and at a rail.

After about six circuits, secure the rush to rail with a spring cramp, and check to make sure that the strands are forming right-angled intersections. If necessary, adjust the strands as in Step 1. Then continue wrapping, stopping periodically to check for right angles.

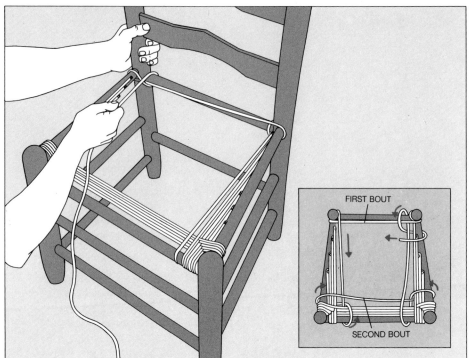

FIRST BOUT

SECOND BOUT

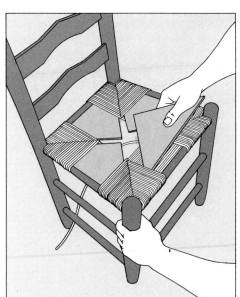

3 **Stuffing the seat.** When the side rails are covered by rush except for about 100 mm, slide a triangle of cardboard into the pocket between the upper and lower layers of rush along each side rail. Continue to weave over the cardboard until about 100 mm of space remains on the front and back rails. Then insert cardboard triangles in the pockets along the front and back rails. If these rails are lower than the side rails, as is the case with many chairs, they will probably need additional layers of cardboard to fill the pocket. When all of the cardboard is in place, cut off the points of all four cardboard triangles to allow more room for weaving. Continue weaving until the side rails are filled.

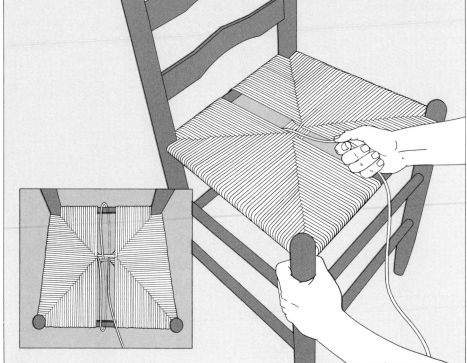

4 **Completing the chair.** To fill the remaining space on the front and back rails, bring the rush up through the centre opening, over the front rail, up through the centre opening again and over the back rail, then up through the centre opening once more to form, in effect, a figure-of-eight *(inset)*. Continue weaving figures-of-eight until the front and back rails are filled, then use a rubber mallet and a small block of wood to flatten the layers of rush where they cross in the centre of the seat. Tack the end of the rush to the back rail, and cut off the excess.

To make sure all the rows of rush lie in the same plane, rub the seat with a block of wood or, if necessary, use a stiff wooden ruler to poke additional cardboard stuffing between strands on the underside of the seat.

Wrapping a Natural Rush Chair Seat

1 **Twisting the rushes.** Pair two rushes, butt to butt, and run a thumb and forefinger along their length to expel air and water—a loud popping noise will be heard. Repeat this process for subsequent pairs. Use string to tie one end of the rushes to the inside of the left rail, about half way along. Then twist a length of the rushes together in order to make the first turn.

2 **Masking the first turn.** Wrap the twisted length over and under the front rail, then over and under the side rail. Pull the loose ends across towards the centre of the front rail.

3 **Joining a new strand.** Tie a new strand to the loose ends of the first pair with a half hitch *(below)*, making sure that the knot falls at the centre and on the top of the frame. Twist the strands together and wrap them over and under the right rail, then over and under the front rail. Tie the ends with string to the inside of the right rail, directly across from where the first strands are tied to the left rail.

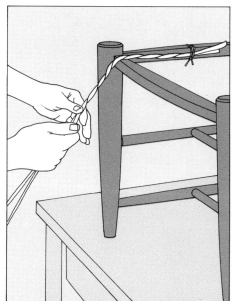

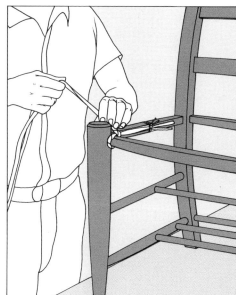

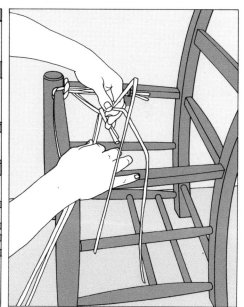

4 **Trimming the ends.** Weave additional rushes, repeating Steps 1 to 3, until the distance between the front corners equals the width of the back rail *(inset)*. If the strands cross the rails too far out, gently tap them back with a block of wood and a rubber mallet; if they cross the rails too close in, flatten them with a mallet to widen the weave. Then trim the excess rush protruding under the string on the side rails *(right)*. After the chair has been squared off, pair two rushes, butt to butt, and tie one end under the string on the left rail. Wrap the rushes round the left front corner, as in Step 1, then round the right front corner, as in Step 3. Continue the pattern to the right back corner, then to the left back corner, and finally to the left front corner to complete an entire circuit.

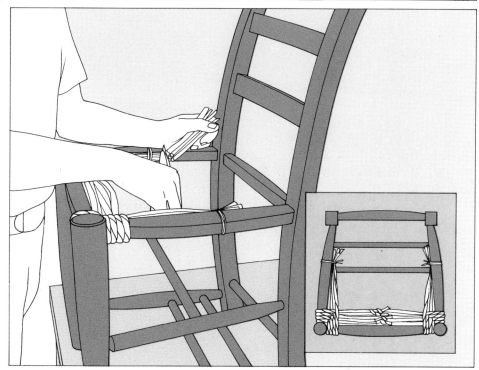

5 **Joining at corners.** After completing a circuit, continue weaving until the strands run out. Join on new strands with a half hitch, positioning the knot so that it falls either at the centre of a rail or at a corner. If joining at the centre of a rail, make sure that the ends of the knot fall on the underside of the seat *(Step 3)*. If joining at a corner, pull the ends up between the last two rows and twist them round new strands.

6 **Packing the seat.** As the side rails begin to fill, turn the chair upside down periodically and pack bundles of damaged rush and rush offcuts firmly into the corner cavities, using a blunt screwdriver to compact the stuffing. The packing will prevent the seat from sagging or becoming loose. At the same time, trim off the ends of knots with a pair of scissors.

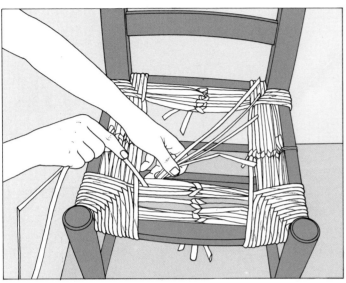

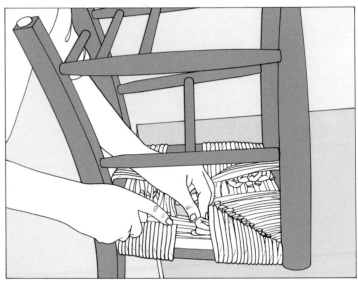

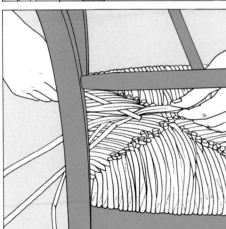

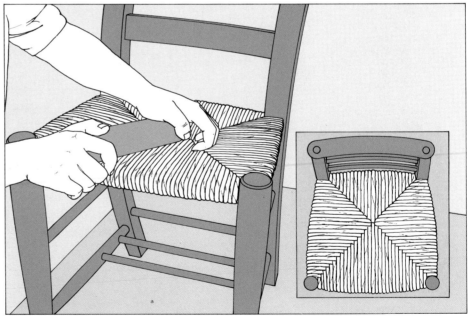

7 **Tying the last knot.** When the side rails are almost filled, cut off the string you used to tie the squaring-off strands. Continue weaving until the side rails are completely filled; wedge the last row into place with a blunt screwdriver. To fill the remaining space on the front and back rails, weave in the figure-of-eight pattern described in Step 4, page 60, again wedging the last row into place with the screwdriver. Turn the chair upside down and tie off the strands.

8 **Rolling for smoothness.** After cutting away any remaining excess round knots, turn the chair right side up again and smooth the seat with a rolling pin, making sure that all the rows are pressed flat. The finished seat should be firm and comfortable, with the two sets of rushes intersecting at right angles to one another *(inset)*.

Restoring a Chair Seat with Pre-Woven Cane

1 Cutting the pattern. After removing all the old cane, tongue and glue from the groove and sanding it clean, tape a piece of paper over the seat. Mark the paper by running a pencil along the inside edge of the groove, then cut along the marked line to make a pattern for the pre-woven cane. Tape the pattern on to a section of the pre-woven cane, positioning it so that one set of double strands runs straight down the centre from front to back, and one set of double strands runs parallel with the front rail (on a square seat) or with a line between the front legs (on a round seat). Cut the caning 25 mm larger than the dimensions of the pattern.

Soak the pre-woven cane for 15 minutes where it can lie flat, then place it across the seat in the correct position. Remove any strands that run along, rather than across, the groove.

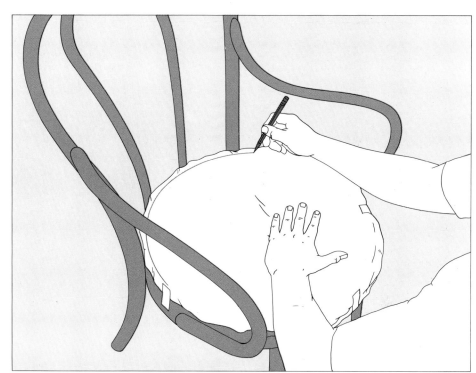

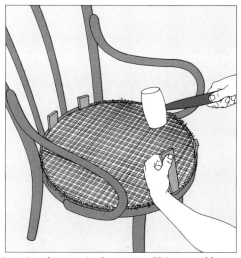

2 Inserting the cane in the groove. Using a rubber mallet and a 100 mm long wedge of hardwood, drive the pre-woven cane into a 50 mm section of the groove at the centre back of the chair. Lock this section in place with a 25 mm long hardwood wedge. Then pull the cane tightly across to the front, and drive it into a 50 mm section of the groove at the centre front, again inserting a locking wedge. Continue working along the groove, first on one side and then on the other, inserting cane in 50 mm wide sections and locking them with wedges, until you have filled the groove all the way round. Sponge the cane periodically to keep it pliable.

Use a sharp knife or a mallet and sharp chisel to trim off any cane ends that stick out of the groove, removing the locking wedges as you go.

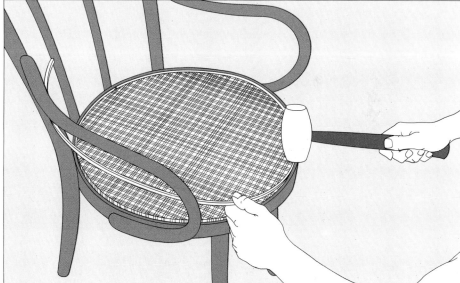

3 Inserting the tongue. Square the ends of a length of reed tongue at least 25 mm longer than the circumference of the groove, and soak it in water for 20 minutes. Run a uniform bead of glue into the groove on top of the cane. If the groove outlines a rounded seat, as here, start the tongue at the back, tapping it lightly with a rubber mallet just enough to position it in the groove. When you have completed almost the entire circuit, lap the tongue over itself, mark the overlap point, and cut the tongue with a sharp knife. Then use a wooden wedge and a rubber mallet to seat the tongue firmly in the groove so that it is flush with the surface of the frame and so that the ends form a butt joint. Sponge off any excess glue and allow the chair seat to dry for at least a day.

If the groove goes round a square-cornered seat, use the same basic techniques to fit the tongue into the groove; but use a length of tongue for each rail, and mitre the ends to fit together at the corners. Take care to cut the mitres so they make neat joints.

Use tweezers or fine sandpaper to remove any whiskers that were raised by the soaking process, and cut off larger filaments with scissors. Pre-woven cane darkens naturally with age, but it can be stained if you choose to do so.

Hand-Caning a Chair Seat

1 Lacing the first vertical row. On a square seat, insert about 100 mm of soaked cane in the centre hole along the back rail—or in the centre hole nearest the left rail if the number of holes is even—and peg it in place with a golf tee or a small wedge of beading cane or wood. Find the corresponding centre hole in the front rail, and pull the strand of cane through it, top to bottom, keeping the glossy side up. Carry the strand along the underside of the front rail, and bring it up through the first hole to the right of the hole just passed through. Then pull the strand of cane across the seat, and thread it through the corresponding hole in the back rail. Continue lacing in this manner, working from the centre to the right, but do not lace through the corner holes. Pull the cane smooth but not completely taut, for it will shrink as it dries.

When a strand is used up, leave about 100 mm hanging below the rail, and peg the end in place; peg a new strand into the nearest hole, again leaving about 100 mm hanging below the rail. If empty holes remain on the front rail after the holes on the back rail are filled, weave an individual strand from each empty front hole to a selected hole on the side rail so that the strands will be parallel and equally spaced (*inset*); leave ends of approximately 100 mm at both front and side. Lace the left side of the seat in the same way, again leaving the corner holes empty.

On a round chair, use these same basic techniques, but take special care to start on corresponding holes in the centre front and back of the seat. In lacing to fill the curved sides, choose holes that will keep the lines of cane parallel and evenly spaced. Do not worry about leaving empty "corner" holes on a round seat.

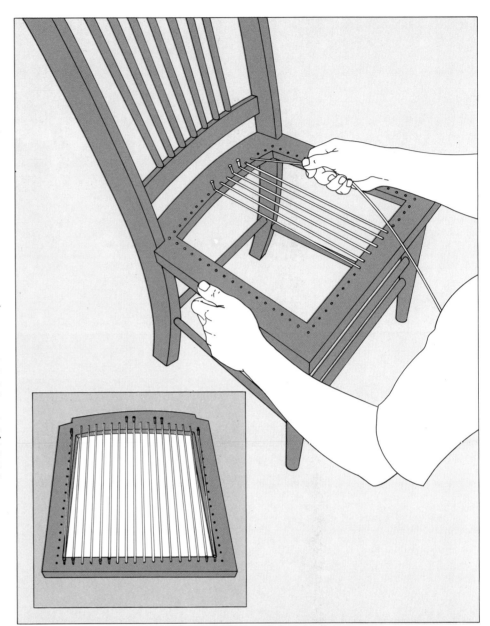

2 Tying off ends. Before continuing the cane weaving, turn the chair bottom up, and tie off any pegged cane ends by knotting them round the loops on the underside of the chair. Thoroughly sponge each end of cane and its adjacent loop, then lift the loop gently with an awl, and slip the end underneath. Keep the rough side of the cane up, and carry the cane under the loop from the inside to the outside edge of the chair rail. Then pass the cane through the new loop it has formed (from the outside of the rail to the inside) and, placing your thumb over the knot, pull the cane tight. Position the knot in the centre of the loop to allow for more than one knot per loop if needed. Trim cane ends to 10 mm.

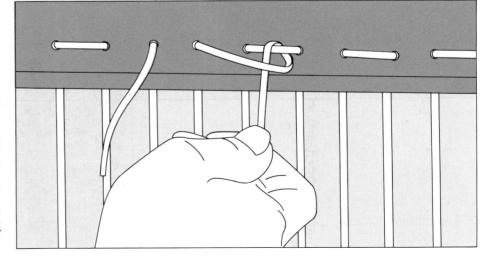

3 **Lacing the first horizontal rows.** On a square seat, begin the horizontal lacing at the back, working between side holes but skipping the holes at the back corners. Peg the end of the cane as in Step 1, and lace it from side to side, over the top of the vertical strands, keeping the glossy side up. Stop weaving after you pass through the last set of holes short of the front corners *(inset)*. Tie off the pegged ends as in Step 2.

On a round chair seat, lace the cane using the same sequence described in Step 1. Begin by lacing from centre side to centre side, then lace from there towards the back. Then return to the centre and lace towards the front.

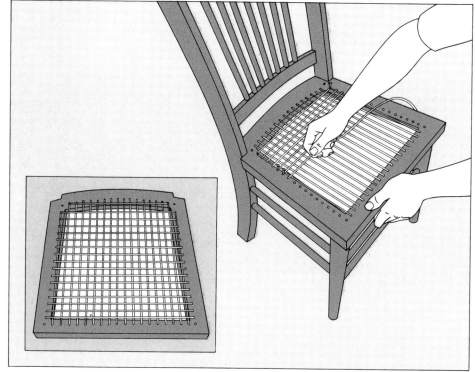

4 **Lacing the first diagonal row.** On a square seat, start lacing diagonal rows at the right front corner; peg the end of the cane in the first hole at the left of the right front corner hole. Thread the free cane down through the first hole on the right side rail next to this corner, and up through the next hole on the same rail. Then carry the cane back to the front rail, going under each vertical strand and over each horizontal strand. Lace the free cane back to the side rail in the same manner. Continue weaving diagonals until you pass through a corner hole. You may find it necessary to weave two diagonals into the same hole on one side, and skip over a hole on the other side, to keep the rows of cane even.

During this step and all subsequent steps that require intricate weaving, frequently dampen the free end of cane, as well as the top and the bottom of the woven seat. To make longer passes across the seat go more smoothly, trim the free cane end to a point, and pull all the excess cane through after every four or five stitches to avoid bending the cane into too many S curves.

Weave diagonals through the second half of the seat in the same manner, starting on the back rail in the hole next to the left back corner hole and running the cane between the back and left rails. When the first diagonals are completed *(inset)*, there should be two strands of cane passing through the holes at the left front and right back corners. Tie off pegged ends. On a round seat, weave the first diagonals following the techniques used for a square seat, using your eyes to judge the appropriate holes for each row.

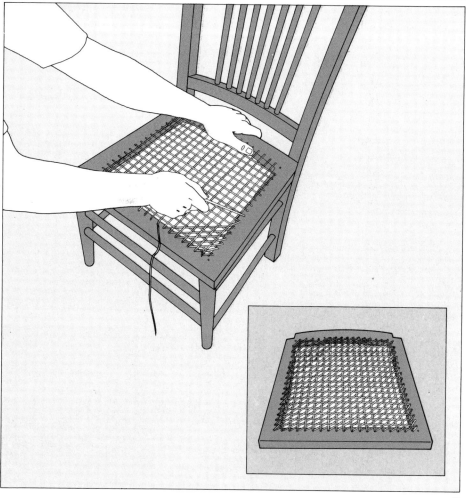

5 Lacing the second vertical rows. Using the same methods as in Step 1, page 64, lay a second set of vertical strands between the front and back rails, placing them slightly to the right of the first vertical canes and stringing them over the top of all work done so far. As before, tie off the pegged ends as shown in Step 2, page 64.

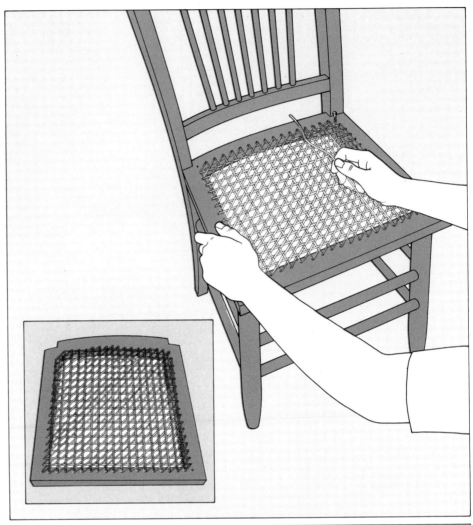

6 Lacing the second horizontal rows. To make this step easier, use two pegs as tools to separate each pair of vertical strands. Beginning in the hole on the right rail next to the right back corner hole, weave a second set of horizontal strands, just behind the first horizontal strands. Follow the same sequence of rows as in Step 3, page 65, but as you weave, go under all the first diagonal rows and the first vertical rows, but over the second vertical rows. Straighten the rows as you work, and check carefully for mistakes. When you have finished weaving a second set of horizontal rows across the entire seat, tie off any pegged ends (page 64, Step 2).

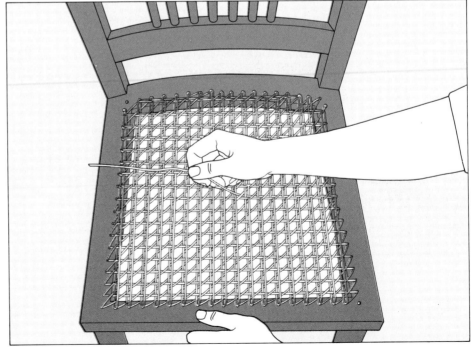

7 **Lacing the second diagonal rows.** With an awl, carefully compact the strands already woven into each hole to make room for additional strands of cane, then weave diagonal rows at right angles to those already laid *(page 65, Step 4)*. Start in the hole in the front rail next to the left front corner hole, and weave under the first diagonal and over the second diagonal that go to this corner hole. Then thread the strand of cane down through the hole on the left rail next to this corner hole, and up through the next hole on the same rail. Continue to weave between the front and left rails, carrying the strands over the vertical rows, under the horizontal rows and alternately over and under the diagonal rows. To avoid possible confusion at the edges, remember that you should never go under or over two consecutive diagonal strands.

To maintain symmetry in the pattern, skip holes or double the rows in a single hole where necessary, as in Step 4, page 65. Stop when you reach a corner hole, then weave diagonals across the second half of the seat in the same way, starting on the back rail in the hole that is next to the right back corner hole and weaving between the back and right rails *(inset)*. Tie off the pegged ends *(page 64, Step 2)*.

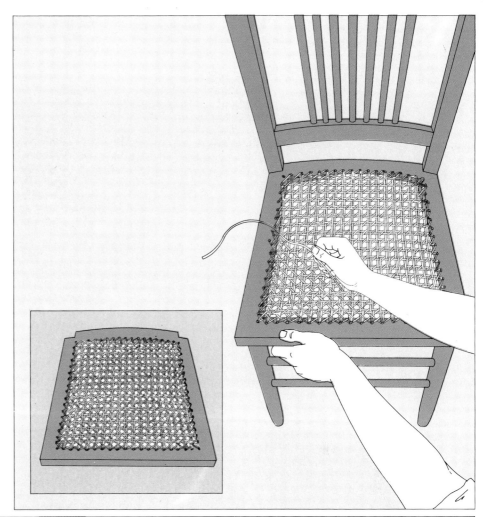

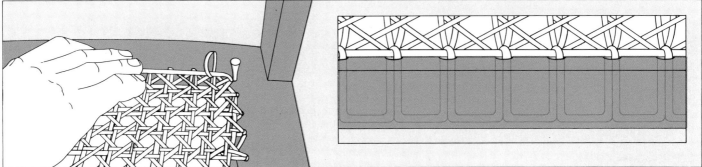

8 **Beading the edge of the seat.** For a square seat, cut a length of beading cane—cane one size larger than the weaving cane—for each rail, making it 50 mm longer than the rail length. Soak the four beading canes and four strands of weaving cane, then peg one end of the cane for the back rail in the hole at the right back corner, allowing about 25 mm of cane to hang beneath the seat. In the next hole along the back rail, thread a weaving strand from under the rail; loop it over the beading from back to front, then push it down through the same hole, anchoring the beading against the rail. On the underside of the rail, tie off one end of the weaver *(page 64, Step 2)* and pull the free end tight, making sure that the weaver is at right angles to the beading and that the beading cane lies flat *(inset)*. Loop in this manner at every hole along the back rail. Insert the beading and the weaver in the left back corner hole and peg them in place.

To start the beading cane for the left side rail, insert one end in the left back corner hole, and peg it in place; then fasten the beading along the left rail as you did along the back rail. Complete the front and right rails in the same way, and insert the last end of beading cane down into the

right rear corner, where you started. To hold the beading ends in place, whittle a softwood plug to fit each corner hole, and hammer the plugs in place from the top with a rubber mallet, making sure that they are flush with the chair frame. Flatten the beading stitches with the wooden handle of an awl, and remove stray hairs from the cane with tweezers or a razor blade.

On curved chair seats, use a single piece of beading cane for the entire seat perimeter. On chairs that have angular back corners and a curved front, use two pieces of beading cane—one for the back and one for the sides and front.

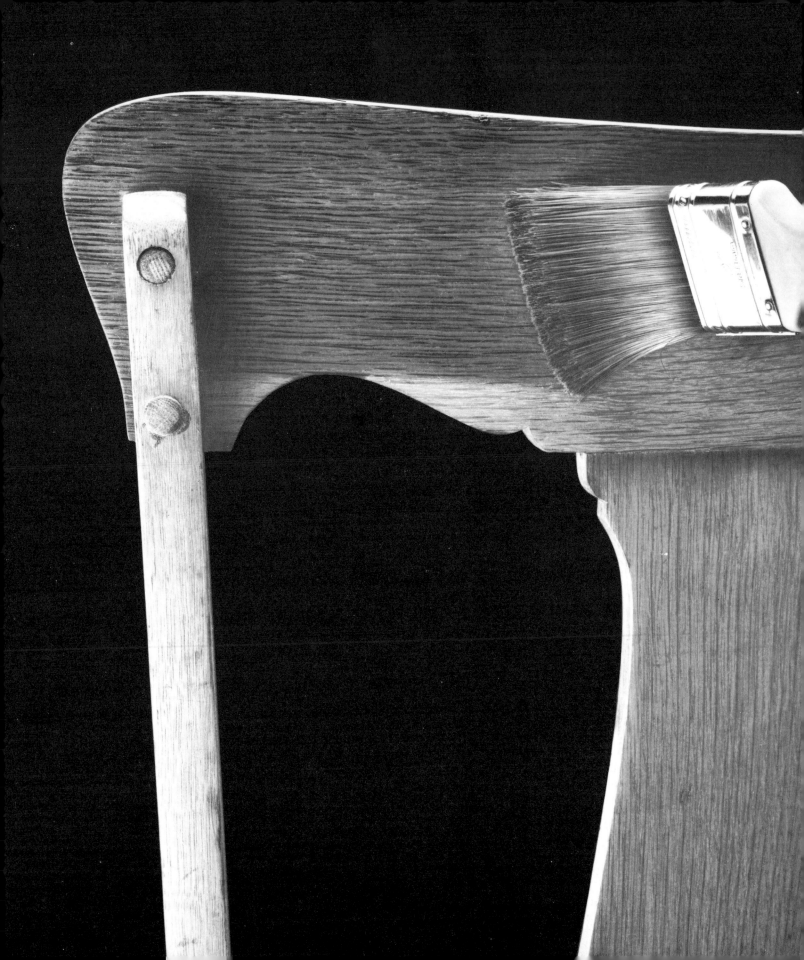

3

The finishing touch. A clear oil finish, brushed liberally on to the bare surface of an oak chair, sinks into the wood and highlights the beauty of the grain. In preparation for this step, the chair was first treated with chemical strippers that removed old paint, layer by layer; then the wood was smoothed with increasingly fine sandpapers. An oil finish is one of the easiest to apply; it can be spread on the surface with a brush or cloth.

For some 5,000 years of furniture-making, wood has been the most popular material—and no wonder. It has been abundantly available and, though strong, it is flexible and light enough to be easily worked. Yet wood has disadvantages: it is susceptible to damage from insects, moisture and misuse. Because it is so vulnerable, most wooden furniture has, through the ages, been covered with a protective coating. In earlier times, this coating was often so extravagantly ornate that it completely hid the wood. King Tutankhamun's wooden throne was plated with gold, and much medieval wooden furniture was encased in gesso, a plaster-like substance. Nowadays, nearly all furniture that is made of fine wood is covered with clear finishes that allow the grain to shine through while also protecting the wood.

Modern finishes guard the wood against moisture, dirt and damage such as scratches or bruises. The most familiar finishes are divided into two groups: those that soak into the wood and those that rest on it in much the same way as skin. Within these groups, each finish performs certain functions better than others. So if you plan to refinish a piece of furniture, your choice of finish will be determined by the use to which the furniture is put, by the visual appeal of the finish and by the ease with which it can be applied.

Common penetrating finishes include boiled and raw linseed oil, and rubbing oils such as teak oil or penetrating-resin sealer, sold under various brand names. All these finishes are usually applied with a rag, and they provide a seal for the pores of the wood without piling up any surface bulk; they emphasize the grain and the colour of the wood rather than obscuring them. They dry quite hard and some of them resist moisture very well, but oil finishes are so thin that they offer little protection from surface abrasion. Although they remain in the pores of the wood, in time oil finishes wear off the surface—so they require periodic reapplication.

Surface-coating finishes include lacquer, varnishes and shellac finishes such as French polish. These are usually applied by brush or, alternatively, they can be sprayed on, often over a sealer that prevents them from penetrating the wood; they dry to form a hard film that lies on top of the wood. The surface-coating finishes form an effective barrier against dirt and damage, but their reaction to moisture varies greatly. Polyurethane varnish is virtually impervious to water, while lacquer and shellac finishes are easily marked by heat, water and solvents. Unfortunately, most surface-coating finishes obscure the natural texture of the wood slightly and impart a coated appearance.

Maintaining the beauty and protective powers of any finish can involve a wide range of procedures, from simple spot repairs to an elaborate process of stripping and refinishing. But no matter how much effort you have to expend, you will have the satisfaction of knowing that, in renewing the finish, you are maintaining an aspect of the furniture that is as essential as its very structure.

Saving a Damaged Finish with Minor Repairs

The original finish on a piece of furniture can sometimes be its greatest asset. It seals the wood against loss of moisture, prevents spills and stains from penetrating the pores and, with age, may take on a mellow patina that enhances the furniture's value. Therefore it may be preferable to correct a flawed finish instead of stripping it.

The corrective measures to be used will depend on the type of finish and the cause of the damage, and often the two are closely related. The white haze that clouds a tabletop, for example, is likely to be the result of a chemical reaction between the shellac or lacquer finish and moisture in the air, which softens both finishes. (The white rings that form when wet glasses sit too long on a shellac or lacquer surface are localized versions of this same phenomenon.)

Both shellac and lacquer belong to a class of finishes called solvent-release coatings. They are solutions of resin in a solvent that evaporates, leaving behind a thin resin film. Solvent-release coatings have the special—particularly useful—property of redissolving readily when an effective solvent is brushed over them. With care, it is sometimes possible to respread such a coating to create a smooth new finish in a process that is called amalgamation.

A second major class of finishes, the chemically reactive coatings, harden through a much more complex process: they absorb oxygen from the air to change from liquid to solid. Two familiar examples of these coatings are varnish and paint, which harden into a thin film; unlike shellac and lacquer, these cannot be amalgamated. Two other reactive coatings are linseed oil and boiled oil, both of which sink into the pores of the wood.

Distinguishing between these finishes requires no particular expertise. Application of an effective solvent *(chart, opposite)* in a hidden spot will cause shellac or lacquer to dissolve and quickly re-dry. If the finish does not respond in this way, it is probably varnish, enamel or paint, which crinkle and soften when remover is applied. Indeed, the finish can sometimes be identified by its response to the materials used in the preliminary cleaning process. The simplest of these cleaners consists of soap and warm water, which are used to wipe away surface dirt. Water should not be left lying on the surface as it may cloud a shellac or lacquer finish.

Alternatively, you can clean the surface with turpentine or white spirit, both useful for deep grime or built-up layers of wax. White spirit, also known as turpentine substitute, may also remedy the flawed finish. If the finish is clouded by a smoky blue haze that disappears when cleaned with white spirit, the problem is one of incompatibility—the furniture has been oiled or waxed over a silicone polish, which repels the other coatings. The silicone, as well as oil or wax, is dissolved by the application of white spirit.

In the normal course of repair, you will need two kinds of refinishing aid—abrasives and chemicals. The abrasives commonly used are extra-fine steel wool, grades 000 and 0000, and silicon carbide paper in grit sizes of 220 to 600, very fine to super fine. Abrasive papers should be used with a sanding block *(page 77)*.

Two other abrasives used in refinishing are rottenstone and pumice, both of which are mixed with mineral oil into a paste. Rottenstone is a very mild abrasive made of powdered limestone; pumice, which is much stronger, is powdered volcanic glass. It should be used only in fine grade or very fine grade and be applied with a well-padded sanding block or a blackboard duster, so that it will not mar the finish. In lieu of either of these two substances, you can use a slightly abrasive car polish.

Chemicals useful in repair work include solvents, dyes, stains, oils and polishes. Solvents combine with the old finish—as methylated spirit amalgamates shellac, and as cellulose thinners will amalgamate lacquer—to remove hazing and to restore a crazed or crackled finish to its original smoothness. Stains, oils and polishes can improve the entire finish, or they can be used for more localized repairs—they will disguise scratches, scuffed areas and similar blemishes.

The simplest remedies for spot repairs are ordinary furniture oils and polishes, which have a wetting effect that may be sufficient to darken minor scratches to match the surrounding finish. When these do not work, coloured furniture polish or an oil-based stain may do the job.

Sometimes makeshift home remedies work almost as well as professional products. Car-paint cleaner or metal polish applied with a cloth will remove the white rings left on furniture by cups and glasses. The kernel of any nut rubbed over a scratch may darken it enough to hide it, and iodine will disguise a scratch in red-stained mahogany. Shoe polish of the right colour will do for a scuffed table precisely what it does for scuffed shoes. With any of these colouring agents, begin with a lighter colour and move to a darker one if necessary, because a scratch that is dyed too dark can seldom be lightened to match its surroundings.

For deep scratches and other blemishes, such as burns and chips, some sort of filler is needed. It may be possible to fill in a scratch by rubbing a child's crayon over it. On painted or varnished surfaces, a slight depression can be built up with successive coats of the same finish, layered on with a fine-tipped artist's brush. But the professional way to patch burnt, chipped or gouged areas is with wax sticks or wood-stopping, both available at hardware shops or artists' supply shops.

A wax stick is held against a hot knife and the wax is then guided into the depression as it melts. Woodstopping, which is sold in paste form in various shades, is applied with a palette knife or flat-bladed scraper. It should be left slightly proud of the surface and sanded smooth when dry.

After any of these spot repairs, the area of the repair should be buffed with a fine abrasive to blend it into the surrounding finish, and then waxed or polished. A hard paste wax, the kind used on cars, provides the best protection and needs renewing only three or four times a year. An oil-based polish imparts a lovely glowing shine, but the polish is not very durable and it must be renewed as often as once a week.

Repairs at a Glance: Local Defects

Material \ Problem	White rings or spots	Minor scratch	Deep scratch	Small burn	Small chip in finish
Furniture polish		Apply to entire furniture surface with a clean cloth; rub well into scratch, then buff.			
Coloured furniture polish		Rub into scratch with cotton wool, and then, if desired, apply to entire surface with a clean cloth.			
Steel wool (grade 000)	Dip in mineral oil or linseed oil, rub over spot with grain in short strokes, wipe away excess with a clean cloth. To restore gloss surface, use abrasive car polish.				
Rottenstone	Mix to creamy consistency with mineral oil, rub into spot with one finger wrapped in a clean cloth. Wipe off excess mixture with a damp rag; dry with a soft cloth.				
Pumice	Mix to creamy consistency with mineral oil, rub gently over spot with grain, using a padded sanding block. Wipe off excess with a damp rag; dry with a soft cloth.				
Furniture-wax stick		Rub into depression to fill it, wipe away excess with a clean cloth.	Choose a colour that matches light grain of finish; melt wax into depression with a hot knife. Cool, scrape smooth. Paint in darker grain with artist's oil paint or watercolours; seal with spray varnish.	Scrape out all charred material with a trimming knife. Choose a colour that matches light grain of finish; melt wax into the depression with a hot knife. Cool, scrape smooth. Paint in darker grain with artist's oil paint or watercolours; seal with spray varnish.	
Polyurethane varnish			Using an artist's brush, fill with successive coats of finish colour. Build up higher than surrounding area, then smooth down with very fine abrasive paper on a sanding block.		Using an artist's brush, fill with successive coats of finish colour. Build up higher than surrounding area, then smooth with very fine abrasive paper on a block.
Methylated spirits (for shellac finish) Cellulose thinners (for lacquer finish)	Wet a small, lintless pad with solvent, wring out. Stroke damaged area, remoistening the pad until the spot disappears.				

Remedies for local damage. Listed across the top of this chart are local damage or spot defects that commonly afflict furniture finishes. Corrective measures for them use the materials in the column on the left. The technique for using a specific material is described in the column beneath the problem. In most cases there are several alternatives, ranging here from mild at the top to more extreme at the bottom. Try the more conservative measures first; for example, to hide a minor scratch in a finish, try using furniture polish before furniture dye.

Repairs at a Glance: General Damage

Material / Problem	Stubborn wax or grease, silicone haze	Scuffed, dull surface, multiple light scratches	White haze	Cracking, crazing
Furniture polish		Apply with a clean cloth; buff.		
Coloured furniture polish		Apply with a clean cloth, working into marred surface to colour it; buff.		
Turpentine or white spirit	Rub in with a clean cloth, changing the cloth as needed until all traces of coating are removed.			
Mixture of 3 parts boiled linseed oil to 1 part turpentine		Rub in along grain with a lintless cloth; wipe away excess with a dry cloth.		
Steel wool (grade 000)		Dip in paraffin oil or linseed oil, rub with grain over entire surface giving special attention to scratched areas. Remove excess oil with a clean cloth. To restore gloss surface where required, reshine with abrasive car or furniture polish.	Dip in paraffin oil or linseed oil, rub with grain in long strokes over entire surface. Remove excess oil with a clean cloth. To restore gloss surface where required, reshine with abrasive car or furniture polish.	
Rottenstone		Mix to creamy consistency with paraffin oil. Apply with a clean cloth, rubbing with grain, giving special attention to damaged areas. Wipe off excess mixture with a damp rag; dry with a soft cloth.	Mix to creamy consistency with paraffin oil. Apply with a clean cloth, rubbing with grain. Wipe off excess mixture with a damp rag; dry with a soft cloth.	
Pumice		Mix to creamy consistency with paraffin oil and apply with padded sanding block. Rub along wood grain with an even touch. Wipe with a damp rag; dry with a soft cloth.	Mix to creamy consistency with paraffin oil and apply with padded sanding block. Rub along wood grain with an even touch. Wipe off excess mixture with a damp rag; dry with a soft cloth.	
Cellulose pullover: mixture of 3 parts white spirit to 1 part cellulose thinners (for lacquer finish)		Apply with chamois leather or pad of soft cloth; rub in hard along the grain with long, even strokes.		

Restoring a generally damaged surface. Across the top of the chart above are listed problems that affect the entire furniture finish. The materials that can be used to correct the damage are listed in the column on the left. The technique for using a specific material is shown in the column beneath the problem. The solutions range from mild at the top to more extreme at the bottom. You can save time and effort by trying the more conservative solutions first. For example, to remove a white haze, try fine steel wool, switching to quicker-cutting pumice if the former does not work.

Patching with a Hot Wax Stick

For this repair to be almost invisible, you need a wax stick that is the exact colour of the lightest grain in the wood, and a tube of artist's paint—oil or watercolour—in the same colour as the darkest grain. If you cannot find a matching wax stick, you can mix your own by melting and blending shavings, pared from several wax sticks of different colours, in a spoon or a metal lid, then allowing them to cool and harden.

Caution: do not melt the shavings directly over a flame or electric burner; they are a combination of paraffin, beeswax, oil and dye and are highly inflammable. Instead, heat the spoon or lid, take it off the heat, then drop the shavings into it; they melt quickly and can be blended before the spoon or lid cools.

Other supplies needed for the hot wax patch are a curved knife, a sootless heat source, a fine-tipped artist's brush, spray varnish and medium-grade steel wool. Professionals use a curved knife called a burn-in knife, but a grapefruit knife or any knife with a slender blade is suitable.

Making an Invisible Plug

1 **Preparing the surface.** To repair a burnt area, as shown here, first scrape away all charred material with a single-edged razor blade or a trimming knife, then clean the depression with white spirit. To prepare gouges or deep scratches for filling, simply clean the blemish thoroughly.

2 **Forming the patch.** Warm the knife over an alcohol lamp or electric hot plate and, holding the end of the wax stick against the heated blade, guide the melting wax into the depression. Reheat the blade as necessary, adding wax to the patch until it is slightly higher than the surrounding surface; the wax will contract as it cools. When the patch is cool, pull a single-edged razor blade across it to level it, and give it a final smoothing with your fingertip.

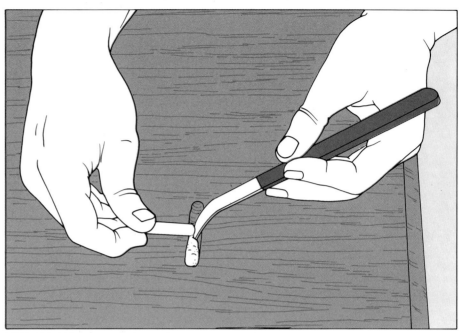

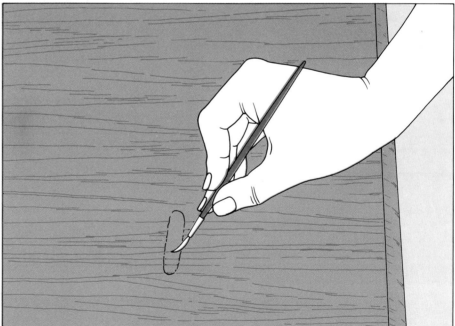

3 **Painting the grain.** Dip a fine-tipped artist's brush into artists' paints that have been squeezed straight from the tube. Wipe the brush over paper, leaving the bristles almost dry. Then paint feathery strokes over the wax patch with the brush, blending them into the pattern of the surrounding wood grain. If the lines look too crisp, smudge the paint lightly with your finger or a cloth for a more natural effect. To fix the patch permanently, seal it with a light application of the original finish.

Caution: if you use a spray finish, spray in a well-ventilated room, away from any open flame, and do not smoke. When the sprayed area is dry, buff with medium-grade steel wool, and wax or polish the entire surface.

Stripping a Finish Down to Bare Wood

Some old finishes, clear or opaque, are worth preserving; after years of polishing, they lend character to a piece of furniture. But many others—bubbled and brittle, or so thick they obscure carving or hide grain—are best removed.

There are three ways to remove a finish: dissolve it with chemicals, heat it so that it bubbles away from the wood, or scrape or sand it away. Speed and potential damage to the wood are the main considerations in choosing a method.

By far the easiest—but not the best—way to strip furniture is to send it to a professional who will dunk it in a chemical dip tank. This process gets the finish off, but it can also bleach the wood and soften glue to loosen joints and veneer; it is not generally recommended for valuable pieces. However, it may be the only practical way to strip furniture that otherwise would require long hours of tedious handwork—wicker, for example.

Several heating devices are excellent for rapidly stripping away many layers of paint. One example resembles a hair dryer and blows air heated to 500℃ on to the paint. But none of these devices is effective on such solvent-release finishes as lacquer and shellac, and may scorch the wood. Propane torches, which are sometimes used for stripping house paint, increase the risk of scorching and should not be used on furniture.

Power sanders used with coarse sandpaper, or sanding attachments for electric drills, speed the job of clearing finished surfaces. But neither is recommended for fine furniture or veneers, and both should be used with caution, as they may gouge the surface and leave scratches that must be removed before the furniture is refinished. Hand-applied chemicals, though slower, allow more control and usually leave the surface ready for refinishing. Sometimes you will have to use more than one of these techniques.

The best all-purpose chemical strippers are solutions containing methylene chloride; other all-purpose chemicals, such as caustic soda and oxalic acid, are more dangerous and difficult to control. Trisodium phosphate, methyl alcohol and lacquer thinner work only on specific finishes. Methylene chloride strippers come as liquids and pastes; the paste type is much easier to use because it clings to vertical surfaces and evaporates more slowly.

Some paste and liquid strippers are labelled "no wash"; others are thickened with wax, which must be removed after use with a wash of white spirit or methylated spirits. A third type calls for a water wash; but this is less satisfactory, as the water is likely to raise the grain of the wood and may separate veneer from its base, making it necessary to sand or reglue.

Although some manufacturers of liquid strippers recommend removing the entire finish with one application, the best technique is to proceed layer by layer. One-step removal requires prolonged soaking with stripper, which may saturate and soften the wood so that the scraper gouges the surface easily and the stripped wood looks bleached and rough. However, because paste is unlikely to produce the same degree of saturation, it can be safely used to remove most finishes after only one or two prolonged applications. Another advantage of paste is that it will not drip or spill.

Chemical strippers can irritate your lungs and skin, so work in a well-ventilated space and wear goggles and rubber gloves. Cover the workroom floor with newspapers and put foil pie cases under furniture legs to catch drips; stripper can dissolve some types of plastic and linoleum flooring, as well as rubber soles on shoes. Work carefully, and allow plenty of time for each job and for cleaning up.

Both heat and mechanical removal require precautions to limit surface damage. Always turn a heating device away from the paint as soon as it softens, to avoid scorching the wood surface or igniting the finish. With a power sander, apply only light pressure, to avoid digging into the surface with the sanding pad. Wear goggles and a mask when using any sander.

Removing a Finish with Liquid Stripper

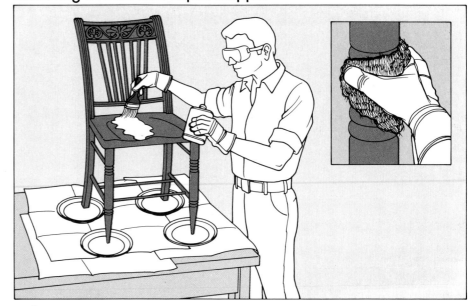

1 Applying the stripper. Beginning with a large horizontal surface, pat the stripper evenly over the wood with an old paintbrush; let it work for five minutes. When the finish begins to bubble, apply a second coat, dabbing it firmly on to the first coat. Wait for 10 minutes and then use a wide putty knife to scrape the stripper and the dissolved finish into a can at the edge of the surface, or wipe it on to an old newspaper with the putty knife. Scrub the surface with grade 2 steel wool, working parallel to the grain, to expose the next layer of hard finish. Repeat until you reach the bare wood. Scrape gently any tiny residue of finish with the putty knife and then scrub the surface smooth with grade 000 or 0000 steel wool, following the wood's grain.

Turn the piece so that another large surface is horizontal and repeat the stripping process. Strip smaller elements by patting on stripper and rubbing with grade 2 steel wool (inset).

2 **Stripping cracks and crevices.** To remove the softened finish from cracks or crevices in a carved surface, position the furniture so that the carved surface is horizontal and pat on stripper, then use a pointed dowel or a small stick to lift out the finish. Work gently, since the wood may be softened by the stripper and easily gouged. Use grade 2 steel wool wadded into a small, tight ball to scrub gently inside the crevices.

If you are doing extensive stripping of heavily carved surfaces, you may need to have special tools. Old toothbrushes, an awl, a small soft wire brush, toothpicks and a penknife *(inset)* are all useful instruments for this purpose.

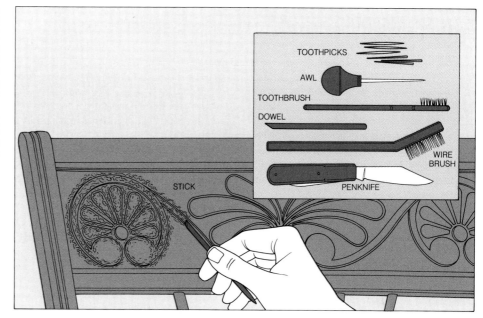

Using a Paste Stripper

Stripping with paste. Use a putty or palette knife to apply the paste. When all surfaces have been coated, wrap them securely in polythene to ensure that the paste remains moist. How long the stripping process takes will depend on the type of finish; manufacturers usually suggest two hours, but periodically you should unwrap a section of the polythene and scrape off a small strip of paste. If the test reveals bare wood, remove all the stripper and rub the surfaces with steel wool *(Step 1, opposite page)*. If the bottom layers of finish have not lifted, rewrap the polythene and wait for another hour. Scrape off the paste and apply a second coating if necessary.

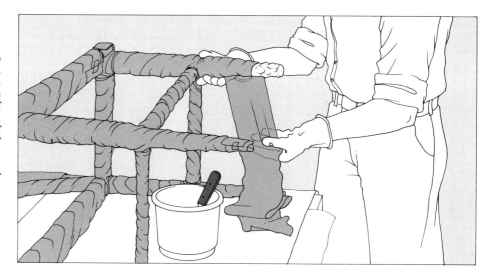

Softening Paint with Heat

Heating and scraping paint. Hold a heat gun designed for paint removal 50 to 100 mm above the paint surface. When the paint bubbles, remove the heat source and gently scrape away the paint, using a wide putty knife. Repeat the process layer by layer until you reach bare wood; finally, smooth with fine steel wool.

Preparing a Smooth Foundation

A good foundation is absolutely essential to any furniture finish, since the tiniest chip or scratch will be worsened by whatever is put on top of it. The key to a smooth base is a series of sanding steps, using abrasive papers suitable for the wood to be finished *(chart, right, below)*. For the initial sanding, power sanders are useful, provided the surface is large and flat. But hand-sanding is needed for the final stages, and for curved or detailed surfaces, followed at the end by a buffing with fine steel wool to remove the last hair-like roughness. (Steel wool for wood finishing is available in grades 00 to 0000.)

The best power sanders for furniture work are finishing and orbital sanders, which allow precise control and reduce the possibility of gouging—a problem encountered when using belt and disc sanders. A finishing sander has a rectangular pad that vibrates in line with the grain of the wood and does very fine work, but it is slower than an orbital sander. The latter has a similar rectangular or square plate that rotates in a 3 mm circle, 9,000 to 12,000 times a minute, but it leaves tiny circular scratches that subsequently have to be removed from the wood with hand-sanding. Sanding discs are available in coarse (grit sizes 36–40), medium (grit sizes 50–80) and fine (grit sizes 100 and above) grades. Some sanders can be operated in either an orbital or a finishing mode.

Hand-sanding to remove the last scratches left by power sanding, as well as to smooth curved or detailed surfaces, uses various sanding blocks to ensure equal pressure over the surface of the wood. For flat areas, the block is usually a rubber-faced rectangle, available at most hardware shops, or a home-made wooden block padded with felt. You can make blocks in different shapes for sanding convex surfaces and inside corners.

Abrasive papers for hand-sanding are used in progressively finer grit sizes. When sanding planed softwood, start with grit size 60 and finish with size 120 for painting and size 280 for polishing or varnishing. On planed hardwood, start with size 60–80 and finish with size 150 for painting and size 280 or 320 for polishing or varnishing.

For the final smoothing, use grade 0000 steel wool. The first step is to wet the wood with a damp cloth so that any loose wood fibres swell and rise. Let the surface dry overnight, then whisk off the fibres with the steel wool. To find remaining rough spots, put your hand inside an old nylon stocking and run it over the surface; if there are fibres that catch, go over the area again with the same steel wool.

After the final smoothing, some open-pored woods—such as oak, walnut, rosewood and mahogany—will need to have the pores filled with a grain filler if you plan to use a glossy clear finish. Fillers usually are thick pastes, made of silica powder mixed with oil, and they come in colours to match most woods. But for an exact match, you can buy a neutral filler and add penetrating stain or oil paint to get the right colour. Test the colour wet; although it will lighten as the filler dries, a clear finish will darken the colour again. When wood is to be stained, apply the stain *(pages 78–79)* before the filler.

To use filler, thin the paste with turpentine to the consistency of house paint, then scrub it on with an old paintbrush, pushing it into the pores. Let the filler dry until the surface is dull, then wipe it off across the grain with hessian or an old bath towel until it is no longer visible on the surface. Allow the filler to dry for 24 hours, then sand lightly to remove surface granules before applying a finish.

A Range of Abrasive Papers for Varied Uses

Grit size	30	36	40	50	60	70	80	100	120	150	180	220	240	280	320
Sandpaper (grades)	3	2½	S2			M2		F2	1½	1		0		FLOUR	
Garnet paper (grades)			1½	1	½		0	2/0	3/0	4/0	5/0	6/0	7/0	8/0	9/0

Choosing the right abrasive paper. Both the above papers are suitable for rubbing down all types of wood and paint. Sandpaper is the common term for abrasive paper coated with ground bottle glass; garnet paper is coated with crushed garnet, and has a softer cutting action which results in a finer finish. Two other common types of abrasive paper are aluminium oxide paper, which is suitable for sanding down hardwood and is available in grit sizes 24 to 400, and wet and dry silicon carbide paper. The latter has the hardest grit of all abrasive papers, and is used on painted surfaces and metals; it is available in grit sizes 60 to 600. Some abrasive papers incorporate a lubricating aid that prevents clogging.

Padded Blocks for Sanding

Making a felt-faced block. Cut a 40 mm block of 100 by 50 mm softwood and a 125 mm square of 2 mm thick felt. Spread rubber cement on one face of the block; then tack an edge of the felt to one side of the block, stretch it across the cemented face and tack it to the other side. When the cement is dry (about five minutes), use a trimming knife to trim overlapping felt. To use the block, tear standard 280 by 230 mm sheets of sandpaper into quarters and hold the sandpaper over the felt with your fingers as you sand.

Make sanding blocks for curves and grooves by cementing felt to dowels or triangular blocks of wood *(inset)*; hold the felt in place until the cement sets. Do not use tacks; they might scratch the surface that is being sanded. Wrap these blocks with small pieces of sandpaper, also held in place with your fingers.

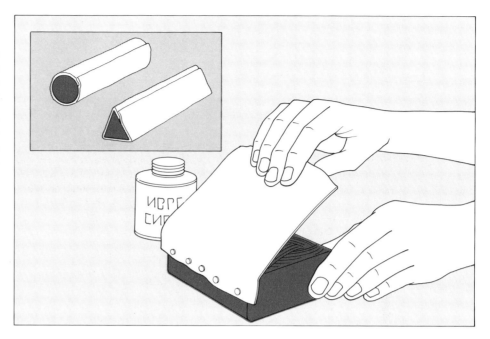

A Sequence of Sanding for Exceptional Smoothness

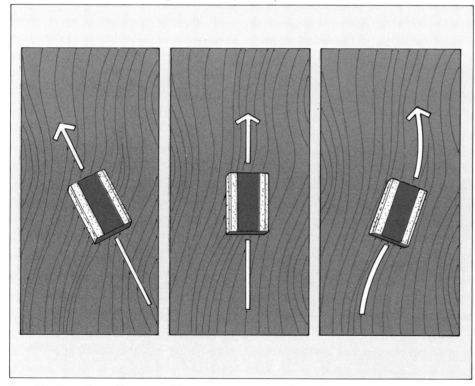

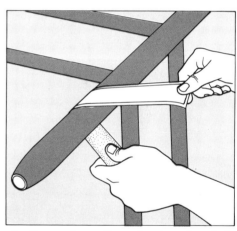

Sanding round parts. To sand parts such as chair legs or spindles, place a length of 25 mm cloth tape against the back of a 40 mm wide strip of sandpaper, to reinforce it. Holding the sanding strip at each end, draw it back and forth round the part as you do when polishing a shoe. Begin with 120 grit paper and progress to 220 grit paper. Finally, sand along the length of the leg or spindle with 280 grit paper or grade 0000 steel wool until surface scratches are smoothed away and raised fibres are removed.

Smoothing flat surfaces. To remove ridges, superficial stains, or damage resulting from stripping, make sanding strokes at a slight angle to the wood grain *(above, left)*. Start with 120 grit paper; if the sanding progresses too slowly, switch to a coarser grade until most of the roughness is reduced, then switch back to 120 grit and continue sanding until the only remaining roughness is from the diagonal sanding scratches. Remove these by sanding with strokes parallel to the grain *(above, centre)*. Use 220 grit paper, and sand until the scratches are entirely removed.

Finally, sand the surface with short back-and-forth strokes following the grain *(above, right)*. Use 240 to 280 grit paper, and sand until the wood is smooth enough to reflect oblique lights.

Changing the Colour of Wood

For most of the thousands of years that furniture-makers have worked with wood, they have used only the innate colours of the materials, sometimes altered slightly with vegetable dyes or the colouring properties of the oil, varnish or shellac finish. But developments in organic chemistry since the mid-19th century have made it possible to achieve a vast array of wood shades and tones easily and safely. Concentrated bleaches can freshen stripped or raw wood darkened by age or even eliminate the natural colour entirely. Stains and dyes can make one wood resemble another or can call attention to the pattern of the grain by tinting it with a colour that is purely decorative.

Bleached wood—with the natural colour chemically removed from its fibres—became popular in the 1930s when blond furniture was in fashion. In the simplest method, ordinary household bleach is used; diluted with water, this will lighten wood, accentuating the pattern of its grain. Oxalic acid, dissolved in hot water, can be used similarly; it is somewhat stronger than household bleach. (Used at full strength, household bleach will also remove dye, ink or water stains from wood. Oxalic acid is especially effective for removing water stains from oak.)

Either of these bleaches should be applied with a synthetic-bristled brush or a plastic-mesh scrubber (natural fibres deteriorate in bleach) and allowed to stand for 15 minutes. Repeat the process until the wood is sufficiently lightened. Then neutralize the bleach to prevent it from attacking whatever finish you apply later. For household bleach, use white vinegar at full strength or a soap and water wash; for oxalic acid, use a wash made of 1 part ammonia in 10 parts water. Allow the bleached wood to dry thoroughly, then sand off the fibres that have risen on the surface (page 76).

The strongest bleaches are sold as a two-part package, a combination of hydrogen peroxide and ammonia or caustic soda. With enough applications, these products can totally eliminate the natural colour of the wood, turning a dark wood white. Because they are so powerful, they must be used with great care, following the manufacturer's instructions. All bleaches are harmful. Wear rubber gloves, and use a dust mask when sanding, because the sanding dust will be impregnated with chemicals from the bleach and neutralizer, which can irritate your eyes.

Stains are used to change the colour of natural wood or to recolour bleached wood. There are two main types. The penetrating stains are made of aniline dye dissolved in water, alcohol or oil; they soak into the wood and colour the wood fibres. The other stains, made of pigments suspended in oil, or in a finish such as varnish, cover the wood with a coloured film and fill the wood pores; a stain in which the pigments are suspended in oil is called a wiping stain. Because they are absorbed differently by the hard and soft parts of the wood, the two stains have different effects. The penetrating stains accentuate the grain, while pigment stains are often used to obscure the grain and disguise cheaper woods.

Stains are available in a wide range of standard colours, and to create other colours you can mix stains that have the same solvent base. You can also make your own stains: artists' oil paints and pigments mixed with linseed oil and turpentine make good oil-based wiping stains, and cold-water-based fabric dyes can be used as penetrating stains, providing a variety of colours from natural wood tones to vivid, if unconventional, rainbow hues. For both of these home-made stains, the proportion of pigment to water or oil depends on the depth of colour desired. Always test the mixture on a hidden or inconspicuous area before you use it, and keep a record of proportions so you can duplicate the stain later if you need to.

Before applying stains, carefully clean and sand the surface, whether unfinished or stripped. Residual wax or rough spots will absorb stain unevenly, making light and dark patches. Begin working on the least conspicuous part of the piece to determine how the wood takes the stain. When applying a penetrating stain, avoid runs, drips and overlaps, which can result in dark spots. For maximum control, thin the stain by adding solvent and apply two or more coats until the desired depth of tone is achieved. If a coat is darker than you would like it to be, you can lighten it by wiping the surface with a solvent-soaked cloth. To avoid staining your hands as well as the wood, be sure to wear rubber gloves.

Applying the Two Types of Wood Stain

Wiping on the stain. Using a sponge or a folded square of muslin as an applicator, wipe on penetrating or wiping stain in broad strokes with the grain, pressing lightly to force the stain into the pores of the wood. Cover a small area at a time, working with the surface horizontal whenever possible. On vertical surfaces, work from the bottom, stroking upwards, to prevent runs that may penetrate unevenly. Keep a clean cloth handy to wipe off excess stain or to rub the surface with solvent if an area is too dark. Wipe the high spots on carved areas to lighten them, which will both emphasize their contours and give them an aged appearance.

When using a penetrating stain, allow each coat to soak into the wood before applying the next. With a wiping stain, wait until the surface is dull (indicating the solvent has evaporated), then wipe away excess pigment with a dry cloth. Usually, wiping stains are applied in one coat.

How to Get the Colour You Want

Standard Colour	Antique Pine*	Brown Mahogany	Red Mahogany	Cherry	Honey Maple*	Antique Maple*	Fruitwood	Dark Oak	Swedish Walnut**
	Colour Sought								
Mahogany	1 part	1 part	1 part	1 part					
Light Oak		1 part		1 part	3 parts	1 part	4 parts	1 part	2 parts
Walnut	4 parts	5 parts	1 part	1 part	1 part	1 part	1 part	1 part	4 parts
Maple					2 parts	2 parts	1 part		

*Thin with enough solvent to lighten the tint.　　**Add a drop of lampblack.

Mixing stains. To obtain wiping stains in the custom colours listed on the top row of the chart, mix the standard stains listed on the left, using the proportions indicated. For more colour variations, add artists' pigment or oil paints in such colours as raw sienna, burnt sienna, raw umber and yellow ochre. Black or white pigments shade the stain or make it paler; additional solvent lightens it. Penetrating stains can be custom-mixed in different colours as long as they have the same solvent base, but proportions vary according to the type of solvent used and the kind of wood being stained. Test any penetrating-stain mixture carefully before using it; wait until the sample is dry to judge the result.

Selecting the Stain Best Suited to the Wood

Stain type	Solvent	Use	Advantages	Disadvantages	Application
Penetrating	Water	All woods; in warm reddish tones is especially good for mahogany, walnut, cherry	Inexpensive and easy to mix; easy to handle; broad range of colours; will not fade or bleed	Raises wood grain; needs 24-hour drying time	Dampen the surface with clean water first. Apply with brush or sponge; wipe off excess
	Oil	Coarse-grained woods such as mahogany, oak, rosewood and walnut.	Does not raise the grain; easy to use; rich tones; long lasting	Saturates soft woods quickly, producing zebra effect. Hard to remove. Will sometimes bleed through varnish unless coated with a sealer	Brush or wipe evenly with no overlaps. Wipe off before it sets; let dry for 24 hours
Non-penetrating	Oil	Close-grained woods such as birch, cherry, maple	Disguises cheaper woods and makes different woods look the same. Lightens coarse-grained woods and tones down grain with uneven colour distribution	Darkens soft, porous woods; does not take well on hardwoods; accentuates dents and scratches	Stir well before and during use. Pre-mix if using more than one can to get even colour. Wipe on; wait until surface dulls, then wipe off
	Varnish Shellac Lacquer	Cheap Woods	Fills, colours and adds gloss in one step. Dries in 3 to 12 hours	Almost completely obscures grain; not a high-quality finish	Apply like varnish

An assortment of stains. Wood stains are classified according to the colouring medium they contain: dye in penetrating stains and pigment in non-penetrating stains. Dye, which is dissolved in water or oil, saturates the pores of the wood; pigment, which is mixed with oil or clear finish, just rests on the wood's surface. Some of the commercial stains are a mixture of both and in addition may contain a sealer that prevents the stain from bleeding into any subsequent finish. Stains vary in their usefulness, as the chart above indicates, and some of them are easier to work with than others. For the amateur, oil or water-based stains are usually the easiest to work with and give the most uniform results.

The Pros and Cons of Five Clear Finishes

If furniture is made of fine, beautifully grained wood, the most desirable finish is generally a transparent one. The clear versions of five types of finish (box, opposite)—shellac, varnish, oil, wax and lacquer—are commonly used, either alone or in combination. Shellac finishes, for example, can be used as a base coat for varnish or they can form a complete finish by themselves. On some fine antiques the finish consists of six or more thin coats of shellac, each rubbed down before the next coat was applied.

The relative merits of the five finishes are partly a matter of aesthetics. Shellac finishes and varnish highlight the grain of the wood, for example; an oil finish mellows its appearance. But other considerations—such as the need to protect the wood against wear and spills, and the relative ease of application of various finishes—also enter into the choice. Shellac, for example, is vulnerable to moisture damage, and varnish is not. On the other hand, varnish is more difficult to apply; it tends to bubble if it is not brushed on carefully with a special technique (page 82, Step 1).

Similarly, though oil finishes are the simplest of all to apply, they take about four to eight hours to dry thoroughly. Lacquer dries in minutes—so fast that it is difficult to apply with a brush without leaving telltale stroke marks. Lacquer is best applied by spraying, but the spray is so volatile that you must take elaborate precautions against fire or explosion.

There also are choices to be made within each category of finish: teak oil versus linseed oil, for example, or, among the shellac finishes, white polish versus transparent polish. Most dizzying of all are the choices among varnishes. These are formulated for floor, outdoor, marine and furniture use, and are labelled as such on the cans. Furniture varnishes are normally less glossy than those made for other uses. They are, nonetheless, also available in a wide range of finishes, from dull to mildly glossy. Furniture varnishes are also somewhat less durable than varnish products made for other uses.

If you want a particularly tough finish, use a high-gloss floor varnish or a two-part cold cure lacquer. These harden by a chemical reaction and have excellent resistance to heat, solvents and abrasion.

With any of these finishes, work where there is no dust, little humidity, uniform light and good ventilation. If you cover the work surface with newspapers to catch drips, as most people do, dispose of the papers as soon as the job is done, for all these finishes are inflammable and their solvents are dangerously so. Be equally careful with oil-soaked rags.

If you plan to do extensive work with spray lacquers, you will have to construct a refinishing booth. An effective spray booth partitions off a corner of the workshop, isolating the potentially explosive spray from any spark or flame. It may be built of either sheet metal or fire-resistant wallboard. All motors and electrical switches

are located outside the booth. In addition one end of the booth must be equipped with a special kind of exhaust fan, one that traps the drifting lacquer spray with filters and expels the lacquer fumes outside the house. The other end of the booth must be open to allow the free flow of air.

To apply varnish, you will need a good brush, such as a varnish brush, with tapered bristles. Pour the finish a little at a time into a clean metal container, such as a coffee can, and reclose the original container. To thin varnish (and to clean brushes), use turpentine or white spirit; avoid thinning and stirring varnish if possible, since this creates bubbles that will mar the finish. To thin shellac finishes, use methylated spirit. To make a linseed-oil finish, you will need to add turpentine.

For the important task of removing sanding dust between coats of finish, one of the most useful pieces of equipment is a tack rag. It can be bought at a hardware shop, but you can easily make your own from a 600 mm square of muslin. Dampen the square with water and wring it out well. Then sprinkle the cloth with a few teaspoons of turpentine, and again squeeze out the excess moisture. Sprinkle the cloth a final time with a small amount of varnish. Fold the four edges towards the centre, and wring the cloth tightly to remove any remaining water; the tack rag should be just damp enough to pick up dust without leaving behind a mark. When not in use, the tack rag should be stored in an airtight screw-top jar.

A Guide to Finishes that Let the Grain Shine Through

The five types of clear finish described below encompass hundreds of commercial products, which vary in their suitability for particular needs. Varnish and oil finishes are the most versatile—they include products formulated for both indoor and outdoor use. Shellac, lacquer and wax finishes are intended only for indoor furniture. But the five also differ in durability, in ease of application and in the qualities that they bring to the natural beauty of wood grain.

Lacquer

Modern lacquer finishes are synthetic compounds made from a cellulose derivative (usually nitrocellulose), a solvent and a plasticizing ingredient (to prevent brittleness). Lacquer hardens on a surface when its solvent content evaporates—a process that happens in a very few minutes. This short drying time has made lacquer the choice of finish in production-line furniture factories.

Lacquers for brushing are available but, because of their rapid drying time, they have a tendency to retain the shape of the brush that is used for applying them. Consequently, lacquer is usually applied as a spray.

For small jobs, lacquer is available in aerosol cans. More extensive work may require a compressed-air gun. When lacquer is to be used with a gun, it must be thinned to spraying consistency with the solvent recommended by the manufacturer. The usual proportions of lacquer to thinner are 2 to 1, but it is best to start out with a slightly thicker mixture and test it on a piece of scrap wood. If lacquer is too thin, it will run; if it is too thick, it will produce a bumpy texture that professionals refer to as orange peel.

Sprayed lacquer dries mirror smooth, but you can tone down the surface shine to a gloss or sheen, if you wish, by rubbing it with very fine steel wool. Several coats of sprayed lacquer can be built up within a few hours. A lacquer finish has fair resistance to wear but little resistance to moisture.

Oil

Oil finishes are the easiest of all to apply and are prized for their soft sheen and subtle beauty. Linseed oil, derived from crushed seeds, teak oil and Danish oil are commonly used in furniture finishing. They penetrate the pores of the wood, and with repeated applications they gradually form a clear, hard film by reacting with the oxygen in the air. Teak oil and Danish oil contain special ingredients that allow them to dry quickly.

Linseed oil can be used undiluted, but more often it is combined with an equal portion of turpentine. Boiled linseed oil is preferable for finishing wood; raw linseed oil dries slowly, taking up to three days.

A linseed-oil finish can be touched up or recoated, but it is not particularly durable and has virtually no resistance to moisture. Teak oil and Danish oil have greater durability and offer good resistance to moisture.

Shellac

Shellac, made from the secretions of a tropical insect, is dissolved in methylated spirits to create a range of finishes known as French, button, garnet, white and transparent polishes. Raw shellac may be obtained in the form of flakes, sticks or buttons, but it is better to buy the made-up solutions. Except for white and transparent polish, which lose their ability to harden after 18 months, all the polishes will keep indefinitely in airtight containers.

Shellac finishes are easily applied with a cotton wool pad wrapped in linen (pages 84–85). They can be built up in successive coats that bond strongly to each other, forming a good base coat for other finishes such as varnish, which are more difficult to apply. But between coats and before varnishing, shellac finishes should be roughened by sanding.

A shellac finish can be rubbed with fine steel wool or polished to modify its gloss or sheen. Though shellac will protect wood from light moisture, it discolours in contact with dampness and dissolves in

contact with alcohol and heat.

Varnish

The term "varnish" encompasses a diverse group of clear, tough, extremely durable finishes for wood, most of which are based on synthetic materials. The types best suited to use on furniture are alkyd-resin, phenolic-resin and polyurethane varnishes.

Both alkyd and phenolic-resin varnishes give a warm, glowing tone to wood and are sufficiently durable for most furniture needs, though less rugged than polyurethane varnish. Alkyd-resin varnish is the type most easily recoated to build up a deep-looking finish; phenolic-resin finish, commonly labelled "spar varnish" or "marine varnish", has a tendency to darken or yellow. It is especially formulated for outdoor use and, even when dry, remains slightly soft to accommodate the shrinking and swelling of the wood beneath it. This softness makes it less suitable for interior use.

Polyurethane varnish is especially prized for its extreme durability and moisture resistance. It produces a glossy or matt finish and is somewhat difficult to recoat. Many polyurethane varnishes are modified with oils or alkyd resins to make them easier to use.

Wax

Simple paste wax is used as a polish over other clear finishes; the wax serves as a buffer against grime and wear. Because wax will yellow if it is allowed to get old, it must be removed once or twice a year and renewed.

Either paste wax or beeswax, melted and then thinned with turpentine, can be used alone as a finish on hardwoods such as maple or oak. If wax is applied to raw, unfinished softwoods, however, it precludes later refinishing because it cannot be removed from the pores. But even a softwood can be given a clear wax finish if the wood is stripped of an old finish that sealed the grain.

Building Up a Varnish Surface

1 Brushing on successive coats. Starting from the centre of a surface and working outwards, brush on a thin, even coat of the finish, lifting the brush slightly at the edge of the wood to avoid run-overs on the adjacent surface. Whenever possible, work horizontally, especially when covering large surfaces. When working on surfaces that rest on the floor or workbench, prop up the piece to keep the finish from puddling around it at the bottom. Props strong enough to support a chair can be improvised from scraps of wood held together with glue and nails.

Dip the brush in the varnish to half the length of the bristles and apply each brush load in a single smooth stroke. Spread the varnish across the grain in a limited area first, then go back over the area, this time stroking with the grain. Finally, smooth the finish by running the tip of an almost dry brush lightly over the entire area, following the grain; during this operation hold the brush almost vertical.

To avoid contaminating your finish supply with particles of dust or dirt, pour a working batch into a clean coffee can. Twist a section of heavy wire through holes that you have drilled or punched near the top of the can, and strike the brush gently on this wire to control the load.

2 Sanding between coats. After each coat of finish dries, rub the surface lightly with grade 000 steel wool or Flour sandpaper *(page 76)*. Sand lightly and evenly, always with the grain; take special care at the edges, where abrasives tend to cut through the finish entirely.

When the surface is smooth and free of imperfections, remove sanding dust with a tack rag. Then apply the next finish coat. Give each coat adequate drying time. To test for dryness, press your thumb against the surface, then wipe the area with a soft cloth; if the thumbprint remains visible, more drying time is needed. For a very deep finish, you may want to apply as many as six coats. When the last coat has dried, polish the finish to a soft sheen with grade 000 steel wool or, for a glossier look, with grade 0000 steel wool.

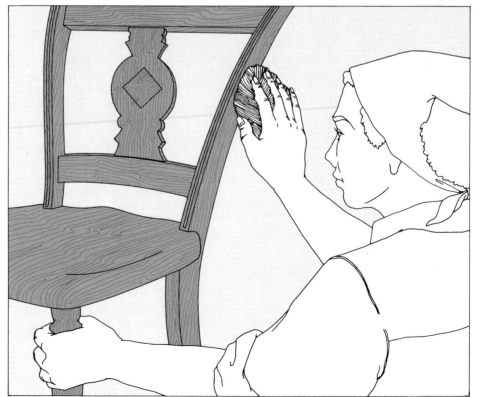

3 **Waxing for protection.** Cover the final coat of varnish with wax, and buff by hand or with an electric drill fitted with a padded buffing wheel. Apply the wax with a soft, damp cloth and leave for 30 minutes before buffing. Use two coats.

Finishing Furniture with Oil

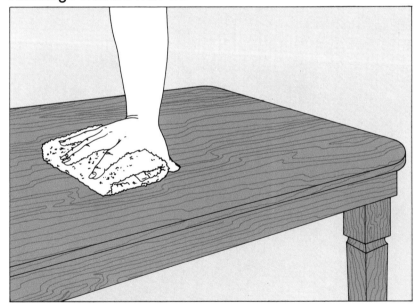

Applying oil finishes. Pour teak oil or Danish oil, or boiled linseed oil mixed in equal portions with turpentine, on to the furniture and rub it over the surface with a soft cloth; alternatively, use a commercially prepared oil. Allow the oil to stand for a few minutes, then wipe away any excess that beads on the surface, and let the wood dry overnight. Apply as many additional coats as desired, depending on the depth and tone you want the finish to have. To add sheen to the final coat, rub the surface with grade 0000 steel wool.

When finishing with linseed oil, continue to apply oil until the surface is saturated and will not absorb any more. Then wipe away the excess and allow the wood to dry for two weeks. Finally, buff the surface with a dry cloth.

Sanding a Panelled Surface

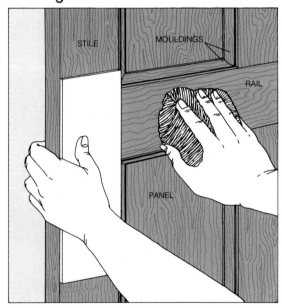

STILE MOULDINGS RAIL PANEL

Sanding complex panels. When you sand furniture panels in which the wood grain runs in different directions, hold a cardboard shield at the point where opposite grain patterns meet, to prevent the sandpaper or steel wool from cutting across the grain of the adjacent panel. If the panelling is contoured, sand the mouldings first, then sand the inset panels, and finally go on to do the rails and stiles of the frame.

The Fine Art of French Polishing

A legacy from the master craftsmen of 17th-century France, French polishing produces a glossy, mirror-like finish which enhances the appearance of almost any wood. However, since the finish is vulnerable to heat, moisture and abrasion, it is not appropriate for furniture which will be subjected to hard daily use. It is best reserved for decorative pieces such as side tables, hall chairs or jewellery boxes.

French polish is the generic name for a range of finishes made by dissolving shellac, a substance derived from the lac insect, in alcohol (page 81). The range includes four main types: garnet, button, white and clear.

Of the four, garnet polish gives the darkest finish; it is suitable for brown woods, such as mahogany, where deep, warm tones are required. Button polish is so called because it is made from shellac in the form of small, transparent discs or buttons that show impurities when exposed to light. It produces a slightly orange hue—ideal for golden-toned woods such as walnut. White polish is made from bleached shellac and is used for lighter-coloured woods, such as oak. There is also clear or transparent polish made from shellac that has been both bleached and de-waxed. It has the least darkening effect of all French polishes and is useful for sealing ash, white beech and other very pale woods.

All types of French polish are built up by applying many thin coats with a pad of soft cloth and cotton wool, known as a rubber. Instead of cotton wool, some professionals use upholsterer's wadding because it makes a firmer pad that can hold a point at one end for polishing details and corners.

Although there are degrees of skill which can be achieved only with practice, the basic polishing procedure is well within the capabilities of the careful amateur. Always work in a clean, dry and warm environment. And try to position your workbench directly in front of a window so that you are facing the light. This will make it easier to see the build-up of polish and to spot any blemishes.

1 Making a rubber. Form a good handful of cotton wool into a pear-shaped wad and place it in the centre of a piece of cotton or linen cloth about 230 mm square. The cloth must be white, so that no dyes can seep on to the work. It must also be plain, since a fancy texture could leave its imprint on the work.

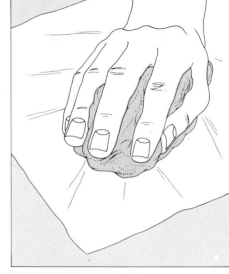

2 Folding the edges. Gather the loose fabric round the cotton wool and fold the edges inwards. The sole of the rubber should be flat, with no wrinkles or creases to prevent the polish from spreading evenly on the surface. Check the sole to make sure that no specks of dirt or loose material have stuck to it.

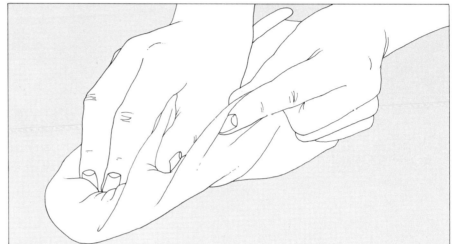

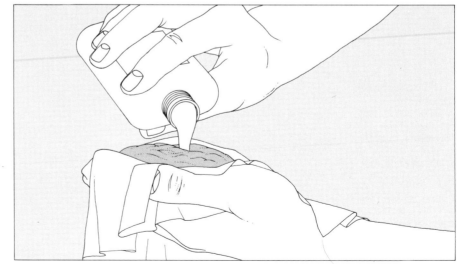

3 Charging the rubber. Unfold the cloth in the palm of your hand and pour French polish, a little at a time, into the cotton wool until it is well charged but not overflowing. Refold the cloth, making sure that it is free of wrinkles, and press the rubber on to a piece of scrap wood to distribute polish evenly over the sole and to squeeze out excess liquid. If no polish at all seeps through the cloth, open the rubber and pour in a little more.

4 Applying the polish. Wet the tip of your finger with linseed oil and dab it on the sole of the charged rubber to act as a lubricant. Apply the polish with overlapping circular strokes *(top inset)*, working from the centre outwards, followed by sweeping figure-of-eight strokes *(bottom inset)*. Only slight pressure is required for the first coat, but as the polish is used up, gradually increase the pressure. Make sure that corners and edges get their full share of polish. Never allow the rubber to rest on a polished surface: keep it moving all the time, sweeping on and off the surface. If the rubber drags, apply more oil.

When the surface has been covered with a thin coat, finish off with straight strokes along the grain and allow the coat to dry—about 15 minutes. If there are any blemishes or dirt particles, gently rub down the surface with the finest grade if silicon carbide paper. Repeat for each coat. Build up four or five coats a day, allowing the polish to harden overnight. Between 10 and 20 coats will be sufficient, depending on the depth of gloss you want.

To obtain a final high gloss, pour methylated spirits into the rubber that has been used for applying the polish, then wring until it is almost dry and just leaves a damp mark when pressed on to paper. Using the rubber, polish with hard, even strokes backwards and forwards along the grain until a shine is obtained.

4 Reupholstering for a New Look

The inner support structure of a seat. Pulled taut with a webbing stretcher and tacked to the underside of the wooden frame, interwoven jute webbing supports the coiled seat springs above. Lengths of cord anchor the spring tops to one another and depress all the coils slightly to give the seat both firmness and bounce.

Few improvements change the appearance of a room more quickly or yield bigger dividends in comfort than newly upholstered furniture. If you do the work yourself, refurbishing old furniture will also introduce you to the fascinating techniques of a centuries-old craft.

The first upholsterers were tent-makers, purveyors of shelter to nomadic peoples of the Middle East and, as such, an élite among craftsmen. Famous among them were the Persian poet Omar Khayyam and the disciple Saint Paul. Although the tent-making tradition continued through the Middle Ages—the coat of arms granted to London's Worshipful Company of Upholders in 1465 bore a picture of three tents—the focus of the craft shifted from shelter to seating as men found more time for sitting still and wanted softer furniture.

The upholders softened their first seats with a covering of leather, but by the middle of the 16th century various hair and fibre stuffings had been introduced; upholstered side chairs, structured in much the same way as they are today, soon became standard household accoutrements. The focus of the upholders then shifted again; this time they turned their attention to the task of embellishing the common side chair with an abundance of jewelled, fringed finery.

Upholsterers of the 16th century received such instructions as these, which came from an occupant of Kenilworth Castle: "A chaier of wallnuttree ... the seate all lozenged with silver twiste, trimmed with fringe of crimson silck and silver; the back of the chaier lyned with crimson sattin." In 1581, Queen Elizabeth 1, not to be outdone by mere noblemen, ordered more than 30 kg of gold and silver fringes to decorate an assortment of 60 chairs and stools; the price of the precious metals alone accounted for more than one-third the total cost of the job.

The following centuries saw such decorative furniture covering carried to extremes and, in some people's opinion, to the point of bad taste. The leg of a Victorian chair, much like the ankle of a Victorian lady, was considered indecent if allowed to be uncovered, so pieces of this period were draped from top to bottom in heavy silks, satins, velvets and damasks. Victorian furniture, in the words of one critic, "shrieks its own agony to all observers".

Today, styles in upholstery range from sumptuous to stark. But the craft has changed very little, because no way has been found to make a more satisfactory seat than the type perfected by the first upholders. Seat springs were introduced around the middle of the 19th century, and more recent innovations have taken the form of synthetic stuffings, paddings and fabrics, but the basic tools and procedures illustrated on the following pages are those that fine craftsmen have used to upholster and reupholster furniture for hundreds of years.

The Basic Upholstery Tools and Supplies

In addition to patience and methodical labour, reupholstering requires a few unique tools and some special supplies. The tools are specifically designed for ripping away old fabric and attaching new. Both tools and supplies are available from hardware shops and upholstery supply merchants.

You will also need a sewing machine equipped with a zip foot. If you do not own a machine, or if you are working with fabric that is too heavy for home models, you may be able to get a professional upholsterer to sew your cut fabric for you. Similarly, farming out button-making chores will avoid the need for a button press, and ready-made piping will save time if you can find a colour suitable for your fabric.

Some tools and materials long used by professionals have begun to give way to innovations. The traditional snout-nosed, magnetized upholsterer's hammer, for example, has been replaced in many commercial shops by the pneumatic staple gun, which is powerful enough to drive a long staple through heavy materials and into a wooden frame.

Electric staple guns are also available. These are relatively inexpensive and work well on softwood frames. They are very fast and may seem a boon to the novice. But because of their speed, mistakes are easier to make, and the staples that they implant are difficult to remove without ripping the fabric. For the beginner, therefore, the upholsterer's hammer and tacks may be a better choice. In any case, tacks and hammer will be needed to pin the fabric to the frame before stapling.

Modern stuffing materials have also largely replaced the traditional horsehair, hog hair, dried moss and tow. Most new chairs and sofas owe their smooth contours to such untraditional stuffings as polyester wadding, foam rubber and polyurethane foam. Sometimes, however, it is better to preserve the original horsehair or hog-hair stuffing of an old piece, both for authenticity and because the stuffing is already shaped to the furniture contours.

Besides the tools shown here and the supplies listed in the chart, you will need other items, such as a knife, a mallet, and PVA and latex glue. Tailor's chalk is best for marking fabric cuts. Sturdy scissors—ideally, 250 mm shears with handles set at an angle to the blades—are used to cut fabric. And if you are rounding cushions by adding an extra layer of polyester wadding, you will need spray adhesive for fastening the wadding to the foam rubber or polyurethane foam stuffing.

Professional upholsterers usually wear a multipocketed carpenter's apron to keep supplies close at hand. They also use padded saw-horses to support pieces while they are being reupholstered.

Tools for Special Tasks

Tools for stripping fabric. A tack lifter, also called a claw chisel, has a V-shaped notch at its tip and is curved to give leverage for prising out tacks. The slotted tip of a staple remover is designed to reach under staples and lift them out. For very stubborn tacks and staples, the ripping chisel is held against the fixing and struck sharply with a mallet to jar the fixing free.

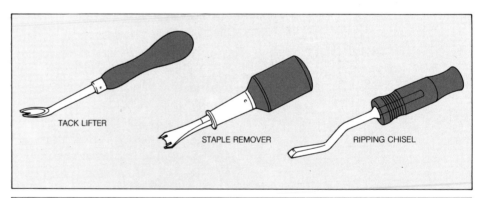

TACK LIFTER
STAPLE REMOVER
RIPPING CHISEL

Tools for attaching fabric. In addition to an upholsterer's tack hammer, which has one magnetized end for picking up tacks, you will need skewers, upholstery needles and a webbing stretcher. Stretchers are available in two forms. One type has sharp spikes and a corrugated rubber tread to grip jute or cotton webbing to pull it tight. The other type works primarily by friction; the webbing is passed through a rectangular aperture, and is secured by a wooden peg. Skewers, sturdy enough to hold heavy materials, have pierced heads for easy removal. A 250 mm straight upholstery needle, pointed at both ends, goes through wadding to attach buttons, gather stuffing and anchor springs; a 75 or 100 mm curved upholstery needle is used for slipstitching from one side of the fabric and also for anchoring springs and stuffing. For large projects requiring much tacking, an electric staple gun is a useful, though not essential, addition to your kit.

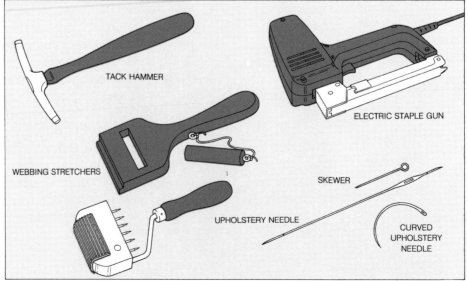

TACK HAMMER
ELECTRIC STAPLE GUN
WEBBING STRETCHERS
SKEWER
UPHOLSTERY NEEDLE
CURVED UPHOLSTERY NEEDLE

Hardware to Hold Coverings

Tacks and ornamental nails. Three sizes of tack are used for different jobs: 10 mm fine tacks for linings and top covers, 12 mm for general upholstery work and 16 mm improved tacks for webbing and hessian. The small, rounded gimp pin secures the decorative braid called gimp. Ornamental nails, available with brass, silver, coloured and hammered heads, are used where the heads are to be exposed. Cardboard tacking tape, with or without embedded tacks, or metal tacking strips are used where they can be concealed. Buckram, a coarse cloth stiffened with gum, can be used in their place.

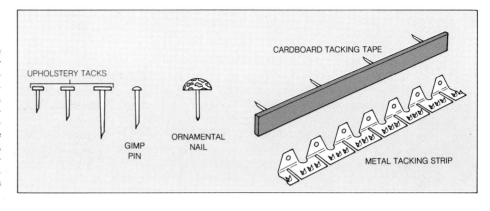

UPHOLSTERY TACKS

CARDBOARD TACKING TAPE

GIMP PIN

ORNAMENTAL NAIL

METAL TACKING STRIP

Supplies You Need and How to Use Them

Determining necessary supplies. This chart lists supplies needed to reupholster a chair or couch. The second column explains the use of each. Where a type, size or material is best suited for the task, it is listed in the third column.

Material	Use	Type recommended
Hessian	Separates springs from stuffing; covers webbing when no springs are used	Medium weight
Cambric	Covers the underside of a couch or chair, shielding it from dust	Glazed, black, tightly woven
Lining	Covers the chair seat under loose cushions	Denim, cotton duck or calico
Edge roll	Prefabricated wadding for front edge of chair seat	Hessian covered, about 40 mm in diameter
Ornamental gimp and edging	Covers tacks holding fabric to edge of frame	Available in many styles and colours to suit upholstery fabric
Wadding	Covers wood-frame surfaces to cushion their edges; covers stuffing to shape it	25 mm thick sheets of long-staple cotton, Dacron-polyester wadding or sheets of high-density polyurethane foam
Stuffing	Covers springs and seat backs; fills cushions	Polyurethane foam or foam rubber in either bulk form or rolls, rubberized hair in rolls; animal hair, coir or other fibres for traditional upholstery; occasionally, down for cushions
Laid cord	Ties down coil springs	Nylon, hemp or jute ply
Stitching twine	Joins sections of cover fabric together, secures stuffing to springs and is used for miscellaneous hand sewing	Flax or linen
Webbing	Tacked across bottom frame to serve as a foundation for springs or wadding	Generally tightly woven 50 mm wide bands of jute or cotton. Occasionally rubber or steel webbing is used
Piping	Ready-made fabric-covered cord sewn into seams	Available in many colours and several sizes to suit upholstery fabrics
Piping cord	Soft cotton cord that can be covered with fabric to make piping	For most purposes 3 to 6 mm in diameter

Removing Old Fabric and Preparing the New

Mystifying as the whole process of reupholstering may seem, it really is nothing more than a methodical layer-by-layer unravelling of the planning and plotting that went into the piece originally. The top layer is the cover, which must be dismantled carefully and with a sharp eye for detail, because the old cover may well be used as a cutting pattern for the new. Even more important, it provides you with valuable information on how the new cover should be assembled.

Rarely are two upholstery covers constructed in exactly the same way. One may have a number of machine-stitched seams; another may consist almost entirely of fabric fitted directly on to the frame, then tacked or stapled into position. As you remove the cover, make a note on paper of which sections are tacked and to what, as well as which sections are sewn together and where. Pay particular attention to the location of piping (the decorative trim that outlines some seams), noting where it stops and starts. To record intricate details, professionals often draw sketches and take step-by-step photographs.

Before beginning the actual stripping, take basic measurements to estimate the amount of upholstery fabric you will need to purchase. Working in an orderly fashion from the outside to the inside, measure the longest and the widest parts of the arm and back sections, as well as the overall dimensions of such elements as wing sections, seat front and arm fronts. On the insides of the arms and back, include the several extra centimetres of fabric that are tucked inside the seat.

When all these basic measurements are taken, make diagrams on graph paper, running vertical measurements vertically and keeping in mind that most upholstery fabrics are 130 cm wide. Add up the vertical centimetres on the diagrams and then divide the total amount by 100 to convert the figure into metres.

To this basic figure you will need to add extra fabric for piping, if you are making your own; usually a metre is enough, since 1 metre of 130 cm fabric will yield more than 17 metres of the 38 mm bias strips that are needed for piping. You will also need additional length in order to match stripes or patterns, to centre dominant design elements or to position napped fabrics. One metre of extra fabric for every 5 metres of basic length is usually sufficient for these purposes.

Napped fabrics, such as corduroy or velvet, are always cut with the nap running in one direction—down towards the floor on the sides and back, to the front on the top of the seat cushion. To check the direction of the nap, run your hand over the fabric; the nap is down when the fabric feels smooth.

For the stripping process, you will need a hammer and a tack lifter or a staple remover to loosen tacked or stapled fabric from the frame, and a trimming knife or single-edged razor blade to open seams. As you strip the fabric away, keep in mind your objectives: if you intend to use the old cover as a pattern when you cut the new, you will need to be more careful with the fabric than if you plan to start with new measurements *(page 95)*.

In either event, label each piece as it is lifted from the chair or sofa. If the section contains a piping seam, leave it attached to the chair until you have traced the outline of the piping on to the new fabric cut for that particular section *(page 96)*. Disturb the underlying wadding as little as possible, and set aside any that falls off; it can often be used again, especially if supplemented with a layer of new cotton.

When all the fabric is removed, check the condition of the frame *(page 92)* and make whatever repairs are needed. This is also the time to renew the webbing and repair the seat if necessary *(page 102)* and to refinish exposed wood on the arms and legs *(Chapter 3)*. That done, you can cut the new fabric, using the notes, sketches and diagrams previously made in the course of plotting fabric requirements and taking exact measurements from the chair frame. In cutting the fabric, as in making the diagrams, line up horizontal measurements with the crosswise grain of the fabric and vertical measurements with the lengthwise grain. Always work right side up, with the design of the fabric facing you.

For most sections of the cover, you will simply rough-cut a rectangle of fabric, which you will later pull and shape to the chair or sofa as the fabric is attached to the frame with tacks or staples. Sometimes, these rough-cut sections are later contoured more precisely. This is usually the case when parts of rough-cut sections are joined by corded piping, for which an accurate seam line must be established. Inner and outer arm sections, for example, are commonly rough-cut, but the seam that joins them is later carefully contoured so that the piping can be inserted.

The choice of fabric for a reupholstery project is largely a matter of taste, though you must also be practical. One of the most popular fabrics for upholstery is an all-cotton drapery fabric; look for one with enough body to stand up to the rigours of stretching and tacking, plus the wearing effects of sitting. Regular upholstery material, usually a mixture of rayon, acetate, nylon and cotton, is somewhat sturdier. It is also thicker, however, and may be difficult for you to work with, especially if the fitting involves pleating and gathering or if you try to stitch through many layers with a home sewing machine.

Almost as strong as cotton is spun rayon, but be sure that it bears the label "spun rayon", not just "rayon"; ordinary rayon wears out quickly. A combination of cotton linen is an elegant, lightweight upholstery fabric; corduroy will take much punishment, though it may be too thick for a home sewing machine. Also hard to work with are the plastics that imitate leather; they tend to be stiff and have little give.

Whenever possible, buy a fabric that has been treated at the manufacturers with a protective, dirt-resistant finishing spray. Ask the retailer for advice. If the fabric has not already been treated, you can spray the piece yourself after the upholstering has been completed.

Finally to save money, you may want to cut some parts of the new cover from less expensive fabric. It is customary, for example, to make the lining (the seat cover under the cushion) from sturdy unbleached cotton or calico. In addition, pull strips of the same material may be sewn to the parts of the inside arms and inside back coverings that are tucked inside the upholstery; these pull strips are used to pull the fabric taut against the frame of the piece for stapling or tacking.

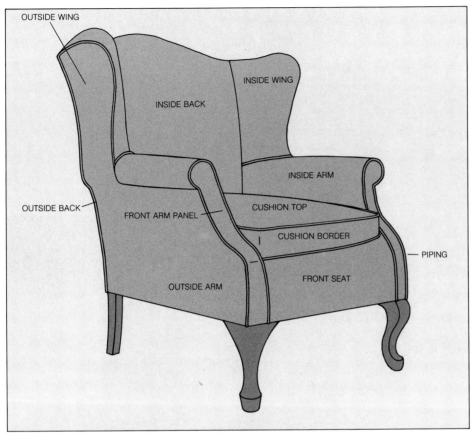

OUTSIDE WING

INSIDE WING

INSIDE BACK

INSIDE ARM

OUTSIDE BACK

FRONT ARM PANEL

CUSHION TOP

CUSHION BORDER

PIPING

OUTSIDE ARM

FRONT SEAT

Complexities Simplified

The parts of an upholstery cover. The labels that identify the parts of the wing chair on the left are the terms used by professional upholsterers. Most fully upholstered furniture will have these same fabric sections, with the possible exception of the wings. Furniture that is more tailored will have additional pieces—called bordering or boxing—at the tops of the arms and chair back.

The upholstery pieces that surround you when you sit on the chair—called the inside sections—are tacked or stapled to the frame in a carefully planned sequence that conceals the fixings. Outside fabric pieces—the front seat, outside arm, outside wing and outside back—are back tacked (hooked on to hidden tacking strips) to adjacent fabric pieces. The curving front arm panels are attached to the inside and outside arm by a combination of machine sewing and back tacking.

The corded piping that outlines the seams between some fabric sections is machine stitched. The cushion sections—top, bottom, and border—are sewn together, edged with piping, and used as a case to hold the stuffing. Hidden beneath the cushion is a square of durable fabric that covers the chair seat; it is referred to as lining.

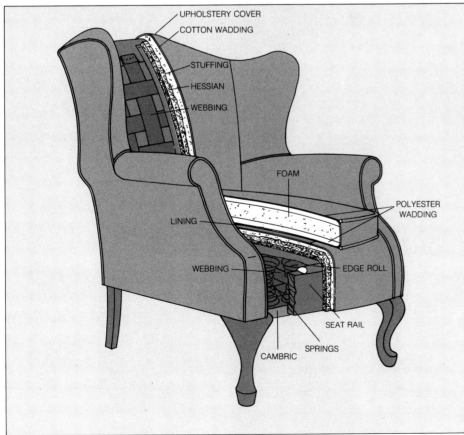

UPHOLSTERY COVER

COTTON WADDING

STUFFING

HESSIAN

WEBBING

FOAM

POLYESTER WADDING

LINING

WEBBING

EDGE ROLL

SEAT RAIL

CAMBRIC

SPRINGS

The chair's puffy interior. The inside of a chair is built up in layers designed to give both comfort and support. The bottom layer is a cambric dust cover, tacked to the bottom edges of the seat rails. Above that, interwoven strips of tightly stretched jute webbing are a foundation for coil springs. The springs are sewn to the webbing and tied together with cord to hold them in position. A layer of hessian is stretched above the springs and serves as a base for the stuffing; a special hessian or felt-covered wadding strip, called an edge roll, cushions the top edge of the seat rail. Top layers of cotton wadding define the final contours of the upholstery.

Although many older seat cushions contain springs, most modern cushions are stuffed with foam rubber or polyurethane foam and shaped with polyester wadding. Many upholstered chairs, such as the one shown here, are built without springs in the chair back.

The chair's rigid skeleton. A typical frame for a piece of upholstered furniture is constructed of hardwood boards cut to size and assembled with conventional chair joints—usually mortise and tenon joints or butt joints strengthened with dowels. The horizontal rails and vertical posts frame the chair and provide the basic support. Corner blocks are added to reinforce the joints between seat rails. The other frame pieces—the arm rails, slats and braces—give shape to the upholstery and provide tacking surfaces for fastening the fabric. The post-and-rail construction of the wings is not essential to the chair's basic structure; the wings are a decorative addition designed to give shape to the seat back.

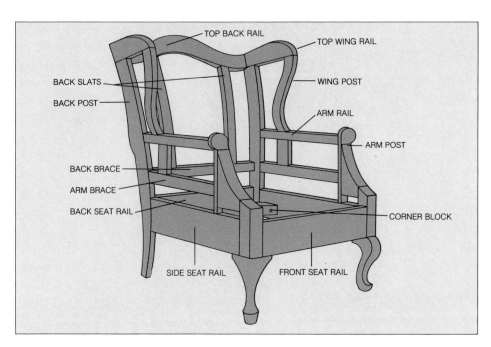

TOP BACK RAIL

TOP WING RAIL

BACK SLATS

BACK POST

WING POST

ARM RAIL

ARM POST

BACK BRACE

ARM BRACE

BACK SEAT RAIL

CORNER BLOCK

SIDE SEAT RAIL

FRONT SEAT RAIL

Step-by-Step Removal of the Old Covering

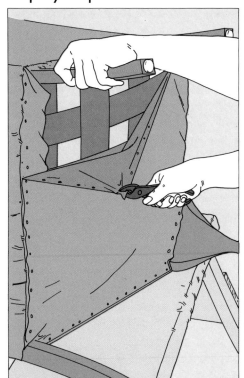

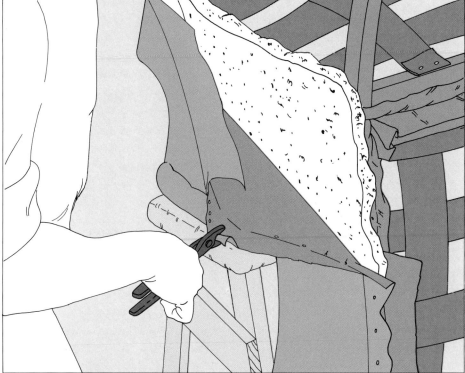

1 Ripping off the cambric dust cover. Place the chair on its back or side on top of two saw-horses, and use pliers to rip away the cambric from the bottom of the chair, exposing the webbing. To rip the cambric in a single motion, grasp an upper corner of the fabric with the pliers and pull it down in a diagonal line towards the opposite corner. Discard the old cambric, but leave the tacks embedded in the frame, to be removed later with a hammer and tack lifter or ripping chisel.

2 Stripping the fabric. With the chair in position upside down on the saw-horses, begin stripping fabric pieces from the outside of the frame. Use pliers for removing sections that have been tacked, again pulling downwards in a diagonal line. For sections that have been hand stitched, use a knife or razor blade to cut the first few stitches. Then rip open the remainder of the seam, cutting the stitches when necessary to avoid tearing the fabric. Leave in place temporarily any curved fabric pieces that are sewn together with piping; use these as a guide for locating the piping on the new piece *(page 96)*.

If you intend to use the old fabric pieces as patterns for the new, label each piece with chalk as you remove it. Indicate where each piece was located on the chair *(page 91)*, and mark the top of each piece with a T.

3 Removing cardboard tacking strip. When a tacking strip does not pull off with the fabric, use pliers to pull it away from the frame; always strip in a downwards motion to minimize the danger of flying tacks. Discard the old tacking strip. Leave in place any loose cotton wadding, and set aside for later use any that falls from the chair.

If you plan to cut the new fabric according to measurements, stop at this point, with the inner fabric pieces still in place, and take exact measurements from the exposed portions of the frame *(page 95, Step 1)*. If you plan to use the old fabric pieces as patterns for the new, omit the measuring step and continue stripping, turning the chair upright to remove the inside fabric pieces from the frame. Identify these pieces with chalked notations, as in Step 2.

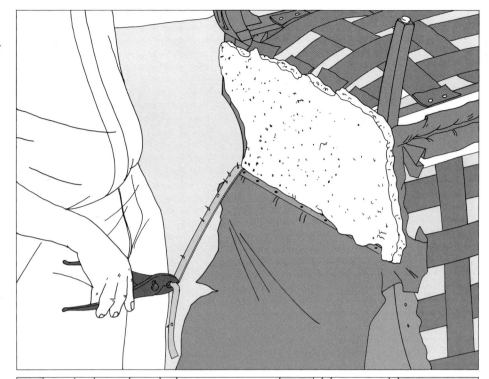

4 Removing tacks and staples. Using the appropriate tools, clear the frame of all fixings. To remove stubborn tacks, lay the bottom of a ripping chisel blade *(page 88)* flat against the edge of the frame, with its tip wedged under the head of a tack. Strike the end of the handle squarely with a mallet to jar the tack out of the wood. For safety, point the chisel away from you; for ease in lifting the tack, point the chisel in the direction of the wood grain. To prise staples out, use a slotted staple remover *(page 88)*.

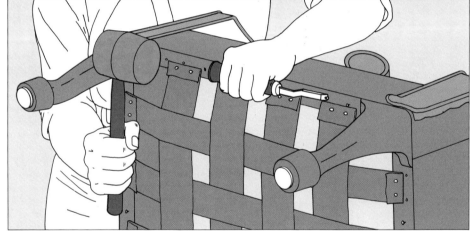

Using the Old Fabric Pieces as Patterns

1 Flattening the pattern pieces. Using a steam iron, smooth each piece of old upholstery removed from the chair. Use the pointed tip of the iron to flatten fabric edges that were folded under to fit round the frame or were joined into seams. Work on the right side of the fabric first, then turn the piece over and iron the reverse side.

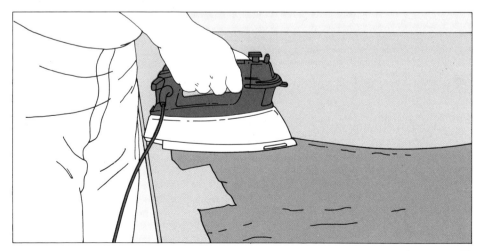

2 **Centring the pattern.** Unroll the new upholstery fabric, right side up, on a worktable or on the floor and lay an ironed pattern piece, also right side up, on it. Shift the pattern piece until the grain lines of pattern and new fabric are aligned, and until the pattern lies directly over the section of design that you want centred on the new piece. Pin the pattern piece for cutting, placing pins 10 mm from the pattern edges.

Continue pinning pattern pieces against the fabric, always lining up the grain and making sure that stripes or other designs match piece by piece. If the new fabric has a nap, check its direction before positioning the pattern *(page 90)*.

3 **Cutting out the new fabric.** Cut round the pinned pattern pieces, following their curves and angles exactly, but adding 50 mm all round to allow sufficient fabric for stretching, tacking and stitching. If the pattern is torn or is missing a corner, cut the new piece a little large, and square off its corners—this will leave room for adjustments when the piece is attached to the frame. As you unpin the old piece from the new, remember to mark the top edge on the back of each new piece, and label its position on the chair.

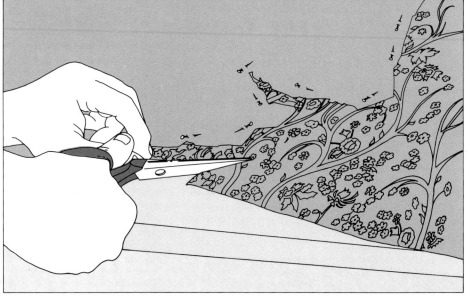

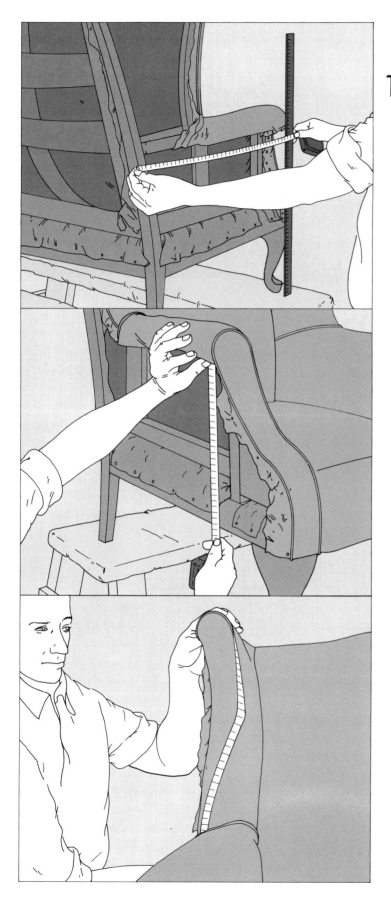

Rough-Cutting New Fabric to Measurements

1 Measuring flat and curved surfaces. For a cover piece that will lie flat, measure the dimensions of the piece after the frame is bare. Measure between the points on the frame that are furthest apart, first horizontally, then vertically *(left, centre)*. When there is a flat surface that is irregularly shaped, such as an outside chair arm *(left)*, prop a bench rule against the widest part on one side and measure across to the furthest point on the opposite side.

When a cover piece will lie over a curved surface, take the measurements for the piece before removing the old fabric. To measure the complex curve of a wing *(left, below)*, hold the measuring tape against the seam at the highest point along the top of the wing, then carry it over the curve and across the rolled front edge, to the point where the wing rail meets the arm rail.

For cover pieces that extend deep into a recess of the chair, as is the case with the inside arm or inside back, insert the measuring tape into the recess as far as it will go. Add 100 mm to the horizontal and vertical measurements for each piece, and note these measurements on the list to be used in cutting new fabric.

2 **Transferring measurements to fabric.** Working systematically from the largest piece to the smallest, measure the dimensions on the fabric with a bench rule. Mark the vertical dimensions first, centring the bench rule over the design element you want centred on each piece and being sure to hold the rule parallel to the selvage—the finished border of the fabric. Using these marks as guides, measure off the horizontal dimensions, half on each side of the vertical centre.

For the initial markings, you can use chalk or pins, but when the outlines of the piece are established, rule them off with chalk lines, using the bench rule. Whenever possible, fit small pieces into fabric remaining along the margins.

Cutting Pieces of Fabric for Stitched Seams

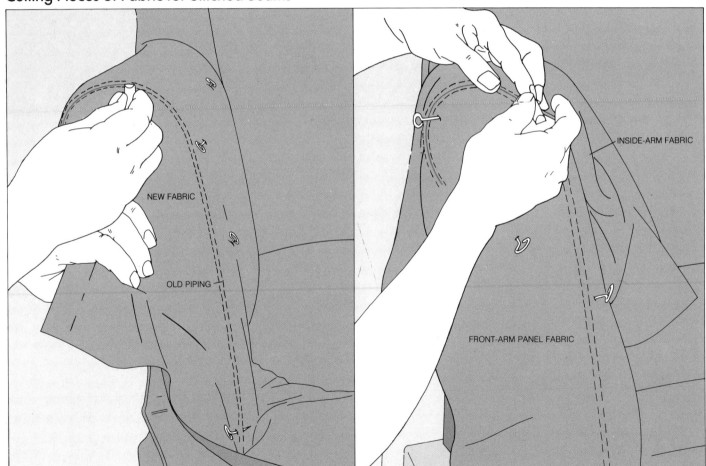

NEW FABRIC

OLD PIPING

INSIDE-ARM FABRIC

FRONT-ARM PANEL FABRIC

1 **Tracing the piping line.** If two cover pieces are joined by a machine-stitched seam, mark the new fabric with an outline for the seam by using the existing piping as a guide. First, smooth one rough-cut section into place over the old cover (still on the chair—*page 92, Step 2*), tucking it into any recesses, as on the inside chair arm above. Secure the piece with skewers. Then pull the fabric over the piping, holding it snug with one hand while you trace the curve of the piping with chalk. Keep the chalk directly on top of the piping, to ensure a precise outline. Unpin and fold back the first rough-cut section, exposing the piped seam that you have just traced on to the new fabric. Then smooth and pin the adjoining rough-cut section in place with its edges overlapping the piped seam; trace the outline of the piping on this section too.

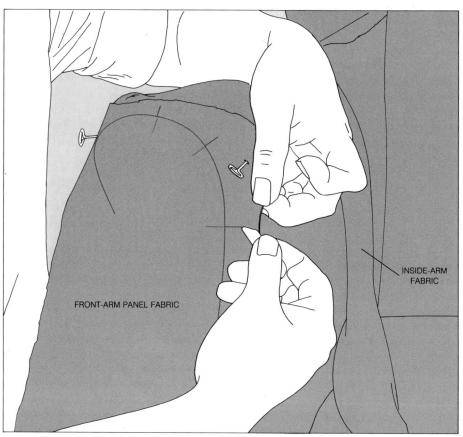

FRONT-ARM PANEL FABRIC

INSIDE-ARM
FABRIC

2 **Marking adjoining pieces for assembly.** Pin the two adjoining pieces into place, lining up their chalked seam line with the piping. So that joining the pieces for stitching will be easier, mark them with perpendicular chalk lines through the seam at several points along its length. To align these marks, flip back the extra fabric at the edge of one section and mark a chalk line across the piping; then hold your fingernail against this line, lift the other section, and make a matching chalk mark across the piping.

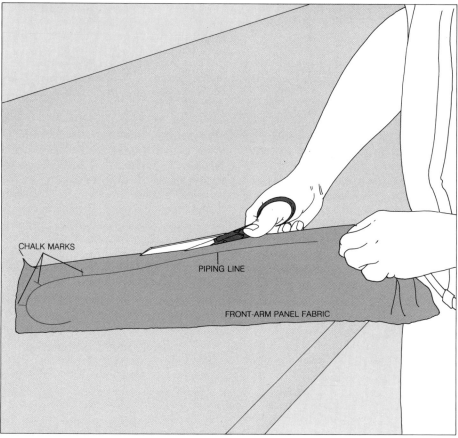

CHALK MARKS

PIPING LINE

FRONT-ARM PANEL FABRIC

3 **Cutting the pieces to shape.** Unpin both fabric pieces and lay them flat on the worktable. Using the chalked outlines as guides, cut each piece to shape, leaving a 10 mm seam allowance along the section of seam to be joined by machine stitching. When you pin the seam in preparation for sewing (*page 108*), line up the perpendicular chalk marks to bring the sections of curve back into their original alignment.

After all the curved sections have been measured and the piping has been traced, strip the remaining upholstery pieces from the chair.

Strengthening the Inner Structure of Old Furniture

Styles in upholstered furniture come and go, but the notion of what makes a chair comfortable to sit on has not changed much since the introduction of stuffings in the 16th century.

Comfort is mainly a matter of softness and springiness. The traditional method of achieving these qualities is with a succession of layers of various materials. They include springs or springy slats of metal or wood; cloth webbing to hold springs or to contribute springiness alone; matted horsehair or hog-hair stuffing to provide cushioning; and cotton wadding to soften uncushioned wooden parts and to smooth the surface under the covering.

For obvious reasons, most of the layering involves the seat. If you lift the fabric cover of an upholstered side chair, for example, you may find a single layer of wadding supported by webbing or a wooden panel. You may also find a layer of some type of stuffing under the cotton wadding. In armchairs and sofas, the number and composition of the layers depend to some extent on the vintage of the piece. In modern furniture, stuffing and wadding or foam rubber cushions are sometimes supported by zigzag springs—flat, curvy strips of steel wire. And underneath the cushions of socalled Danish modern furniture you are likely to find strips of rubber webbing.

But the most conventional arrangement, tested by time and the weight of countless tired bodies, is the multilayered assembly of webbing, springs, stuffing and wadding found in the comfortable armchair or sofa that occupies a place of honour in many homes. This arrangement usually consists of nine or more coil springs tied together and sewn to supporting criss-cross strips of jute webbing. In some modern construc-

tions, the jute webbing itself is reinforced with several strips of flat steel webbing which span the underside of the chair or sofa frame.

Under the webbing is a protective cover of cambric, and above the springs is a layer of hessian on which rests the stuffing. The stuffing is topped by wadding and the seat is finished off with calico or denim, called lining, on which the cushion rests.

Such a seat is used to illustrate the upholstery repair techniques that follow. The techniques are standard and are easily modified to suit the structure of any chair or sofa, as well as the different configurations that may underlie various parts. Springs, for example, may or may not be found in the back of a chair and are almost never present in the arms. Here, the support normally provided by webbing may, instead, be a panel of stretched hessian.

The first step in restructuring a seat is to check the condition of the webbing. Look underneath the chair for sagging, which indicates that the webbing has stretched. Press up against the cambric covering; if the surface yields easily, the webbing has lost its tension. Then turn the chair upside down and remove the cambric covering for a closer inspection of the webbing itself, which may simply be slack or may have begun to fray or even come loose along the wooden frame.

It is not always necessary to replace worn or loose webbing; sometimes you can simply reinforce the existing webbing by adding a new strip over it. On the other hand, if further inspection shows that the frame needs structural repairs or the springs need retying *(pages 104–105)*, or if you are planning to put a new cover on the chair, it is better to remove loose webbing

completely and replace it with new.

A chair or sofa may also contain steel webbing strips beneath the jute webbing. If steel webbing has sagged, it can be restretched with the aid of a special tool that you may be able to borrow or rent from a professional upholsterer.

To reinforce old jute webbing or replace it with new, you will need a roll of webbing that matches the width of the original, and a supply of 16 mm improved tacks. You will also need a webbing stretcher, an upholsterer's tack hammer and, to sew new webbing to the springs, a 100 mm lightgauge curved needle and stitching twine. To hold tacks at the ready, you may find it useful to make a tack holder by sawing 25 mm deep cuts in a scrap of wood and lining up tacks, heads up, in the cuts.

Before tacking new webbing to the frame, fill in small cracks and holes left by previous repairs, using PVA glue or wood filler. If the edge of the frame has been weakened by too many tack holes, you can coat the splintered rail with PVA glue, working it into the damaged wood. Then lay a piece of hessian over the whole rail and brush glue over it. Press the hessian firmly in place with a sanding block. Allow the glue to dry before resuming work.

When you stretch webbing, certain general rules apply. Webbing on a seat is always stretched first from back to front; on the back of a chair it is stretched from bottom to top. The first strip is always placed in the centre of the frame, with additional strips placed alternately on either side. When all the strips in one direction are attached, perpendicular strips are woven through them, again placing the first strip in the centre and then working outwards on alternate sides.

New Webbing for Reinforcement

1 Reanchoring loose springs. A temporary repair can be carried out if one or two strips of webbing have stretched to lose their tension, or the coils have loosened or moved out of position. Clip away any bits of loose or broken cord anchoring the springs to the existing webbing, then reattach the affected springs to the webbing with a pattern of stitches that forms a square over two intersecting strips of webbing. Using a 100 mm curved needle you have threaded with a 1 metre length of stitching twine, make the first of four stitches at one corner of the intersecting strips, being sure to plot this first stitch so that the last stitch will finish as close as possible to the next coil that requires sewing. First, push the point of the needle down through the webbing on the inside of the coil *(below, left)*, then bring it up again through the webbing outside the coil *(below, right)*. Tie a slip-knot in the twine *(bottom, left)* and pull the knot down until it rests against the webbing.

Make a second stitch in the square at the adjacent corner, again pushing the needle down through the webbing inside the coil and bringing it up outside the coil; lock this stitch by drawing the needle underneath the twine carried from the first stitch *(bottom, right)*. Complete the third and fourth stitches in the same fashion, then move on to the next loose coil. If the two coils are adjacent, do not cut the twine: if they are some distance from each other, cut the twine and tie a knot. Continue until all the loose springs are firmly attached to the webbing.

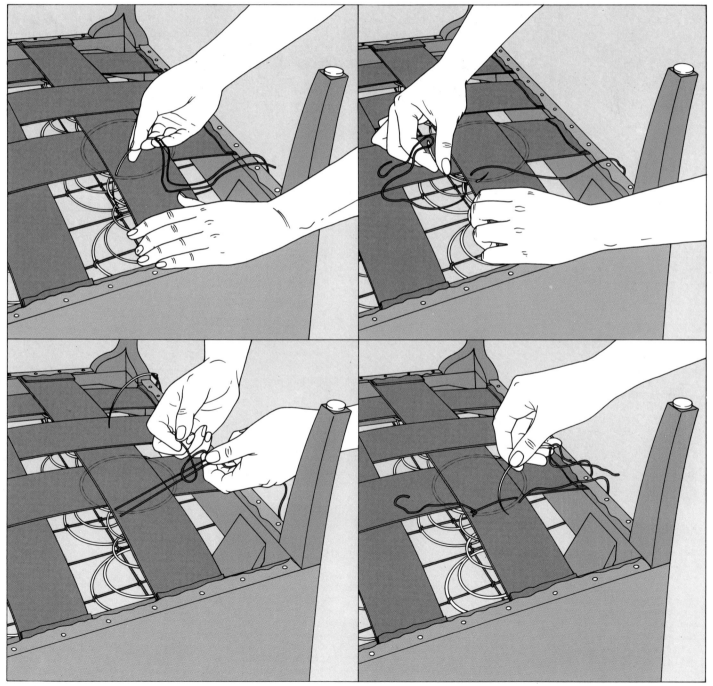

2 **Adding new webbing.** Unroll new webbing over the existing webbing and fasten it to the back seat rail with 16 mm improved upholstery tacks spaced roughly in a line *(box, below)*; allow an overlap of 40 mm. If the folded edge of the existing webbing falls slightly in from the edge of the seat rail, try to place some of the upholstery tacks in that narrow strip of wood.

3 **Stretching new webbing.** Unroll a length of webbing to reach across the chair frame. Slot the loose end through the aperture in a webbing stretcher, and fasten it with the retaining peg. Holding the stretcher at a 45 degree angle against the front seat rail, pull the webbing taut. To tighten it further, push down on the stretcher handle until it is horizontal.

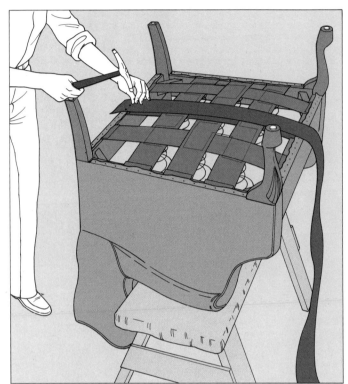

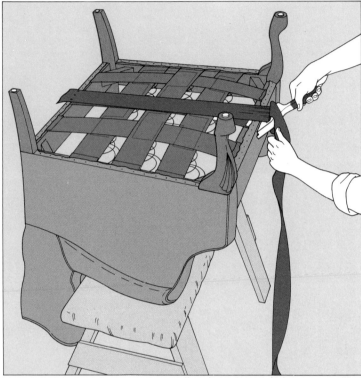

A Pattern of Tacks

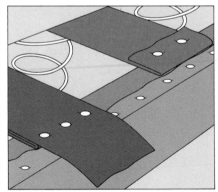

Spacing the tacks. To ensure a firm, even grip, upholsterers generally tack webbing in a staggered pattern. The first tack is hammered into a webbing strip about 18 mm from the outer edge of the chair rail. The next two are placed on either side of the centre tack, 5 mm from the side edges of the strip. The loose end is folded over, trimmed and pinned along the inner rail edge, with two more tacks spaced between the first row.

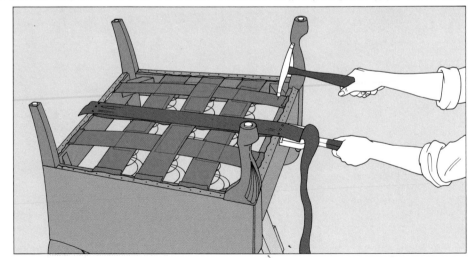

4 **Tacking stretched webbing.** As you hold the stretcher horizontal with one hand, use the magnetic end of the hammer to pick up a tack. Position the hammer about 150 mm above the webbing strip and, with a sharp blow, drive the tack down through the webbing, half way into the rail. Turn the hammer and, with the non-magnetic end, drive the tack all the way into the wood. Hammer in two more tacks on either side of the first. Cut the webbing. Fold it over and secure with two more tacks *(box, left)*. Repeat for the other loose end.

To insert more than two pieces of webbing, it is necessary to remove the old webbing and tacks; too many tacks may split the wood. The new webbing should be tacked to the frame as shown here. Lay the back-to-front strips, then interweave them with side-to-side strips.

Repairs for Back and Arm Supports

Restretching loose back webbing. After freeing the top end of the centre webbing strip on the back with a ripping chisel and mallet, fasten a 200 mm extension to the original webbing with two skewers, overlapping the ends of the strips by 10 mm. Pull the extension across the top of the rail and secure it in the stretcher, then push the stretcher flush with the back. Retack the original webbing to the inside face of the rail. Remove the extension and use it to restretch the remaining strips of webbing. Fold the loose ends over and tack them in place.

Tightening sagging hessian on an arm. If all of the old upholstery is being replaced and the frame is bared, you can tighten hessian by removing it from the frame and retacking it. First, attach the top edge of the hessian to the inside face of the arm rail with tacks spaced at 50 mm intervals. Then pull the hessian taut and tack its bottom edge to the inside face of the arm brace. Finally, stretch and tack the side edges.

Once the new upholstery has been added to the inside of the frame, place a layer of wadding over the hessian and hold it in this position by stretching and tacking a single strip of webbing across it and the frame *(inset)*.

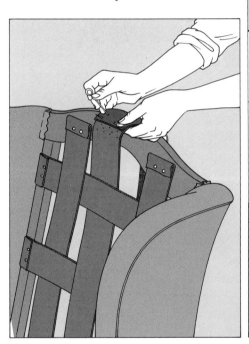

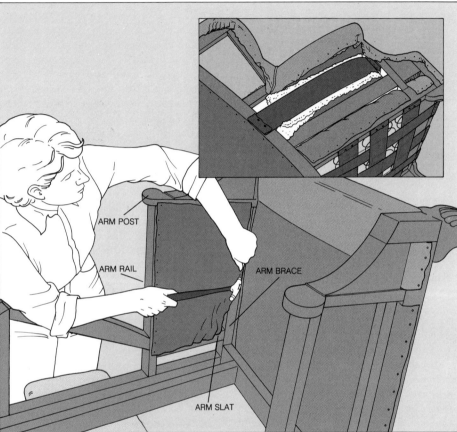

ARM POST

ARM RAIL

ARM BRACE

ARM SLAT

Replacing Worn-out Rubber Webbing

Fastening new end clips. Slide the old strips of rubber webbing out of the grooves on the seat rails and use them to cut out new rubber strips, 10 mm shorter. Fasten new clips to both ends of the new strips by pinching the jaws of the clips round the webbing with pliers *(inset)*. Slide the clips back into the grooves in the frame.

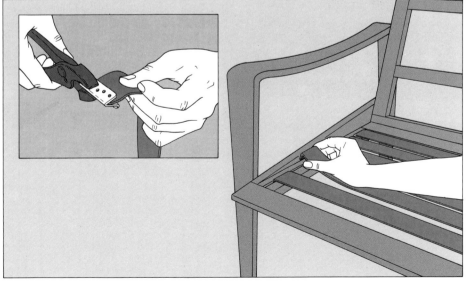

Putting Bounce Back in Springs

The coiled wire springs that give upholstered seats their bounce rarely wear out. It is the webbing that supports the springs, the thread that anchors them to the webbing and the cord that ties them to one another that break, stretch or fray.

If the only problem is stretched or frayed webbing, or broken thread, you will be able to reinforce the bottom of the seat without actually exposing the springs. But if the springs are popping through the fabric, either above or below, or if they are so loosely joined to one another that they are easily pushed out of alignment, it is time to restructure the entire seat. This means taking apart all the old layers from top to bottom—the hessian, the springs, twine and cord, the webbing, the cambric—and installing a complete new support system for the old springs.

Before you tear the seat apart, remove the cambric and mark the positions of the old webbing strips on the bottom edges of the seat rails with chalk; the marks will serve as a guide for installing new webbing. Then, working from the top of the seat, clip the stitches that anchor the hessian to the springs and strip off the hessian, using a tack lifter and mallet to prise out the old tacks from the seat rail. Next, cut the cord that fastens the springs together at the top, as well as cutting the stitches that anchor the bottom of the springs to the webbing. Then take out the springs and remove the old strips of webbing.

The springs that you find inside the seat of a well-made chair or sofa will be of 8 to 12 gauge wire. They will have a double-helical shape, with wide coils at the ends and narrow coils in the middle.

If the chair or sofa has been comfortable, there is no need to replace springs. However, if you want either a softer or a firmer seat, buy new springs of the same height as the old ones, but with more or less springiness. Double-helical springs are rated as hard, medium or soft: the smaller the waist coil—the narrowest coil in the middle of the spring—the harder the spring. No matter which degree of firmness you choose, look for springs with at least seven coils; springs with fewer coils are weaker and less efficient.

If you find that the seat has conical springs, each with a large coil at the top tapering down to a small coil at the bottom, you may want to replace them with double-helical springs. Conical springs are very rigid and cannot be attached to regular jute webbing. They must be mounted on metal bars and arranged as a single unit to fit over the seat frame.

You may also find cylindrical coil springs in the chair back or cushions and, occasionally, inside arms. These springs are usually shaped of lighter-gauge wire and are encased in hessian, calico or foam rubber to form a single unit. Since they are rarely defective, such spring units can be reused just as you find them.

Restructuring a coil-spring seat takes time but does not call for any special expertise. First you stretch a new layer of jute webbing across the bottom of the seat (*page 100*). Then stitch the bottom coil of the springs to the webbing with twine, using a 250 mm double-pointed upholstery or mattress needle. Finally, you tie together the spring tops, using laid cord.

In some modern upholstered furniture, you may find flat zigzag-shaped springs instead of coil springs. Such springs are fastened to the frame with metal clips and always run across the frame in one direction only—back to front on the seat, bottom to top on the chair back. On a seat, the spring strips are slightly longer than the frame and they arc upwards to provide support with resilience.

Zigzag springs do not require webbing and they are sometimes referred to as sagless or no-sag springs. They are usually fastened to one another with metal connectors instead of cord. However, if such springs begin to slip from side to side because their connectors are broken or lost, the simplest remedy is to tie them together with laid cord or twine (*page 105*).

Sewing the Springs to New Webbing

1 Anchoring the first spring. Centre the first spring over the intersection of the front and middle strips of webbing, making sure that the interlocked finish of the spring is facing towards the centre of the seat. Plot four equally spaced stitches round the bottom coil so that the last stitch will fall at the back of the coil. For the first stitch, push a double-pointed needle that is threaded with twine straight down through the webbing just inside the coil *(top left)*. Bring the needle up through the webbing on the outside of the coil *(top right)* and pull the twine through this stitch, leaving a 300 mm end.

Secure the first stitch with a slip-knot, doubling the loose end over the length of twine and back through the loop in the loose end *(bottom left)*. Tighten the knot against the coil *(bottom right)*, then push the needle down, outside the coil, through the original hole in the webbing.

Move 90 degrees round the coil and make a second stitch, pushing the needle up through the webbing inside the coil and back down outside the coil. Then repeat this procedure to make the third stitch. Neither the second nor the third stitch is secured with a slip-knot.

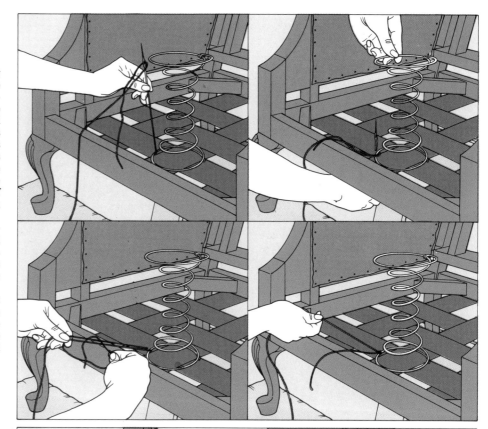

2 Running stitches between springs. For the fourth stitch, reverse the procedure for the second and third stitches: push the needle up through the webbing outside the coil, then down through the webbing inside the coil *(top)*. Place a second spring behind the first, again at the intersection of two webbing strips. At the point where this coil is nearest the first, bring the needle up through the webbing on the inside of the coil *(bottom)* and down on the outside.

Complete the second and third stitches, pushing the needle up on the inside and down on the outside of the coil. Complete the fourth stitch as before, pushing the needle up on the outside and down on the inside, but with this stitch in place, move on to a third spring placed to the side of the second spring, adjacent to this stitch.

When your stitching takes you into a corner *(inset)*, fasten off the twine by using the needle to draw the twine underneath the last stitch you made; then remove the needle, pull the twine taut and tie a knot. Continue anchoring springs at every intersection of the webbing strips until all the intersections are covered.

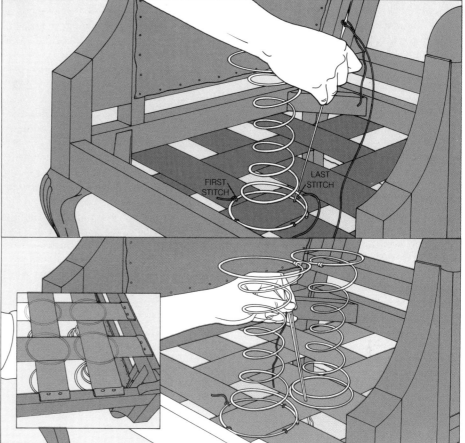

Tying Springs in Place with Lengths of Cord

1 Anchoring the cord. For each row of springs, front to back and side to side, cut a length of laid cord 1½ times the distance between the rails, and anchor the cord to the rails with pairs of upholstery tacks. Along each of the four rails and in line with the centre of each row of springs, drive a 16 mm improved tack half way into the top edge of the frame. Then loop one end of the first length of cord round the middle tack on the back rail and drive the tack all the way into the wood *(top)*. Drive a second tack half way into the rail 3 mm away from the first tack; loop the cord in the opposite direction round this tack, forming a figure-of-eight *(bottom)*. Then drive the second tack all the way into the wood *(inset)*.

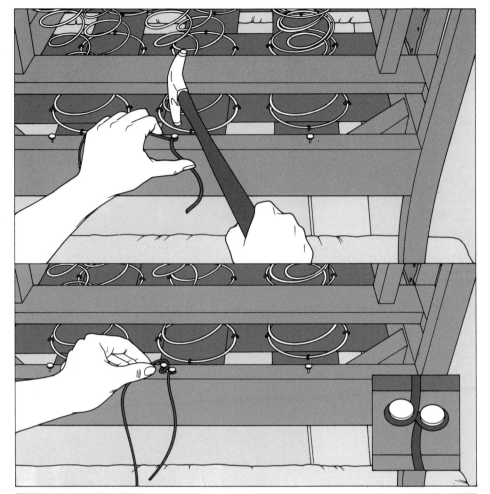

2 Tying the coils. Standing at the front of the frame, draw the anchored cord up under the back brace to the second coil from the top on the back spring. Pass the cord under this coil, pull the cord taut and hold it against the coil with your thumb to maintain tension while you tie a simple knot round the coil *(inset)*.

Draw the cord across this same spring and with your thumb hold it taut against the underside of the top coil while you tie a knot round that coil. Continue working from the back to the front, tying down the rest of the springs in the centre row. At each spring, knot the cord round both sides of the top coil until you get to the front spring; at that point, tie the second knot against the second coil from the top.

Some professional upholsterers, if working with traditional materials, do not knot the first string but merely wrap it round individual coils so that the springs can be adjusted at a later stage to give a good curve to the seat.

BACK BRACE

3 **Securing the cord.** At the end of the row, push the front spring down firmly and loop the cord on the centre tack of that rail. Pull the cord tight and drive the tack into the wood. Add a second tack and loop the cord in a figure-of-eight.

Tie down the rows of springs on either side of the centre row in the same fashion, alternating sides until all the rows running back to front have been tied. Then tie the side-to-side rows, again beginning with the centre row and working out on alternate sides *(inset)*.

Cut a secondary set of cords, but this time cut one cord fewer of each length. Drive tacks half way into the frame round all four sides, between those used to anchor the existing cord.

4 **Tying the secondary cords.** Starting with an inner cord on the back rail, anchor the first end as in Step 1, then draw the cord under the back brace and, knotting as in Step 2, tie the cord to each piece of cord it crosses. Anchor the cord end on the opposite rail. Tie all back-to-front cords first, then side-to-side cords.

Cut cords that are 1½ times the length of each diagonal row. Anchor and tie these cords as in Step 2, placing the first and last knot in each row one coil from the top of the spring *(inset)*. Start with the centre diagonals and work towards the corners, first doing all the rows in one direction, then crossing them with rows running the other way. On the corner springs, tie both of the knots on the second coil from the top.

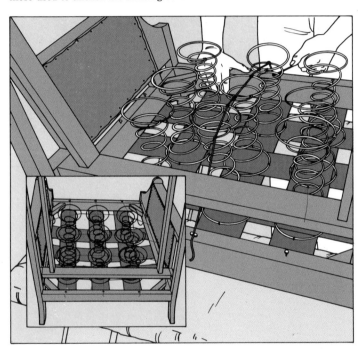

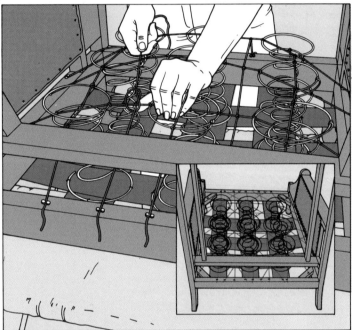

A Fix for Zigzag Springs

Tying for zigzag springs. To secure zigzag springs that slip out of line, tie them with lengths of laid cord or twine running between the side rails. Space the cords 150 to 200 mm apart. Anchor the cord ends and tie the knots as for coil springs.

To tighten metal spring clips that have worked loose from the rails, ease the spring out of the clips, keeping a firm hold on the spring to prevent it from snapping out of control. Release the relaxed spring, then remove the tacks anchoring the loosened clip, fill the holes with PVA glue and allow the glue to dry. Reposition the clip at a spot free of tack holes but as close as possible to its original position. Refasten the clip, then move the matching clip on the opposite rail so that it is in line with this new position. Slip the spring ends back into their clips.

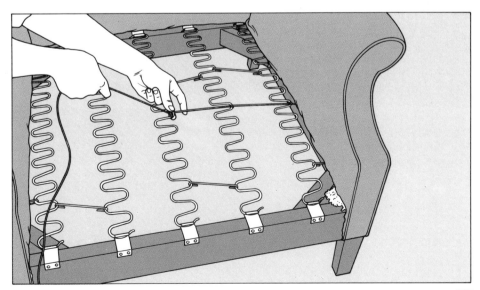

Stuffing for Softness and Shape

Hessian and stuffing top off the springs in upholstered seats and constitute the complete inner structure of most chair backs and arms. The hessian provides a support for the stuffing and keeps it from falling down into the springs. Stuffing gives the furniture softness and shape.

The standard hessian used weighs at least 300 g per square metre. It is stretched by hand over the area to be covered and fastened to the frame with 16 mm tacks. When stretched over springs, the hessian is sewn to the top coil of each spring with a 100 mm light-gauge curved needle and hessian stitching twine. As a finishing touch, a hessian-encased cylinder of either cotton or felt, called an edge roll, is tacked along the edge of the front seat rail to pad and shape the front edge of the seat. For a traditional finish, edge rolls may be formed by stitching through the layers of upholstery to compress the stuffing and give a firm edge. One or two rows of slip-stitches are inserted, and then one row of through-stitches.

Stuffing materials are available in bulk form or in prefabricated sheets. The most widely used of the loose stuffings are horsehair, cattle hair or hog hair and other natural substances such as coir or grass fibre. Hair is preferable to fibre stuffings—it is more resilient, cleaner and longer lasting. Most hair stuffing lasts indefinitely, and only rarely needs to be replaced.

If you do need new stuffing, the most convenient form is rubberized hair, which is sold in sheets or rolls and is easy to use because it forms a smooth, symmetrical surface without the coaxing and rearranging needed for loose stuffings. This pre-shaped material is more expensive than loose stuffing, but its excellent resilience and time-saving qualities make it the choice of many professionals.

Adding a Layer of Hessian over the Springs

1 **Slitting the hessian for a neat fit.** Cut a rectangle of hessian 150 mm longer and wider than the seat frame and lay the hessian over the springs, folding the 150 mm overlap back towards the centre of the seat. Make a diagonal cut from the back corners of the hessian to the fold so that the hessian will fit round the back posts when it is pulled down and tacked to the back and side seat rails. Make similiar diagonal cuts at the arm posts in front, and a perpendicular cut to any other vertical section of frame that the hessian must pass round.

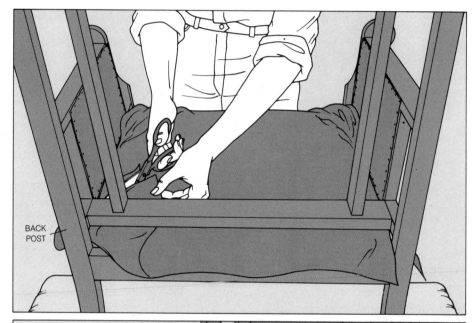

BACK POST

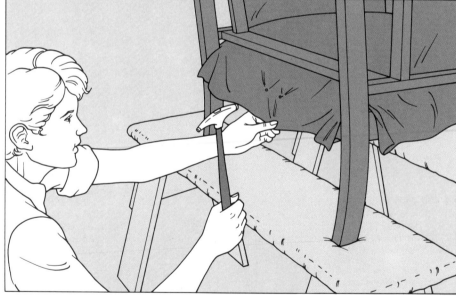

2 **Tacking the hessian edges.** Draw the overlapping edge of the hessian down between the back brace and back rail, and fasten it to the outer face of the rail with 16 mm tacks at 100 mm intervals. Then pull the hessian taut over the springs and tack the front edge to the front rail. Place the first tack at the centre of this rail, then work out towards the corners, stretching and smoothing the hessian as you go. Repeat this procedure for the sides.

Stretch and tack rectangular pieces of hessian to the inside of the arms, wings and back of the chair, but do not pull these coverings over the frame. Instead, tack them to the inside faces of the frame. Trim away the excess hessian, leaving a 10 mm edge beyond the tacks.

3 **Sewing the hessian to the springs.** To anchor the hessian to the springs, stitch it to the top coil of each spring at three places. Begin at a corner spring and, using a curved needle threaded with twine, stitch down through the hessian on the outside of the coil and back up inside the coil. Tie a slip-knot *(page 103, Step 1)* to anchor the first stitch. Plan the positions of the second and third stitches so that the third stitch will be close to an adjacent spring *(inset)*. Lock each of these stitches in turn by drawing the needle back under the twine running from the previous stitch. Move on to the top coil of the next spring. When you reach the end of a length of twine, tie it off with a slip-knot and rethread the needle.

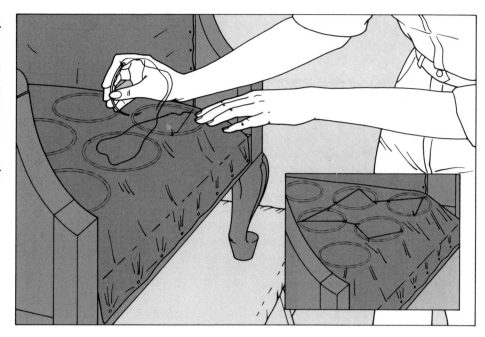

Padding to Cushion the Front Seat Rail

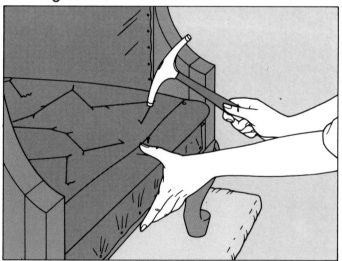

Tacking on the edge roll. Measure and cut a section of edge roll the same length as the front seat rail; hold it in position over the hessian and tack through the seam allowance into the top edge of the seat rail. Use 16 mm tacks and space them at 100 mm intervals along the rail.

Stitching a Layer of Stuffing to the Hessian

LINING FABRIC

Stitching down new stuffing. Shape the stuffing to fit the area bounded by the inside edges of the side seat rails, the inside edge of the back seat rail and the line where the lining will be sewn to the hessian *(page 117, Step 1)*. Stitch the stuffing in place with twine, guiding the curved needle down through the stuffing and hessian and under the outer curve of the top coil of a spring. Work round the perimeter of the stuffing and make one stitch per spring. Sew stuffing to the outer ends of zigzag springs in the same way.

Cut wadding or position stuffing for the inside back, arms and wings, shaping each piece to fit between the inside edges of its frame. Stitch the perimeter of the stuffing to the hessian pieces already attached to the frame.

Using a Home Sewing Machine for Upholstering

A home sewing machine that is powerful enough to stitch through four thicknesses of light to medium-weight upholstery fabric will perform all the machine stitching needed for reupholstering a chair or sofa. This stitching includes only a few seams: one to join the lining under the cushion to the seat front *(page 117)*; three to join the pull strips used to stretch fabric against the inner arms and back *(pages 119 and 121)*; and the seams to shape the cushion.

With a home sewing machine that has a zip foot, you can also attach the piping that outlines various pieces of upholstery and strengthens the edges. Moreover, instead of buying the piping, you can make it yourself by stitching bias strips of fabric over lengths of cotton cord—some home machines have a cording attachment that makes this job even easier.

For the extra strength needed in upholstery, and to help the covers withstand hard wear, use special upholstery thread and heavier-than-average needles. The strongest thread, size 20 cotton wrapped in polyester, has the advantage of being thin; but 4-ply cotton thread will also serve. The best needle size is 16 or 18. Generally, the density of the fabric calls for a fairly long stitch, about 4 stitches per centimetre, but you should shorten the stitch length round curves and at corners to provide extra strength. You can also stitch each seam twice, for additional reinforcement.

Seams on upholstery are customarily stitched 10 mm from the edge of the fabric. To maintain this distance as you guide the fabric under the needle, a seam gauge is handy. Many machines have attachments for this purpose; if your machine does not, a strip of masking tape placed on the throat plate of the machine, 10 mm away from the needle, works just as well.

After stitching the seam that joins lining to the seat front and the one that joins pull strips to arms and back, spread the seams open and press them to lie flat. When the seam joins many layers of fabric, the seam allowance should be graded after stitching, to reduce bulk. To grade a seam, cut each layer of the seam allowance a slightly different width, graduating from 10 mm on the bottom layer of fabric to 5 mm on the layer at the top of the seam.

Sewing a Straight Seam

1 **Using a seam gauge.** With the right sides of fabric together, secure the seam with pins placed at right angles to the seam line, a technique known as pin-basting. Then align the outer edges of the fabric against the seam gauge.

2 **Backstitching to secure a seam.** Beginning about 10 mm from one end of the seam, and with the machine set to reverse, stitch backwards to the top of the seam, then forwards for the length of the seam. Guide the fabric with your hands, butting its outer edges against the seam gauge. When you reach the other end of the seam, backstitch again for about 10 mm.

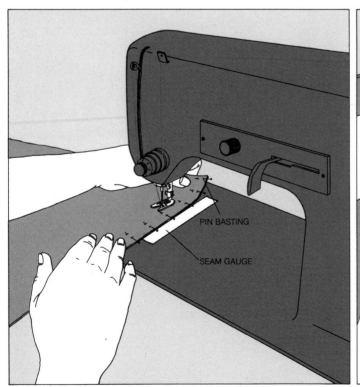

PIN BASTING

SEAM GAUGE

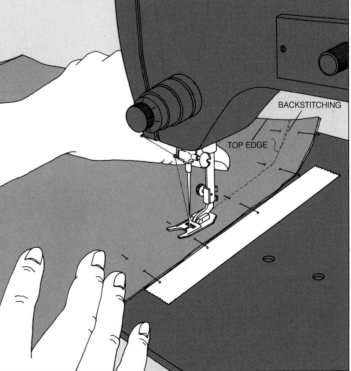

BACKSTITCHING

TOP EDGE

Making Piping from Bias Strips

1 **Finding the bias.** On a flat surface, fold the fabric diagonally, so that the lengthwise grain of the bottom layer parallels the crosswise grain of the folded-over portion. Iron along the diagonal fold, then spread open the fabric. Using the fold line as a guide, draw parallel lines, 40 mm apart, on the wrong side of the fabric, using a straightedge and tailor's chalk or marking pencil. Cut along these lines to make the bias strips.

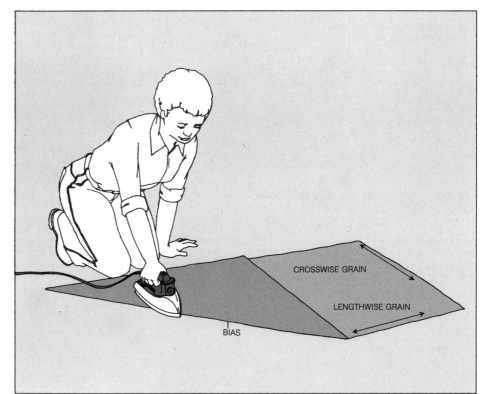

2 **Joining bias strips.** Pin-baste the end of one bias strip at right angles to another, right sides facing, and double-stitch them together, using the seam gauge as a guide. Press the seam open and clip off corners of seam allowance that protrude beyond the edges of each strip *(inset)*. Continue adding strips in the same way, creating a single length of bias strip. Lay cord along the middle of the strip, on the wrong side of the fabric, so that about 25 mm of cord extends beyond each end of the strip. After folding the fabric over the cord, align the edges and pin-baste them together.

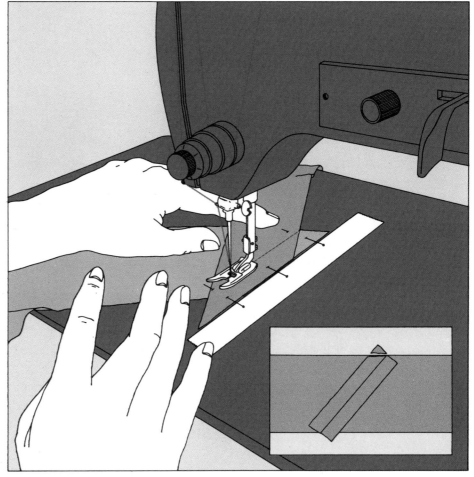

3 **Covering cord.** If you have a cording attachment for your machine, follow the manufacturer's instructions. Otherwise use the zip foot to sew through the folded piping, close to but not directly against the cord inside it. Guide the strip with your hands to keep the stitching line straight. If the finished seam allowance is uneven, trim it so that it is an even 10 mm.

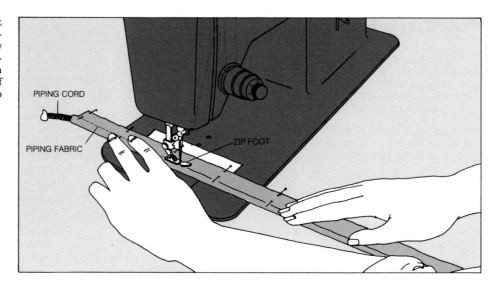

PIPING CORD

PIPING FABRIC

ZIP FOOT

Attaching Piping to Fabric

Stitching piping in place. Pin-baste piping to the right side of the upholstery fabric, keeping the seam allowances aligned, and stitch with a zip foot just inside the piping seam line. If a second piece of upholstery fabric is being joined to the first, pin-baste the two pieces together, right sides facing, with the piping sandwiched between them and all three seam allowances aligned. Turn the pieces so that the previously stitched seam is visible and, using the zip foot, sew through all layers of fabric, between the seam line and the cord *(inset)*. Grade the seams.

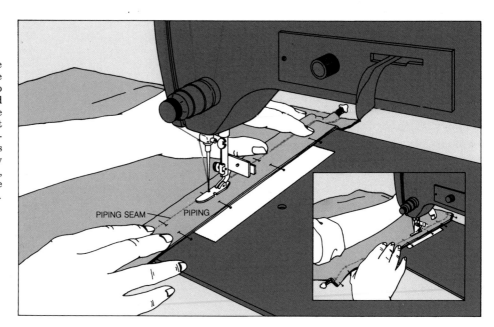

PIPING SEAM   PIPING

Special Techniques for Applying Piping

Fixing piping to curved and squared seams. On a curved seam *(near right)*, anchor the piping with a pin just short of the curve, keeping seam allowances aligned. Pull and pin the piping round the curve, clipping several V-shaped notches in the seam allowance to permit the piping to lie flat. Stitch with a zip foot as for a straight seam, but shorten the stitch length along the curve. To turn a sharp corner *(far right)*, pin piping to the fabric to within 25 mm of the corner, then notch the seam allowance at the corner; pin and stitch.

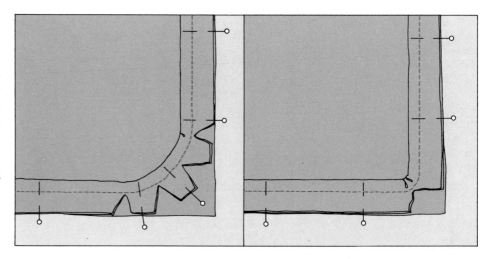

Rejuvenating a Loose Cushion

The loose cushion that covers the seat of most upholstered furniture is commonly made of identical top and bottom pieces, separated by a border the height of the cushion. Usually the cushion is square, as in the illustration here, but sometimes the back is rounded to fit the chair.

Inside the cushion you will usually find a stuffing of polyurethane foam or foam rubber. Older cushions may be filled with animal hair or fibre; some even contain springs. In expensive furniture and some antiques, the cushion may be filled with down, encased in an inner cover of down-proof ticking.

Restoring a loose cushion usually means simply replacing the cover, although you may want to discard the stuffing and springs of an old cushion and substitute a slab of foam. If the cushion is filled with down that has matted with age, you may be able to revive it. Sometimes you can do so by pinning the cushion on a clothes line and beating it with a broom. Twirling it in a clothes dryer set at a low temperature may also restore it to its original shape.

Another way of reviving a down cushion is to add more down, although you must do this with care, using a funnel, to avoid creating a blizzard of tiny feathers. If all the down must be removed, either for cleaning or to replace the cover, pass the job over to a professional; large quantities of down are difficult to handle.

Fashioning a new cover for a cushion involves cutting the pieces, machine-stitching the seams and piping, and inserting a zip fastener. The easiest way to ensure a perfect fit is to use the old top and bottom pieces as patterns for the new. When this is not possible, lay a rough-cut piece of fabric on the chair platform and trace the outline on to it with a piece of tailor's chalk. If the fabric has a dominant design element, such as a large rose, centre it on the cushion. When all the seam lines have been marked, cut the fabric 10 mm outside the chalk outline.

For the borders, cut three strips on the lengthwise grain of the fabric, the height of the cushion plus an allowance for 10 mm seams all round. Cut one strip long enough to cover the combined length of the front and the two sides (this strip will later be recut). Each of the other two strips should be the length of the back, plus 200 mm.

If the cushion has a rounded back, cut one border the length of the front plus 125 mm, and two strips of back border 25 mm longer than the zip length. (This zip is usually about half the length of the entire curved edge.) Cut two more borders long enough to span the space between the back and front borders plus 75 mm.

To make it easier to join the pieces, locate the centre front and back of the top and bottom pieces by folding them in half and marking the fold line with tailor's chalk. Similarly mark the centre top and bottom of the back corner.

Apart from the standard reupholstery supplies *(pages 88 and 89)*, you will need an upholstery zip—stronger than a dressmaking zip—as long as the back border strips. This zip will lap several centimetres on to the sides, to make it easier to insert the stuffing. If you are adding new stuffing, you will also need a piece of polyurethane foam or foam rubber.

Polyurethane foam, also called polyfoam, is available in many grades and should be judged by its density and compressibility: the denser and heavier it feels, the longer it will last. Polyfoam with a density of 21 to 23 kg per cubic metre is ideal; it can be found at upholstery supply shops or in stores that specialize in foam. If you are using foam rubber, choose a medium density. A thickness of 75 or 100 mm is suitable for the size of cushion shown here.

If possible, have the supplier machine-cut the foam to the desired size, since the result will be more even. If you must cut the foam yourself, an electric carving knife is the best tool. A serrated bread knife may also be used.

To round the contours of the cushion, you may want to add a layer of polyester wadding to the top and bottom of the foam; glue it on with aerosol adhesive. Layers of the same wadding can also be used to refurbish the contours of an old cushion or can be stuffed into the corners of a cushion whose foam slab is somewhat too small.

Anatomy of a Cushion

Creating the borders. In this square cushion, the long front border has been cut into three pieces—one piece 125 mm longer than the cushion front, the remainder cut into two even lengths for the borders at the sides. The two back borders have been folded in half lengthwise, right side out, and each stitched 6 mm from the open edges, creating two double-thick back strips to hold the zip along the folds *(page 112)*. The edges of the cushion have been outlined with lengths of piping, cut 50 mm longer than the total measurement of the cushion's perimeter.

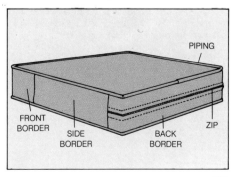

PIPING

FRONT BORDER

SIDE BORDER

BACK BORDER

ZIP

Circling a Cushion with Piping

Joining piping ends. Pin-baste the piping to the cushion top *(page 110)*, beginning at the centre back and clipping the fabric at the corners so that the piping lies flat. Open the stitching at one end of the piping and cut the exposed cord so it butts against the covered cord at the other end of the piping. Trim the opened piping cover 10 mm longer than the exposed cord, fold under 5 mm of the fabric, and lap it over the other end of the piping. Pin the joint to the cushion top, then sew the piping in place with a zip foot. Repeat this procedure for the cushion bottom.

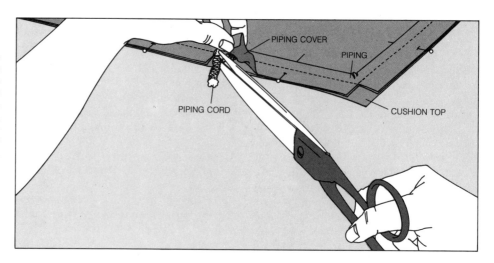

Installing an Access Zip

1 **Setting the zip in borders.** Line up one end of both back borders with the top of the zip tape, folded edges against the edge of the zip teeth; pin the zip tape in place, open the zip and machine stitch along one folded edge, 5 mm from the fold. Begin stitching at the top of the zip, closing the zip as you near its base. At the base, pivot and stitch across the tape; pivot again and stitch along the other folded edge to the top of the zip, 5 mm from the fold. With the zip still closed, pivot and stitch across its top, just above the glider.

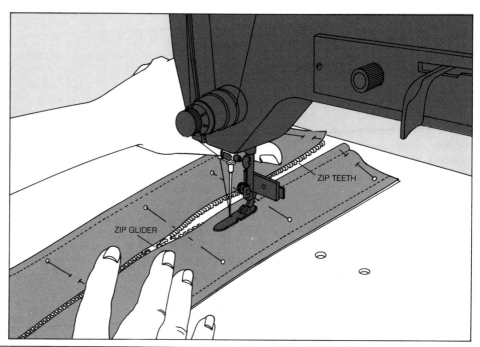

2 **Attaching the back and side borders.** Pin the back border to the side borders, right sides together *(below, left)*, and stitch 5 mm seams. Then, with the border right side out, fold 50 mm of one side border over the glider end of the zip *(below, right)*, creating a pocket. Pin the pocket edges to the back border and stitch along the seam lines to hold the pocket in place.

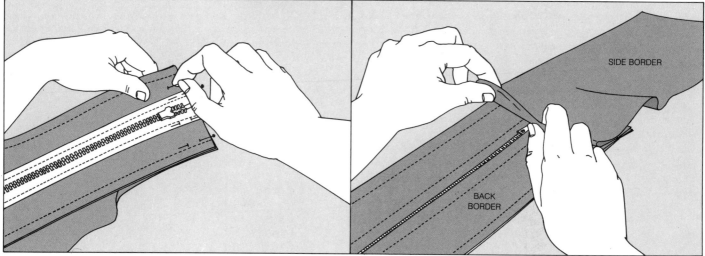

Attaching the Borders
to Top and Bottom

1 **Pinning borders to the cushion top.** Pin the back border to the cushion top, right sides together. Begin at the centre back, and work out to the ends of the border, clipping the border for a smooth fit at the corners. Then pin the front border to the cushion top, beginning at the centre front and clipping at the corners.

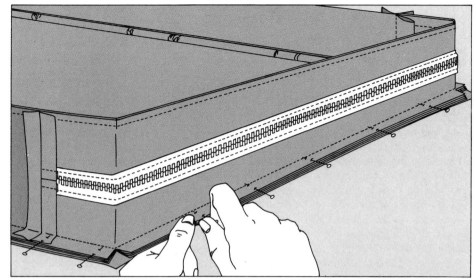

2 **Joining front and back borders.** Pin together the front and back borders along the side of the cushion, taking up in the seam any excess border fabric so that the border fits smoothly round the cushion. Stitch the seam that joins the two borders, then stitch the border to the cushion top, 10 mm from the edge. Pin and stitch the borders to the bottom in the same fashion.

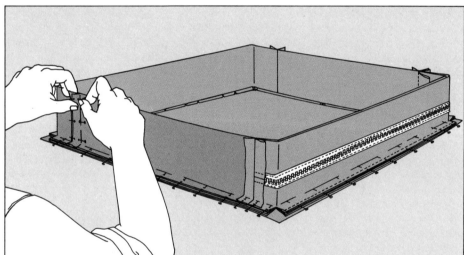

Stuffing the Cushion

Creating rounded contours. Using an aerosol adhesive suitable for polyurethane or foam rubber, coat the top of the foam and lay a sheet of polyester wadding on top; press the sheet into place and trim it with scissors to fit the block. Repeat on the bottom. Slide the cushion into the cover, compressing the foam and reaching inside to push it into the corners. Close the zip.

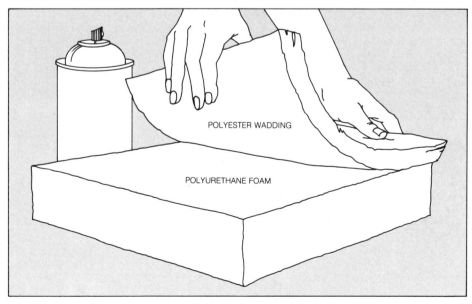

POLYESTER WADDING

POLYURETHANE FOAM

Attaching a New Cover to Finish the Project

The fabric that covers an upholstered chair or sofa is a true cover-up—outwardly it appears to be almost as seamless as skin, with few visible signs of construction. Yet actually there are several pieces of fabric that have been joined to one another in a special overlapping order to simplify the fitting task and to minimize the chance of error. One basic rule governs the job of upholstering from beginning to end: work from the inside of the chair to the outside, first attaching the inside cover pieces to the wooden frame, then covering their edges with the outside pieces.

Although there are hundreds of furniture styles, you can cover almost any chair or sofa by following the procedures used for the wing chair shown on these and the following pages. For sofas, the sections of fabric simply are larger. On antiques, the procedures are actually easier because there are fewer upholstered parts and more "show wood"—sections of exposed and finished wood. Many modern chairs are not really upholstered at all: they are an assemblage of cushions attached to an exposed frame, and you can simply remove the cushions and make new covers for them *(pages 111–113)*.

When professionals re-cover a chair or sofa, they usually try to duplicate the techniques used in the original covering. As they remove the pieces of fabric *(pages 92–93)*, they note how each piece was trimmed and fitted round curves and frame parts; and where it was fixed. You need not, however, duplicate precisely the fixing techniques used originally, many of which may have been superseded by newer, less time-consuming methods and even by new hardware.

The easiest way to join two pieces of upholstery fabric is to tack one piece directly to the frame and then fasten the other piece over it, using a technique known as back tacking *(below and opposite, top)*, so called because the tacks are hidden by a fold of fabric. Where this is impossible because there is no wood beneath the joint, the two pieces of fabric must be sewn together—by machine if possible *(pages 108–110)*, by hand if necessary.

To hand sew two pieces together, upholsterers use a nearly invisible stitch called a slip-stitch *(opposite page, bottom)*, which buries almost all of the thread beneath the fabric. In some instances, as on the front of a chair arm *(page 119)*, where stitching produces a neater joint than back tacking, upholsterers prefer to machine sew as much of the seam as possible, then to finish the remainder by hand.

Ordinarily, the new cover will be attached directly over a layer of cotton wad-ding. But in stripping an antique chair, you may find an undercover of calico; decades ago, most fine pieces were covered first with calico, then with fabric of the buyer's choice. If the stuffing and frame of an old chair are in good condition, you can leave most of the calico in place, but you may have to remove some of it to expose frame parts that the new cover will be attached to. These critical parts include the framing at the bottom of the chair and also the outer faces of the arms, the back and the wings.

On all of these surfaces, you will have to remove the calico undercover if the shape of the wooden framing members is not apparent. You may also have to untack the calico cover if it obstructs the gaps in the frame through which you must pull the new length of fabric; usually you can re-tack the calico to a part of the frame where it will not be in the way.

Professional upholsterers rarely discard existing wadding when re-covering a chair. Instead, just before fastening the new cover, they add a layer of cotton wadding over the old. This new wadding does not need to be shaped; the cover will shape it. Since wadding is inexpensive and can only improve the resilience of what lies beneath it, use it wherever the old wadding seems to be thin or worn.

Techniques for Achieving a Snug Fabric Fit

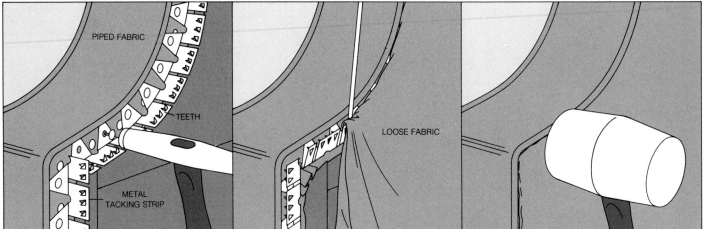

Back tacking along a curve. Most seams on a chair or sofa are made by back tacking the edge of one piece of fabric over the piped edge of a piece already in place. For back tacking along a curve, tack a length of flexible, L-shaped metal tacking strip to the frame, setting the base of the L against the piping, with the toothed half of the strip facing out *(above, left)*. Fold the toothed half towards the tacked half, leaving a 5 mm gap. Tuck the edge of the loose fabric into this gap with a 250 mm straight needle *(above, centre)*. Then hammer the tacking strip shut with a soft rubber mallet *(above, right)*. The teeth in the tacking strip will fasten the fabric against the piping, and the strip will be invisible.

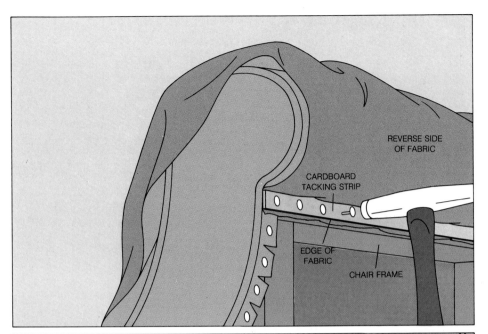

Back tacking along a straight line. To back tack along a straight line use a strip of cardboard tacking tape or a strip of buckram. Position the loose fabric, reverse side out, against the piped fabric, aligning the piping edges. Hold the tacking strip against the corded piping and fasten the tacking strip to the frame, tacking through both layers of fabric. Then fold the loose fabric down over the tacking strip, so that the strip is hidden.

REVERSE SIDE OF FABRIC

CARDBOARD TACKING STRIP

EDGE OF FABRIC

CHAIR FRAME

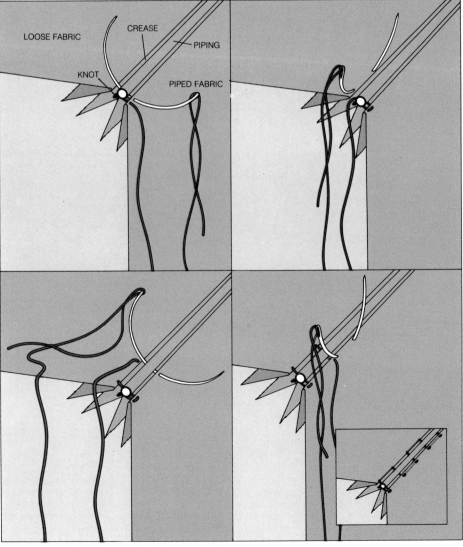

LOOSE FABRIC

CREASE

PIPING

KNOT

PIPED FABRIC

Slip-stitching. Where a loose piece of fabric cannot be back tacked to a piped piece, you can sew it by hand with a slip-stitch, using a curved upholsterer's needle. To make a slip-stitch, first crease the loose fabric along its seam line, then cut a length of thread twice the length of the seam to be sewn. Tie a knot in one end of the thread, and hide the knot by stitching through the corded piping, close to the cording, bringing the needle up through the piped fabric, close to the piping. To make the first stitch, push the needle back through the piping fabric and corded piping *(far left)*, and carry it inside the crease of the loose fabric, bringing it up 10 mm farther along *(left)*.

Return the needle to the piped fabric by passing it through the corded piping *(far left, below)*. Then carry the stitch inside the piped fabric, bringing it back out 10 mm farther along *(left, below)*. Pull the thread tight to draw the pieces together, and repeat the stitch, forming a pattern of crenellated stitches against the piping *(inset)*. To anchor the thread at the end of the seam, slip-stitch backwards about 50mm and use scissors to cut the thread off close to the piping.

115

Fitting the fabric to curves. If fabric must lap over an outside curve, relieve pressure on the fabric by slashing the edges at 25 mm intervals, cutting to within 5 mm of the visible edge.

Where fabric must lap over an inside curve, fold the fabric edges into 10 mm pleats. To keep pleats even, put the first one at the middle of the curve, and work out towards the ends.

Fitting round exposed corner framing. Fold the fabric diagonally back from the corner of the frame, leaving about 10 mm betweeen the corner of the frame and the fold line. Cut from the corner of the fabric in as far as the fold line. Then unfold the fabric, tuck the triangular sections under so that they fit against both sides of the frame (inset), and secure the fabric to the underside of the frame with tacks.

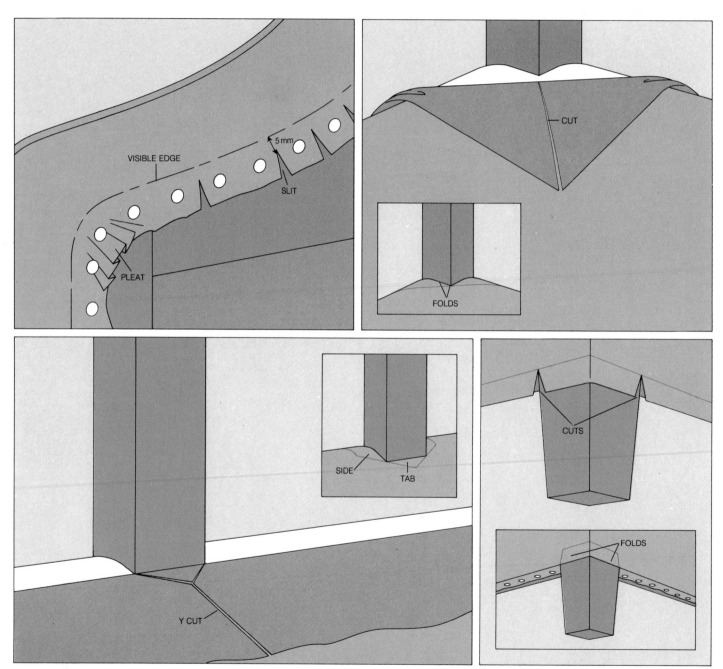

Fitting round three sides of a post. Fold the fabric back, parallel to the inner side of the frame, leaving a narrow space between the frame and the fold line. Make a Y-shaped cut that reaches the corners of the post; the throat of the Y should be about 25 mm from the post. Fold under the tab at the top of the Y (inset), aligning it with the inner side of the post. Then fold the two sides of the Y under, fitting them neatly against the two adjoining sides of the post. Finally, tack the bottom edge of the fabric to the underside of the frame.

Fitting fabric round a leg. Cut into the seam allowance of the fabric at the corners where the leg meets the frame, ending the cuts at the bottom of the frame. Fold the fabric under at the top of the leg (inset); tack it securely to the underside of the frame to hold the folds in place.

Attaching the Cover Fabric

1 **Sewing the lining to the seat.** Machine stitch the lining—the rough fabric under the seat cushion—to the front seat cover *(page 108)*. Then hand sew the joined pieces to the hessian-covered seat along the seam line, positioning the seam 125 mm behind the edge roll (the padding at the front of the seat). Pin the lining to the hessian with skewers, then fold back the front seat cover to expose the seam allowance. Hand sew the seam allowance to the hessian with 25 mm stitches, using a curved upholsterer's needle and stitching twine.

Return the front seat cover to its place, then fold the lining forwards, along the seam line. Sew a piece of stuffing to the hessian behind the seam *(page 107)*, and cover it with cotton wadding. Fold the lining back across the seat.

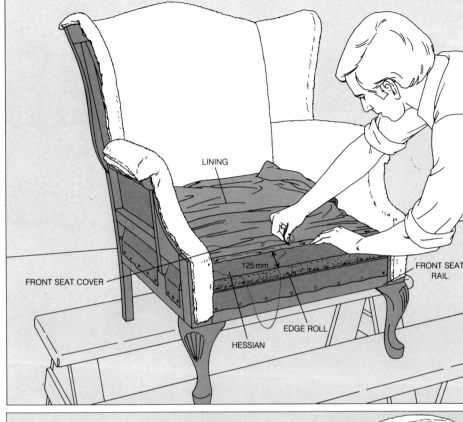

LINING

FRONT SEAT COVER

125 mm

FRONT SEAT RAIL

HESSIAN

EDGE ROLL

2 **Tacking the lining to the frame.** Slit the rear corners of the lining *(opposite, top right)* so that you can fit it round the back posts of the chair frame, and pull the lining through the back sides of the frame—between the seat and the back and arm braces. Holding the lining taut, drive tacks half way in at the middle of the back seat rail and the middle of each side seat rail. Then, working from the middle to the end of each rail, tack the lining permanently to the rails at 25 mm intervals.

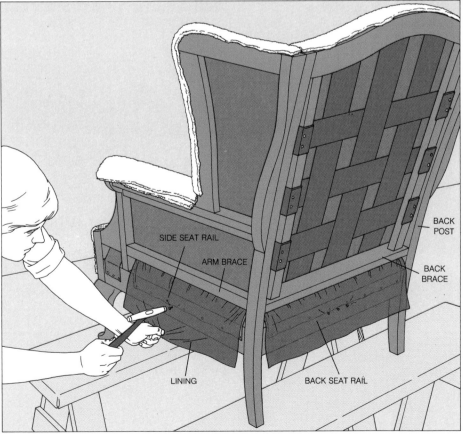

SIDE SEAT RAIL

ARM BRACE

BACK POST

BACK BRACE

LINING

BACK SEAT RAIL

3 **Padding over the edge roll.** Again fold back the front seat cover along the seam line, and cut a piece of cotton wadding to fit between the edge roll and seam. Lay the wadding loosely in place. Then cut a second, larger piece of wadding *(inset)* to extend from the seam, over the edge roll, down to the bottom edge of the front seat rail. Tack this second piece of wadding to the front seat rail, leaving it loose along the seam at the top.

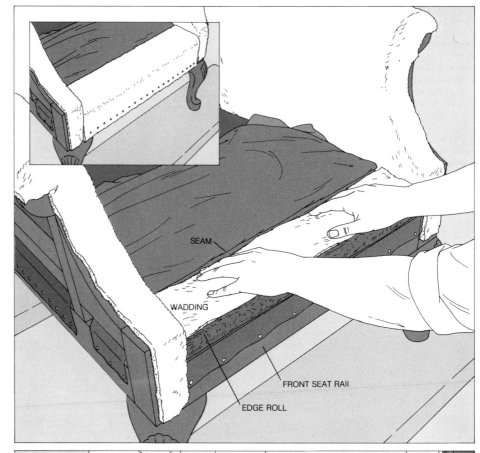

4 **Covering the front of the seat.** Pull the front seat cover down over the two layers of cotton wadding and the edge roll; hold it taut and tack it temporarily to the underside of the front seat rail. Then pull at the sides of the cover, slit it to fit round the arm posts *(page 116)* and tack it temporarily to the outsides of the arm posts and to the side seat rails *(inset)*. Cut and fold the cover so that it fits neatly round the front legs *(page 116)* and then tack it permanently to the lower edge of the front seat rail and to the arm posts and the side seat rails.

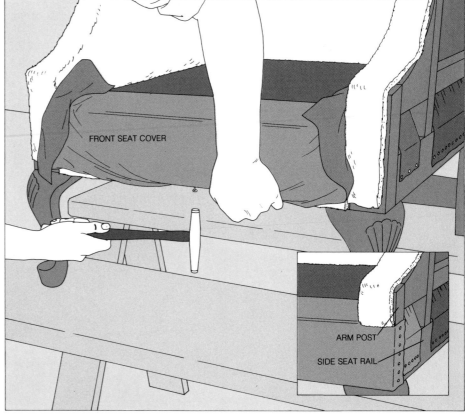

5 **Covering the inside arm.** Machine stitch an inside arm cover to the inside edge of a front arm cover, with piping already attached (*pages 96–97*); leave the unpiped outer edge of the front arm cover loose. Place the joined pieces on the chair (*inset*) and pull the top of the inside arm cover over the arm, tacking it temporarily to the outside of the arm rail. Pull the back edge of the inside arm cover through to the back of the frame, at the gap between the back slat and the back posts, and tack it temporarily to the back post. Then slit the bottom edge of the cover to fit through the arm frame, pull it down through the gap between the seat and the arm brace and tack it temporarily to the outside of the side seat rail, over the front seat cover and the lining.

Adjust the cover to fit smoothly over the arm stuffing, slitting it at the edges to eliminate wrinkles and bunching. Tack the cover permanently to the chair frame at 25 mm intervals.

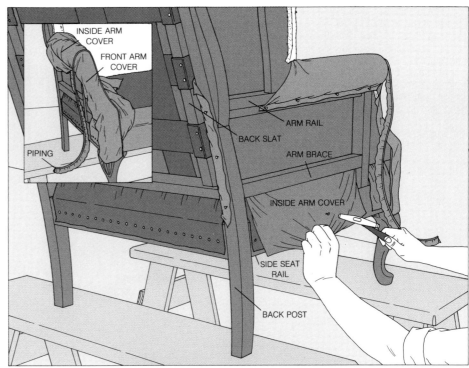

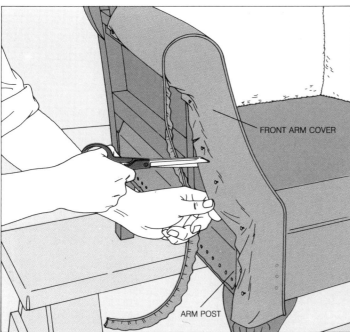

6 **Fitting the front arm cover.** Attach the bottom inside edge of the front arm cover to the arm post by folding back the cover and tacking the piped seam allowance to the post; place the last tack about 25 mm above the top of the chair leg. Then draw the cover tightly over the stuffing, tacking it temporarily to the outside of the arm post to hold it in place. Using scissors, slit and pleat the fabric to fit neatly round the curve of the arm post, and attach it permanently to the post with tacks spaced at 25 mm intervals down to within 25 mm of the top of the chair leg.

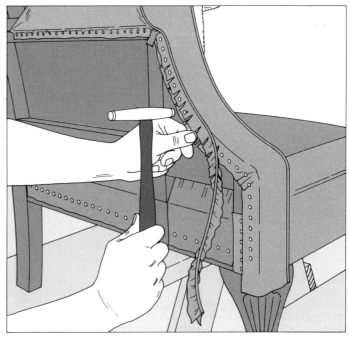

7 **Fastening the arm piping.** Hold the loose end of the piping against the curve of the front arm cover, checking that the previously stitched seam matches the curve of the upper arm; if it does not, open the seam with a razor blade where it does not fit. Then tack the piping to the outside of the arm post down to within 25 mm of the top of the chair leg, clipping and folding it for a neat fit. Finally, finish fastening the inside arm cover— still loose along the sharp curve at the top of the arm—by slip-stitching it (*page 115*) against the piping of the front arm cover.

8 **Ending the piping.** Grasp the end of the cord inside one end of the piping and slide the fabric back to expose more of the cord. Snip off the end of the cord so that it is even with the top of the chair leg and pull the excess fabric back over the cord. Repeat this step at the other end of the piping. Then fold the fabric under, so that it is even with the top of the leg, and tack it to the arm post just above the leg.

Following Steps 5 to 8, attach the inside arm cover, front arm cover and piping to the opposite chair arm in the same way.

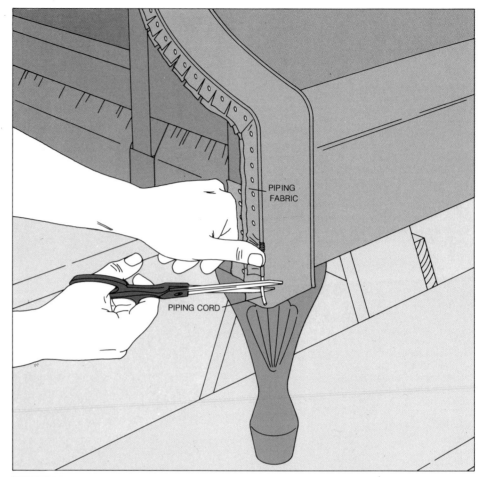

9 **Covering the inside wing.** Place an inside wing cover against a wing, centring the dominant design element if there is one, and mark the line where the bottom of the wing meets the arm; machine stitch piping along this line *(page 110)*. Begin to fit the cover at the top of the wing, temporarily anchoring the bottom by tacking the piped bottom edge to the outside of the wing frame. First, make a large V cut at the top rear corner, where the top back rail meets the back post. Pull the upper edge of the V-cut fabric over the top back rail and tack it to the rail temporarily *(inset)*. Pull the lower edge through the gap between the back post and back slat, and tack it temporarily to the back post.

Lap the fabric over the top of the wing and, holding it taut against the stuffing, pleat it so that it fits round the sharp curve along the front of the wing top; drive tacks permanently through the pleats into the top wing rail and into the wing post. Slash the fabric to fit along the gentler curves at the top and front of the wing, and tack it temporarily. After adjusting the fabric to eliminate wrinkles and bunching, tack it permanently to the front, back and top of the wing frame at 25 mm intervals. Slip-stitch *(page 115)* the piped bottom edge to the inside arm. Attach the other inside wing cover in the same way.

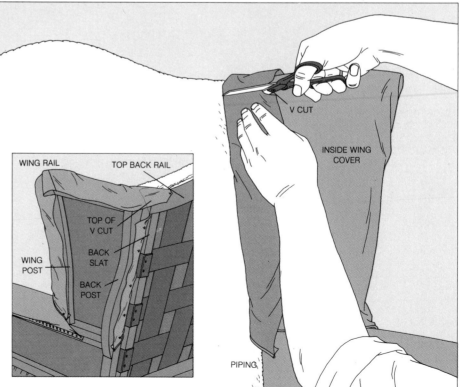

10 Covering the inside back. Lay the cover for the inside back over the stuffing, centring the dominant design element if there is one, and make four V cuts in the corners of the cover—two at the top, where the top back rail meets the back posts, and two at the bottom, where the back posts meet the back brace. Pull the cover over the top of the back and through the gaps in the sides and bottom of the frame *(inset)*. Temporarily tack the cover to the outside of the top back rail for several centimetres along the middle of the rail. Pull the sides of the cover over the back posts and tack them temporarily at the middle of the posts. Pull the bottom edge downwards and tack it temporarily to the back seat rail at the middle. Starting from the mid-point of each post or rail, tack the cover permanently to the frame at 25 mm intervals. If you want buttons on the back, attach them now *(page 123)*.

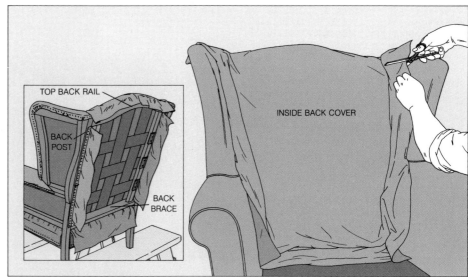

11 Tacking on the wing piping. Cut a length of piping—called the wing piping—to fit the outer edge of the two wings and the back, adding 50 mm at each end for finishing. Slide back the fabric at each end, and clip the cord to fit the exact measurement of the wing piping. Tack one end of the piping to the underside of the arm rail just below the wing, to hide the loose end. Then tack the piping to the entire edge of the combined wings and back, placing the tacks at 25 mm intervals and clipping or pleating the piping seam allowance for a smooth fit round curves. Hide the end of the piping under the opposite arm rail as at the beginning of the tacking operation.

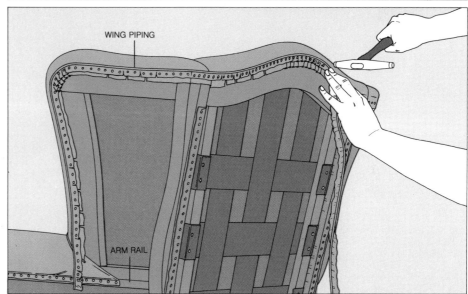

12 Fastening the outside wing cover. Tack a length of metal tacking strip to the outside of the wing frame, beginning at the bottom of the wing post, following the line of the wing piping, and ending at the upper rear corner of the wing. Then tack a piece of hessian over the outside wing, doubling the edges of the hessian to keep it from tearing, and tack a layer of cotton wadding over the hessian. Place the outside wing cover over the wing, and tack it temporarily over the back post and under the arm rail. Back tack the cover to the frame at the front and top of the wing *(page 114)* and tack it directly to the frame along the back and bottom of the wing *(inset)*, placing the tacks at 25 mm intervals. Attach the opposite outside wing cover in the same way.

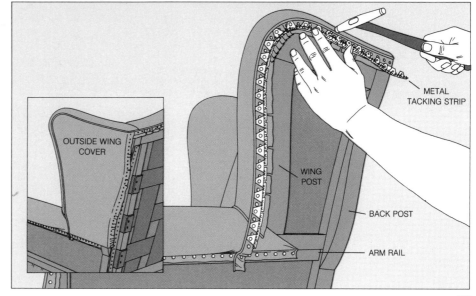

13 **Fitting the outside arm cover.** After turning the chair on its side, fasten a metal tacking strip along the piping that outlines the front of the outside arm. Cover the entire outside arm with hessian and cotton wadding, as in Step 12, page 121. Place the outside arm cover on the chair, matching its pattern to that of the outside wing cover so that the two appear to be one continuous piece of fabric. With a row of pins, mark the seam line where the inside and outside arm covers join. Then carefully fold the outside arm cover up over the inside arm cover, using the row of pins to align their common seam. Using a cardboard tacking strip, back tack the outside arm cover in place on this seam line, driving the tacks into the side of the arm rail *(inset)*.

Temporarily tack the back and bottom edges of the cover to their respective sections of frame—the rear of the back post and the lower edge of the side seat rail. Then, using the metal tacking strip, back tack the front edge against the piping, and cut and fold the bottom edge of the cover to fit round front and back legs *(page 116)*. Finally, fasten the back and bottom edges permanently with tacks at 25 mm intervals.

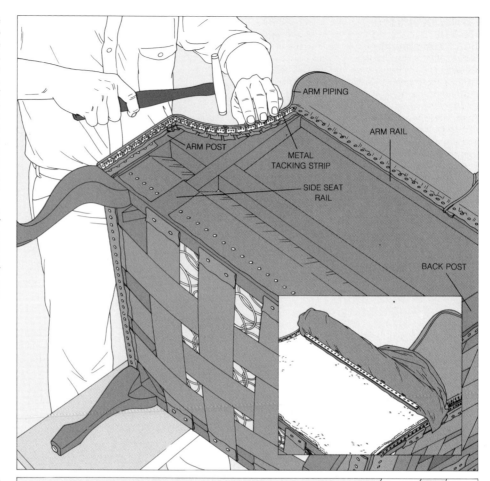

ARM PIPING

ARM RAIL

ARM POST

METAL TACKING STRIP

SIDE SEAT RAIL

BACK POST

14 **Covering the outside back.** After resting the chair on its arms, tack two vertical strips of piping down the full length of the back (one on each side) and finish off their ends, top and bottom, as in Step 8, page 120. Outline the top and sides of the back with a continuous length of metal tacking strip. Cover the entire back with hessian and cotton wadding. Using the metal tacking strip, back tack the cover to the back, centring the dominant design if there is one. Then tack the bottom edge of the cover to the underside of the back seat rail at 25 mm intervals, folding and fitting the cover at the rear legs *(page 116)*.

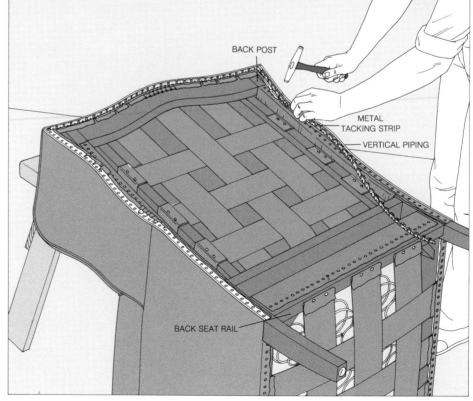

BACK POST

METAL TACKING STRIP

VERTICAL PIPING

BACK SEAT RAIL

15 **Covering the bottom with cambric.** Turn the chair upside down and cut a piece of cambric that is 10 mm wider than the outer dimensions of the bottom of the chair frame. Fold under 15 mm on all four sides of the cambric, and tack it temporarily to the frame at the mid-points of the seat rails at the front, sides and back; leave 5 mm between the fold line and the edge of each rail. Then, working out from the middle to the end of each rail, tack the cambric permanently to the frame at 25 mm intervals, fitting it round the legs as shown on page 116.

Attach any remaining finishing decorations, such as braid or decorative tacks (below). Make a seat cushion, as described on pages 111–113.

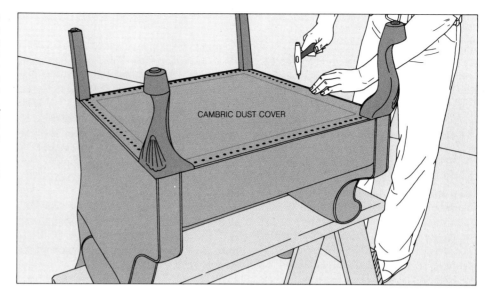

CAMBRIC DUST COVER

Finishing Touches for Different Styles

Hiding a bare edge. If fabric is tacked to the out-side instead of the underside of the frame, con-ceal the tacks with gimp—ornamental trim—or with decorative nails, or both. To fasten gimp, spread a bead of PVA glue along the fabric edge and hold the gimp in place for several minutes, until the glue dries. To hold the gimp more se-curely, you may also tack it to the frame with small gimp pins 25 mm apart. If the gimp pins are too conspicuous, hide them by placing broad-headed decorative nails next to them (inset). To hide tacks with decorative nails alone, cover the edge with a row of nails, heads touching.

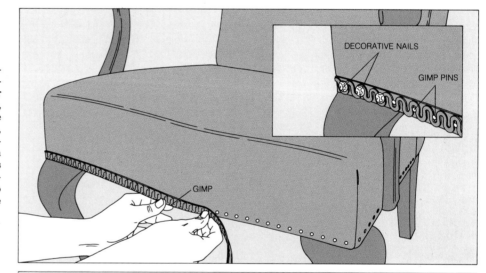

DECORATIVE NAILS

GIMP PINS

GIMP

Attaching buttons. If you use buttons, fasten them to the inside back cover (page 121, Step 10) be-fore attaching the outside cover. Using chalk, mark locations for the buttons on the inside cover of the chair back. For each button, cut a length of stitching twine about 450 mm long, and thread the twine through the eye on the back of the button. Then bring the two ends of the twine together, and thread them through the eye of a 250 mm straight needle. Push the needle through the inside cover of the chair back at a mark, and pull it through to the outside.

From the rear, fasten the button twine to the webbing of the chair back with a knot made with the two ends of the twine; before tightening it, insert a small roll or toggle of leather or cover fa-bric into the knot (inset). Secure the twine and roll with two additional knots.

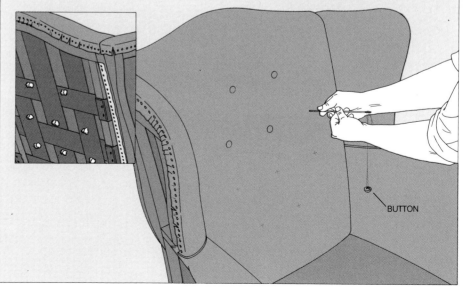

BUTTON

Picture Credits

The sources for the illustrations in this book are shown below. Credits for the illustrations from left to right are separated by semicolons, from top to bottom by dashes.

Cover: Fil Hunter. 6: Fil Hunter. 8, 9: Drawings by Forte, Inc. 10–17: Drawings by Frederic F. Bigio from B-C Graphics. 18–25: Drawings by John Massey. 26: Drawing by Jackson Day Designs. 27: Drawings by Walter Milmers Jr. from MJ Commercial Art. 28: Drawings by Walter Milmers Jr. from MJ Commercial Art, except bottom right: Drawing by Jackson Day Designs. 29–31: Drawings by Walter Milmers Jr. from MJ Commercial Art. 32: Fil Hunter. 34–37: Drawings by Elsie J. Hennig. 38–41: Drawings by John Massey. 42–47: Drawings by William J. Hennessy Jr. 48–49: Drawings by John Massey. 50–55: Drawings by Eduino J. Pereira. 56, 57: Drawings by Forte, Inc. 59, 60: Drawings by Eduino J. Pereira. 61, 62: Drawings by Jackson Day Designs. 63: Drawings by Eduino J. Pereira. 64–67: Terry Atkinson. 68: Fil Hunter. 73, 74: Drawings by Frederic F. Bigio from B-C Graphics. 75: Drawing by Frederic F. Bigio from B-C Graphics—Drawing by Jackson Day Designs—Drawing by Frederic F. Bigio from B-C Graphics. 77, 78: Frederic F. Bigio from B-C Graphics. 82, 83: Drawings by Walter Milmers Jr. from MJ Commercial Art. 84, 85: Drawings by Jackson Day Designs. 86: Fil Hunter. 88: Drawing by Frederic F. Bigio from B-C Graphics—Drawing by Frederic F. Bigio and Jackson Day Designs. 89: Drawing by Frederic F. Bigio from B-C Graphics. 91–97: Drawings by Snowden Associates, Inc. 99: Drawings by Frederic F. Bigio from B-C Graphics. 100: Drawings by Frederic F. Bigio from B-C Graphics except bottom left: Drawing by Jackson Day Designs. 101, 103–107: Drawings by Frederic F. Bigio from B-C Graphics. 108–110: Drawings by Forte, Inc. 111–113: Drawings by Melissa B. Poore. 114–123: Drawings by John Massey.

Acknowledgements

The editors would like to extend special thanks to Anthony Ritter, Bellou le Trichard, Orne; Emily Brandt-Clarke, Hamburg; and Tim Fraser, Sydney. They also wish to thank the following: Anthonies Upholstery and Furniture Repairs, Sydney; Kate Cann, London; Ernst Diekgraefe, Altena; Firma Werkmeister, Norderstedt; Firma Wilhelm A.C. Wessel, Lübeck; Firma Zweihorn, Hilden; Anthony Handley, Oxford; William Jousselin, Mauves-sur-Huisne, Orne; Wulf Kappes, Hamburg; Aquila Kegan, London; Eberhard Köhnke, Lübeck; René Marie, Saint-Mard-de-Reno, Orne; Werner Nehring, Hamburg; Vicki Robinson, London; R. Rustin, Rustins Ltd., London; Sewing Thread Specialists, Sydney; Heinrich-Otto Wulf GmbH, Hamburg.

Index/Glossary

Metric Conversion Chart

Approximate equivalents—length

Millimetres to inches		Inches to millimetres	
1	1/32	1/32	1
2	1/16	1/16	2
3	1/8	1/8	3
4	5/32	3/16	5
5	3/16	1/4	6
6	1/4	5/16	8
7	9/32	3/8	10
8	5/16	7/16	11
9	11/32	1/2	13
10 (1cm)	3/8	9/16	14
11	7/16	5/8	16
12	15/32	11/16	17
13	1/2	3/4	19
14	9/16	13/16	21
15	19/32	7/8	22
16	5/8	15/16	24
17	11/16	1	25
18	23/32	2	51
19	3/4	3	76
20	25/32	4	102
25	1	5	127
30	1 3/16	6	152
40	1 9/16	7	178
50	1 15/16	8	203
60	2 3/8	9	229
70	2 3/4	10	254
80	3 1/8	11	279
90	3 9/16	12 (1ft)	305
100	3 15/16	13	330
200	7 7/8	14	356
300	11 13/16	15	381
400	15 3/4	16	406
500	19 11/16	17	432
600	23 5/8	18	457
700	27 9/16	19	483
800	31 1/2	20	508
900	35 7/16	24 (2ft)	610
1000 (1m)	39 3/8	Yards to metres	

Metres to feet/inches		1	0.914
2	6' 7"	2	1.83
3	9' 10"	3	2.74
4	13' 1"	4	3.65
5	16' 5"	5	4.57
6	19' 8"	6	5.49
7	23' 0"	7	6.40
8	26' 3"	8	7.32
9	29' 6"	9	8.23
10	32' 10"	10	9.14
20	65' 7"	20	18.29
50	164' 0"	50	45.72
100	328' 7"	100	91.44

Conversion factors

Length		
1 millimetre (mm)	= 0.0394 in	
1 centimetre (cm)/10 mm	= 0.3937 in	
1 metre/100 cm	= 39.37 in/3.281 ft/1.094 yd	
1 kilometre (km)/1000 metres	= 1093.6 yd/0.6214 mile	
1 inch (in)	= 25.4 mm/2.54 cm	
1 foot (ft)/12 in	= 304.8 mm/30.48 cm/0.3048 metre	
1 yard (yd)/3 ft	= 914.4 mm/91.44 cm/0.9144 metre	
1 mile/1760 yd	= 1609.344 metres/1.609 km	

Area		
1 square centimetre (sq cm)/100 square millimetres (sq mm)	= 0.155 sq in	
1 square metre (sq metre)/10,000 sq cm	= 10.764 sq ft/1.196 sq yd	
1 are/100 sq metres	= 119.60 sq yd/0.0247 acre	
1 hectare (ha)/100 ares	= 2.471 acres/0.00386 sq mile	
1 square inch (sq in)	= 645.16 sq mm/6.4516 sq cm	
1 square foot (sq ft)/144 sq in	= 929.03 sq cm	
1 square yard (sq yd)/9 sq ft	= 8361.3 sq cm/0.8361 sq metre	
1 acre/4840 sq yd	= 4046.9 sq metres/0.4047 ha	
1 square mile/640 acres	= 259 ha/2.59 sq km	

Volume		
1 cubic centimetre (cu cm)/1000 cubic millimetres (cu mm)	= 0.0610 cu in	
1 cubic decimetre (cu dm)/1000 cu cm	= 61.024 cu in/0.0353 cu ft	
1 cubic metre/1000 cu dm	= 35.3146 cu ft/1.308 cu yd	
1 cu cm	= 1 millilitre (ml)	
1 cu dm	= 1 litre see **Capacity**	
1 cubic inch (cu in)	= 16.3871 cu cm	
1 cubic foot (cu ft)/1728 cu in	= 28.3168 cu cm/0.0283 cu metre	
1 cubic yard (cu yd)/27 cu ft	= 0.7646 cu metre	

Capacity		
1 litre	= 1.7598 pt/0.8799 qt/0.22 gal	
1 pint (pt)	= 0.568 litre	
1 quart (qt)	= 1.137 litres	
1 gallon (gal)	= 4.546 litres	

Weight		
1 gram (g)	= 0.035 oz	
1 kilogram (kg)/1000 g	= 2.20 lb/35.2 oz	
1 tonne/1000 kg	= 2204.6 lb/0.9842 ton	
1 ounce (oz)	= 28.35 g	
1 pound (lb)	= 0.4536 kg	
1 ton	= 1016 kg	

Pressure		
1 gram per square metre (g/metre^2)	= 0.0292 oz/sq yd	
1 gram per square centimetre (g/cm^2)	= 0.226 oz/sq in	
1 kilogram per square centimetre (kg/cm^2)	= 14.226 lb/sq in	
1 kilogram per square metre (kg/metre^2)	= 0.205 lb/sq ft	
1 pound per square foot (lb/ft^2)	= 4.882 kg/metre^2	
1 pound per square inch (lb/in^2)	= 703.07 kg/metre^2	
1 ounce per square yard (oz/yd^2)	= 33.91 g/metre^2	
1 ounce per square foot (oz/ft^2)	= 305.15 g/metre^2	

Temperature	
To convert °F to °C, subtract 32, then divide by 9 and multiply by 5	
To convert °C to °F, divide by 5 and multiply by 9, then add 32	

Phototypeset by Tradespools Limited, Frome, Somerset
Printed and bound by Artes Gráficas, Toledo, SA, Spain
D. L. TO: 1671 -1984